## ACKNOWLEDGEMENTS

The author would like to thank the following people for their assistance in the preparation of this work: George W. Slade, Professor Emeritus, University of Baltimore; Dr. A. J. Sullivan, Professor Emeritus, School of Public Communication, Boston University; Norman Bryden , School of Public Communication, Boston University; Frank Swartz, who photographed the techniques prior to their being drawn; Michael Campbell, who portrayed the "suspect" in all the techniques; John McHugh and DockxDesign, the artists who transformed the photographs into professional works of art; Al Harrington, the "wizard" who served as the production coordinator; without his help we would still be talking about this book; Massad Ayoob, internationally-recognized expert on impact tools and on officer survival training, who graciously wrote the Foreword to this book; Harry L. Temple, Executive Director of the United States Combat Judo Association, who kept many of these techniques alive during the years; A. D. Swartzbaugh and Lawrence T. Kessler, also of the United States Combat Judo Association, whose insight and philosophy were invaluable; David Maxwell, Washington Public Power Supply System, whose valuable input shall never be forgotten; J. D. Myers, (he knows where he is), who originally advised us to use line drawings; Steve Campbell, Northern Virginia Criminal Justice Academy, whose questioning of various techniques led to small, yet significant, changes; Gary Egan, Executive Director, Massachusetts Criminal Justice Training Council, who helped pioneer defensive tactics training in Massachusetts; William E. Lavash, Director, Waltham (MA) Police Academy, who was the first to adopt our defensive tactics program as an integral part of recruit training; J. W. Simmons, Director of Extension, Sampson (NC) Technical College and Neil Monroe, Chief, Cumberland County (NC) Alcohol Beverage Control for blazing a "new" trail for defensive tactics in North Carolina; Garry Wegner, Assistant Director, Washington Criminal Justice Training Commission; Sheriff Frank Kanekoa and Deputy Michael Kestner of the Clark County (WA) Sheriff's Department, and Deputy David Tameno, Kitsap County (WA) Sheriff's Department for pioneering our program in the state of Washington; Larry Plott, Director and Michael N. Becar, Regional II Training Coordinator, Idaho Peace Officer Standards and Training, for advancing defensive tactics training in the state of Idaho; Jerry Hamilton, Idaho State Police, for blazing a trail in the Northwest for defensive tactics; Arnold Bernstein, Albuquerque (NM) Police Department, who blazed a trail for professional defensive tactics training in the state of New Mexico; Judith Panora and John Quirke, Massachusetts Criminal Justice Training Council; M. Gary Patton, Los Angeles Police Department; Thomas J. Archambault, Defensive Tactics Institute; Typotech, Inc. for typesetting; and Wendy, who spent countless hours typing "rough drafts". Finally, thanks to the hundreds of police, court, military and security personnel who have "street-tested" and who have definitely proven the safety and the effectiveness of the techniques contained in this book.



Defensive Tactics DTI Institute, Inc.



Published by: Reliapon Police Products
P.O. Box 14872
Station G, NE
Albuquerque, NM 87111

ISBN #: 0-935878-02-5

First Printing: December 1981
Second Printing: December 1982

## FOREWORD

Defensive tactics is a field that is all too tragically limited in its exposure to the people who need it most: America's police. In some police academies, an officer may get sixty hours of firearms training, but only a few evenings of unarmed self defense, perhaps after supper when his learning capacity is ebbing. Is is unlikely that the young officer will have to fire his service revolver once in his career, if that— but he or she will be involved in many, many unarmed combats during that period.

Surely, firearms training must never be sacrificed, for when you do need the gun, life is on the line. What many fail to realize is that life and limb can also be lost if the officer doesn't know how to protect himself with his hands or feet. Near where I live, we saw the following deaths in one year:

—An officer carrying no sidearm had his heavy duty flashlight taken away, and was bludgeoned to death with it.

—A 33 year old officer was DOA after a struggle with two men who used only fists and feet.

—A fortyish policeman was punched in the solar plexus by a younger, stronger street punk. He made his way to the emergency room...and died there.

I won't second guess those officers, and say that they died because they weren't able to swiftly restrain their assailants with defensive tactics maneuvers. That may be left to the reader's conclusion.

Consider, too, the many more cases each year where the officer survives...sort of. The men in wheelchairs with broken backs from being thrown or stomped, or who see double after being kicked in the head, or who suffer the sometimes permanent agonies of groin injury. Today's street cop is probably older than the offender he faces, often smaller and less powerful, and less likely to be able to work out and stay in shape, given the extraordinary demands of his job. Perhaps one cop in a hundred is seriously into the martial arts.

It is for such officers that defensive tactics training is most important, and if the Academies— especially in this day of budget-cutting mentality— cannot afford to deliver that training, it behooves the officer to seek his own. Many officers, with their low salaries, topsy-turvy schedules, and necessary second jobs, find it impossible to enroll at a martial arts studio. For them, learning from textbooks is the only answer.

No book will equal the hands-on training one can receive from a good instructor, but a good "DT" manual will go a long way toward closing the gap. The trick is to find a really good book.

I spent many years on the martial arts scene, writing for magazines like BLACK BELT, KARATE ILLUSTRATED, and OFFICIAL KARATE. I spent more teaching police officers how to defend themselves. I saw many, many books on how to fight...and few that were much good to a novice by themselves.

The book you hold in your hands is an exception. It was written especially for the police officer, learning alone. The instructions are clear and concise. Instead of shadowy, half-tone photographs, starkly simple line drawings are used so as to leave no doubt of proper hand, foot, and hip positioning. Virtually all the techniques can be effectively learned with only a book and a practice partner.

The book's real secret, though, is not its manner of presentation but the men who wrote it. John Peters, Jr. is indisputably one of the best DT instructors in the country, and in some areas of the discipline, the best. Head of the US Combat Judo Association, he has distilled his formal training in judo, jiu-jitsu, and aikido into simple, highly efficient techniques that can be learned and retained even without an instructor, and even by a reader who is not athletically inclined.

I have seen John teach. I have studied with him, and later, I taught for him. This gave me an opportunity to interface privately with a number of officers, street cops and instructors alike, who have worked with him. Virtually all were deeply impressed by his techniques and his methods of teaching. The techniques were easy to learn, they were well retained by the patrol officers with a minimum of basic and refresher training, and most important, they worked on the street!

Peters' co-author, Shihan Takayuki Kubota, is a living legend in the world of karate. Steeped in the lore of the martial arts since his *sensei* father initiated him at the age of four, the Shihan holds advanced black belt rank in numerous arts, and has gone on to develop many techniques of his own. He has taught police from Tokyo to Los Angeles and eastward, where his methods remain in daily and successful use among thousands of police officers on the street.

The book you are about to read is not strictly a martial arts manual. It deals with practice instead of theory, with the street instead of the *dojo*. It contains elements of escalation of force, and civil liability concern—two of the inescapable elements of fighting in real life. Peters was a pioneer in developing police DT programs that encompassed these vital elements of using force under the mantle of law. He well understands that an officer hasn't really won a street fight if his career, pension, and reputation are sacrificed in the aftermath of an excessive force charge, and he teaches officers how to prepare for survival in this arena.

It is because of this uncompromising approach to reality, as well as a host of simple, effective, street-proven techniques that are easily learned and retained, that this book offers so much to the professional police or security officer. I predict that in the years to come, it will save the men and women of the law enforcement sector from injury, from maiming, and even perhaps from death.

I recommend it highly.

Massad Ayoob
Concord, NH 1981

Defensive Tactics DTI Institute, Inc.

## INTRODUCTION

Remember those seemingly worthless self-defense classes at the police academy? Weren't very interesting, were they? After all, who would attack a police officer? Things like that only happened in the movies. And besides, if someone did attack you, that's why the department issued you a gun and then taught you how to use it.

We're sure that if this attitude ever existed, you have replaced it with the truth. You have since learned that people do attack police officers. You have also learned many other things upon leaving the academy: that your word didn't always please people or make them listen; that people will push you to the limit; that the catch-all solution isn't the use of a firearm or a baton; and that your self-defense training was inadequate for most of today's street confrontations.

Unfortunately, you, like most other law enforcement officers, are given extensive firearms training, but are given little, if any, training in self-defense. Basically, you are better trained to kill someone with a firearm than you are to protect yourself with defensive tactics. And, by now, you certainly know that shoot-outs are far less frequent (you may never see one), than are unarmed encounters. Like Massad Ayoob, we believe that firearms training is a necessity, but not at the expense of defensive tactics training.

You can most likely recall incidents where the knowledge of a few simple defensive tactics techniques would have saved an officer from getting injured; saved an officer from needlessly beating a suspect because (s)he didn't know what else to do; saved an officer (or maybe yourself) from embarrassment because a drunken patron knew more self-defense than those sent to remove him/her; saved an officer from ridicule from his/her peers because (s)he could not handle the whimpy-looking suspect; saved an officer or the department from a long and costly criminal or civil law suit; and finally, saved an officer from injury when (s)he attempted to apply a martial arts technique on a drunk, only to wind up on the receiving end of a punch because the technique failed.

Our files contain many incidents where officers have successfully used our techniques. For example, the Chief of one department, used one of our disarming techniques, to relieve a shotgun-wielding gunman of his deadly weapon, while he and other patrons of a bar were being held at gunpoint. In another case, a young officer who had responded to a call-for-assistance found seven frustrated colleagues who had tried unsuccessfully to remove a demonstrator who was firmly holding onto an auditorium seat. Quickly and effortlessly, he successfully removed the demonstrator as his fellow officers watched in bewilderment. In addition to defending themselves, many officers—both male and female—have told us that their confidence and self-image was enhanced after training with our techniques.

Our contemporary defensive tactics system is based upon the use of technique rather than the use of brute strength. The results: female and small-framed male officers have both been able to use the techniques with success. In fact, many people have found that our system of training is a natural fit for both the smaller and the weaker officer. For example, David Maxwell of the Washington Public Power Supply System told us that the techniques are the most "common sense" movements that he had ever seen. "Each technique is a natural extension of a normal defensive reactionary move. The techniques are simple, yet extremely effective and control the suspect better with less injury and danger to both the suspect and the arresting officer."

In addition, our techniques can be applied from a "cold start." That is, you do not need to perform lengthy warm-up exercises before you can use or can apply these techniques. In our opinion, any technique which cannot be effectively applied without first warming-up is ineffective for the street and has no place in defensive tactics. And our system's techniques dovetail making it easy to go from one technique into another.

As you know, a combative situation is constantly changing. The unknown thoughts and actions of your aggressor all too soon become intimate knowledge and reality. The defensive tactics techniques which you study and learn, therefore, must also provide you with a chamelion-like quality; the flexibility to change, to modify or to integrate movements to match the demands and the changes of combat.

Our techniques possess these inherent qualities; however, you must first learn and then practice them. Practicing various combinations will give you the range of response necessary for combat. Our techniques are the ingredients from which you can make construct a good defense.

Our defensive movements are not traditional martial arts techniques. While some of our techniques are derived from the martial arts, they have all been designed to keep you safe on the street. The techniques contained in this book are for use in the street to safely, to effectively and to quickly control or to restrain an individual. Today's street survival tactics are no place for the traditional martial arts such as judo and karate.

Judo, for example, is a sport and is practiced as such. While there may be rules governing the judo contest, there are no "rules" on the street where survival is the "trophy." Also, with all the equipment you must carry on your belt, throwing techniques are made most difficult.

Karate, too, doesn't give you the range of techniques needed for the subduing of an offender. The kicking of or the punching of a suspect who refuses to leave a bar would, most likely, generate both brutality claims and criminal and civil law suits.

The serious study of the martial arts also involves a total commitment from the student. It may take months or even years to acquire the necessary skills to readily defend yourself. Few police officers have the time or the desire to make such a committment.

Finally, to become and to stay proficient in most martial arts techniques, you must continuously practice. Many of our techniques can be used effectively with very little practice; other techniques require more study. Regardless of the frequency of your practice sessions, we have found that the movements in our defensive tactics system are easily remembered. Many of our students have told us about how easy the techniques were to learn and to remember. And to help you learn our techniques, we have included balance lines in each movement. These lines will give you a "third dimension" regarding proper body positioning. Remember, however, that the single most important factor affecting your safety is *professional training*.

To avoid getting injured or injuring the suspect because you didn't know what you were doing, and to avoid needless litigation and law suits, we suggest that you complete a Defensive Tactics Institute certified program. Books and training manuals, regardless of their quality, can never replace actual training under the helpful eye of a professional instructor. The Institute's instructors are former police officers who have had street experience and who are dedicated and trained to give you the best training available in the field of defensive tactics. All of us subscribe to the philospophy that the classroom is the best place to learn, and the *only* safe place to make mistakes.

To be notified of our next defensive tactics course in your area, please send your name, address and phone number to the Defensive Tactics Institute. You may also desire to arrange for training in your area; if so, write to the Institute. Finally, you may visit one of the Institute's regional training centers.

We hope that you will never need to use the techniques contained in this book. Should you be forced to use them, however, we know that you won't be disappointed in their effectiveness. Practice them. They work.

John G. Peters, Jr.
Boston

Takayuki Kubota
Los Angeles

JOHN G. PETERS, JR. is president and founder of the Defensive Tactics Institute. He is also president and director, respectively, of the Defensive Tactics Institute's two sister organizations: the PR-24 International Institute and the Kubotan Institute (co-founder with "Tak" Kubota).

Involved in the study of martial arts and police tactics since 1965, Peters holds a second degree black belt in Jiu-Jitsu and a first degree black belt in Kodokan Judo. He is also a certified Instructor Trainer in the Kubotan, in the the PR-24 baton, in the straight baton, in the flashlight, in the Immobilizer, in the Action Control Grip, in the 36" riot baton, in handcuffing techniques and applications, in firearm retention and disarming and in defensive tactics.

Educationally, Peters was awarded an Associate in Applied Science degree and a Certificate in Corrections, both *Cum Laude* from the Northern Virginia Community College; a Bachelor of Science degree, *Summa Cum Laude*, from the University of Baltimore; a Master of Science degree, from the School of Public Communication, Boston University; and a Master of Business Administration degree, *With Honors*, from Babson College. He has also done post-graduate work in governmental finance and accounting at Suffolk University.

Peters began his law enforcement career in 1969 when he was appointed to the FBI as a clerical employee. While there, he received a *Letter of Commendation* for his Judo instruction from then FBI Director, J. Edgar Hoover.

In 1972, Peters joined the Northern York County (PA) Regional Police Department as a Police Officer/Self-Defense Specialist. Later, he transferred to the York County (PA) Sheriff's Department as a Deputy Sheriff. While there, Peters spent three years on the District Attorney's Fugitive Squad.

In 1978, Peters became the Staff Executive (Civilian equivalent of Deputy Chief) of a Massachusetts police department, where he headed the Administrative Bureau (seven divisions) and the Planning and Research Unit.

Peters also served as Senior Research Associate for a Massachusetts-based criminal justice research firm. While there, he conducted extensive research into the area of management of criminal investigations, and became one of the nation's leading authorities in this field.

A noted author of many articles, book chapters and training manuals, Peters has served as a training consultant to many criminal justice, military and security agencies, including: the Los Angeles Police Department; the California Highway Patrol; the Las Vegas Metropolitan Police Department; the Seattle Police Department; the Salt Lake City Police Department; the Massachusetts Criminal Justice Training Council; the Washington State Criminal Justice Training Commission; the New Mexico Law Enforcement Academy; the Idaho POST Academy; the Ohio Peace Officer Training Academy; the Northern Virginia Criminal Justice Academy; the United States government; the Staff Training College, Montreal, Canada; and Australia.

Peters has also served as an instructor in the Security Program, Northern Essex Community College. He is currently a member of the college's Security Advisory Board, and also a member of the American Society of Industrial Security. A member of *Who's Who in the East*, he is serving his third year on the Braintree, Massachusetts Finance Committee.

TAKAYUKI KUBOTA, inventor of the widely-adopted Kubotan, is vice president of program development for the Defensive Tactics Institute. He is also vice president and executive director, respectively, of the Defensive Tactics Institute's two sister organizations: the PR-24 International Institute and the Kubotan Institute (co-founder with John Peters).

Born in Kumamoto, Japan, in 1934, he began studying the arts of Karate and Jitsu at the age of four. His teaching career began at the age of 14 and has flourished since that time. He has been teaching police techniques for over 25 years; courses ranging from handcuffing to his world-famous baton techniques. For over 22 years he has been training law enforcement personnel in the use of batons, and in his own personal techniques known as Kubo Jitsu, or the *Pen Technique*.

Holding an eighth degree black belt in Karate, a fifth degree black belt in Aikido Jitsu, a third degree black belt in judo and a first degree black belt in Kendo, Kubota served as instructor for the Kamata-Tokyo (Japan) Police Department from 1949-1959. While there he taught Karate, baton techniques, self-defense and "tai ho jitsu". Later, with the Kamata-Tokyo Police Department, he actively participated in the day-to-day activities of the police. It was during this period that Kubota developed, tested and refined many of his techniques.

As Kubota's reputation grew, so did his teaching. From 1958 to 1964, he instructed United States Military Police and other personnel in self-defense techniques at military bases in Japan. Kubota also served as bodyguard for the United States Ambassador to Japan. In 1964, he moved to the United States, and has since trained criminal justice, military and security personnel from various federal, state and local agencies.

In 1969, the Los Angeles Police Department (LAPD) placed Kubota under contract to train its instructors at the Los Angeles Police Academy in baton, in self-defense and in apprehension techniques. In 1974, he introduced a new police baton Kendo technique to the LAPD. From October 4, through December 16, 1977, Kubota trained a special group of LAPD female police officers in his Kubotan self-defense system.

In 1974, the Federal Bureau of Investigation (FBI) sent personnel to his school to learn various self-defense and baton techniques. That same year, the FBI Academy made a 150 page manual of his techniques which is used to assist in the training of its agents, law enforcement officers and instructors. In 1975, Kubota presented the FBI with a film on knife defensive tactics.

Kubota has also been an instructor in weaponless defense in the Police Science Program at Fullerton (CA) Junior College.

Although busy instructing, Kubota has found time to write many articles and books. His publications include: *Baton Techniques and Training* (Charles C. Thomas, publisher); *The Art of Karate* (Peebles Press, publisher); plus, *Advanced PR-24 Baton Techniques, Handcuffing Techniques* and others too numerous to list. Kubota has a forthcoming book on Kubo Jitsu, a work showing the uses of the tonfa, the bo, the staff and other forms of stick fighting. He has also published several articles which have appeared in a variety of national and international magazines.

In addition to his writing, Kubota has also appeared in over 200 movies, commercials and television shows which include: *The Mechanic, The Killer Elite, MacArthur, Shaft in Africa, Operation Petticoat, Baa Baa Black Sheep*, "Dinah Shore Show" and numerous others.

A United States citizen since 1974, Kubota devotes much of his time to the teaching of Karate at his Glendale, California dojo (school). President and general instructor of the International Karate Association, he has affiliated schools throughout the world. In 1970, two of Kubota's students joined the U.S. Team in the entry to the World Tournament in Tokyo, Japan. In 1972, three of his students entered the World Tournament in Paris, France. Kubota has also had his students in other national and international tournaments.

In 1967, 1968, and 1969, personnel from the LAPD, all of whom were trained by Kubota, entered the following Police Olympic Tournaments and took first place: San Diego, California, Orange County, California and Phoenix, Arizona (individual champions in the National Olympics).

...

## DEFINITIONS

APPROPRIATE FOLLOW-UP PROCEDURES. Those techniques based upon departmental policy, rules and regulations or other legal guidelines which you select and use after effecting the arrest of an individual.

STRONG HAND. As used in this book, your gun hand. That is, if you are right handed, then your right hand is your strong hand; the opposite if you are left handed.

STRONG LEG (FOOT). As used in this book, your right leg or foot if you are right handed; the opposite if you are left handed.

WEAK HAND. As used in this book, your non-gun hand. That is, if you draw and shoot your service weapon with your right hand, then your left hand is your weak hand.

WEAK LEG (FOOT). As used in this book, the leg or foot on the opposite side of your strong side, as previously defined.

(1) USE of FORCE
chapter 9 penal
(A) defense of person

(2) be able to justify the use of force to include deadly force.

Defensive Tactics
DTI
Institute, Inc.

# CONTENTS



three things if taken away

(1) BALANCE
(2) sight
(3) BREATH

weakest part of hand

three places to stay away

CHAPTER ONE

# PERSONAL WEAPONS

In addition to the weapons issued to you by the department, you also possess many personal weapons which can be used to help defend you during a confrontation. Your personal weapons include your head, your elbow, your forearm, your hands and fingers, your knee and your foot.

Personal weapons are generally used when a firearm, a baton or a chemical agent cannot be used (e.g., crowded store, bus, etc.); when you do not have your firearm, baton or chemical agent (e.g., you've been taken hostage, or you're off duty); or when you are suddenly attacked, finding yourself unable to obtain your firearm, baton or chemical agent (e.g., you are jumped from behind, or you are unexpectedly attacked).

Your personal weapons and how they are used are described below. Learn how to use them, so that they can aid you in successfully defending yourself.

HEAD. If grabbed from the front or rear, forcefully smash your head into the attacker's face. Striking the attacker on the nose, lips, eyes and so forth should make him/her release his/her grip allowing you to use an appropriate defensive tactics technique.

ELBOW. If grabbed or choked from the rear, forcefully strike the person with the flat section of your elbow (it's just above the elbow at the base of your bicep). DO NOT USE THE TIP OF THE JOINT OF THE ELBOW AS THE ELBOW MAY BREAK. An elbow strike may be delivered to the person's head, chest, stomach, rib, abdominal and leg areas.

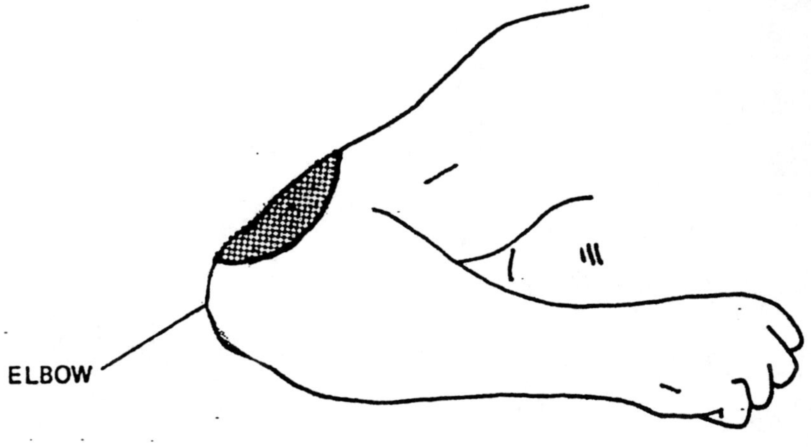

HANDS AND FINGERS. The fleshy edge of your hand can be used to "chop" or to strike the person. You can use the edge of your hand or fist to strike the person's head, shoulder, chest, arm, rib, stomach, abdominal or joint areas. The palm of your hand can also be used to strike these areas. Your fingers can be used to grasp the person's body, or to thrust into the person's eyes to temporarily blind him/her so that you can escape or use an appropriate defensive tactics movement.

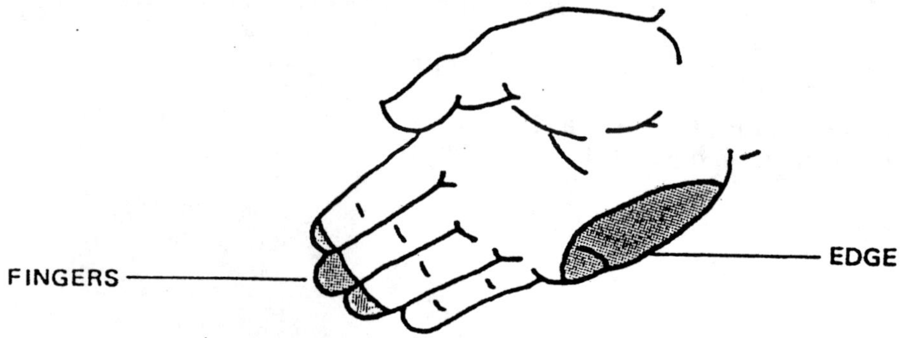


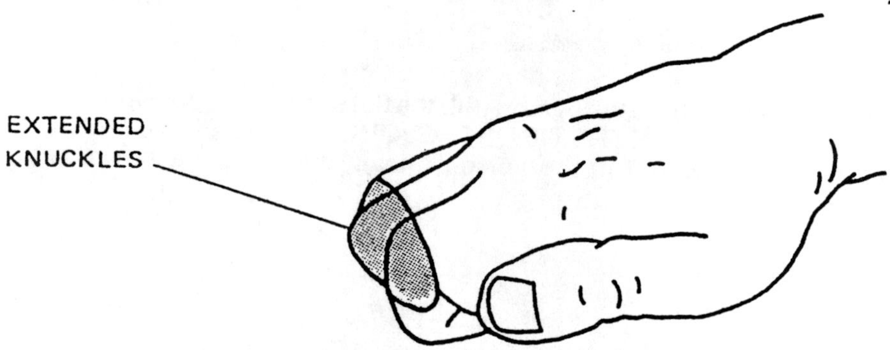


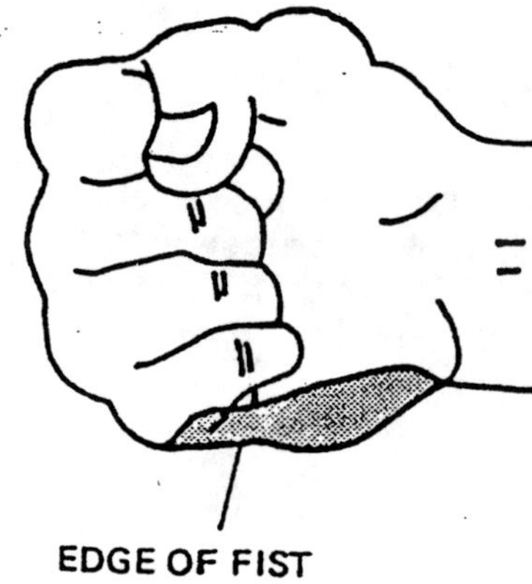


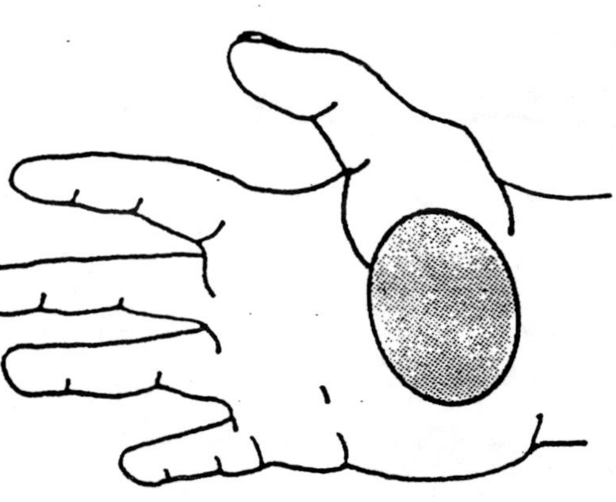
HEEL OF THE HAND

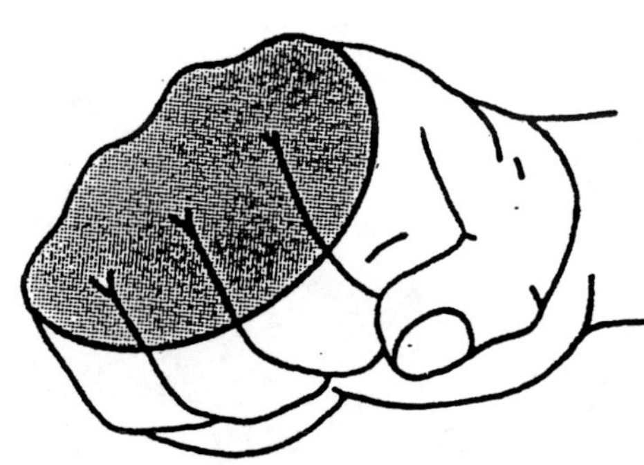
CLOSED FIST

FOREARM. The meaty portion of your forearm can be used to block punches or similar type blows. You can also use it to strike a person in the head, shoulder, chest, rib and abdominal areas.

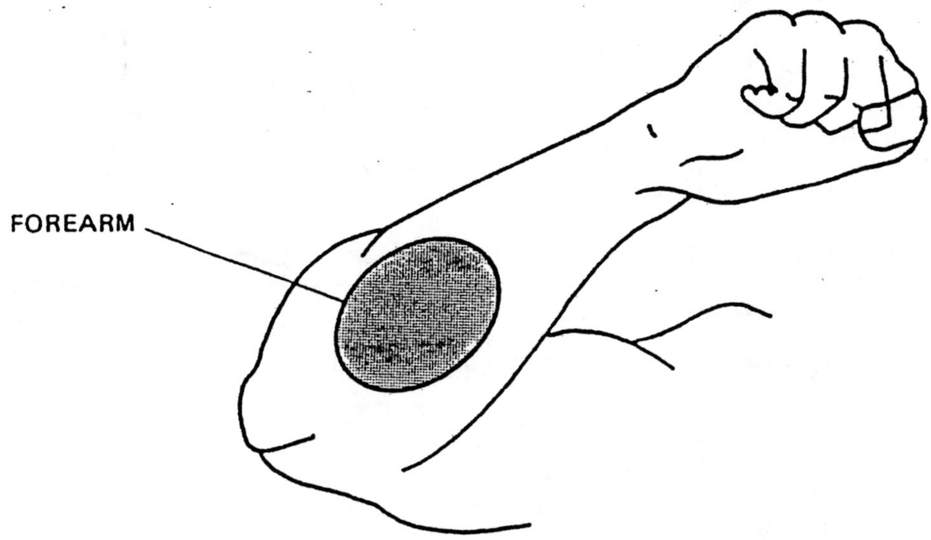


KNEE. The top of your knee (just above the knee joint) can be used to forcefully strike a person in almost any part of the body. DO NOT USE THE FRONT OR THE HINGED SECTION OF THE KNEE AS IT MAY BE BROKEN.

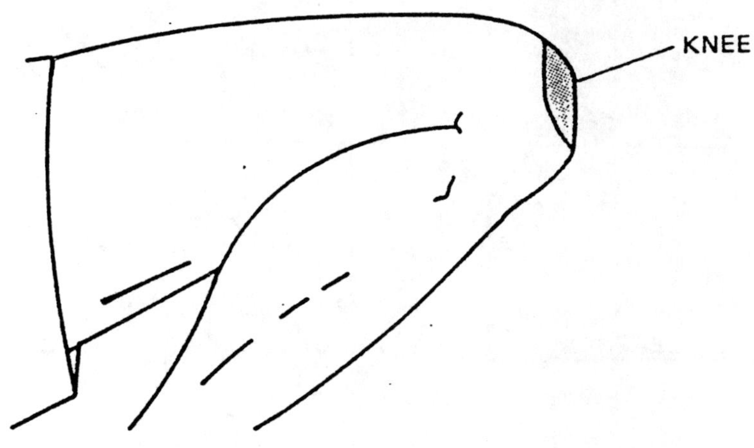


FOOT. You can use the heel of your foot to stomp on a person's foot, or use your foot (shoe) to kick the person on the shin area. In most cases, these actions will cause the person to release his/her grip.

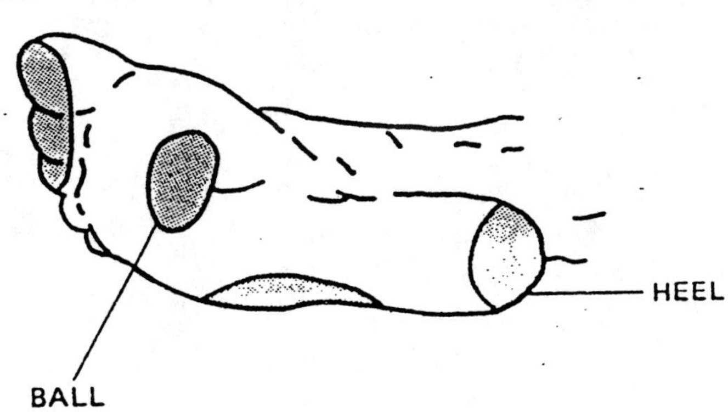

# CHAPTER TWO

## BALANCE

Most everything that you do in life begins and ends with balance. For example, you cannot walk, sit or stand if you cannot keep your balance. It is very important, therefore, that you retain good balance before, during and after a combative confrontation. Keeping good balance will help to keep you safe, and also give you greater mobility. Conversely, by keeping the suspect off balance it will minimize his/her mobility and his/her ability to fight back. You safety is once again enhanced.

BAL-1 shows the basic eight points of balance. In all, there are 360 points of balance; one for each degree of a circle. However, you need to only concern yourself with the basic eight points, since these are primary ones which you will use in your daily activites.

These points are illustrated and are discussed in BAL-2 through BAL-12.

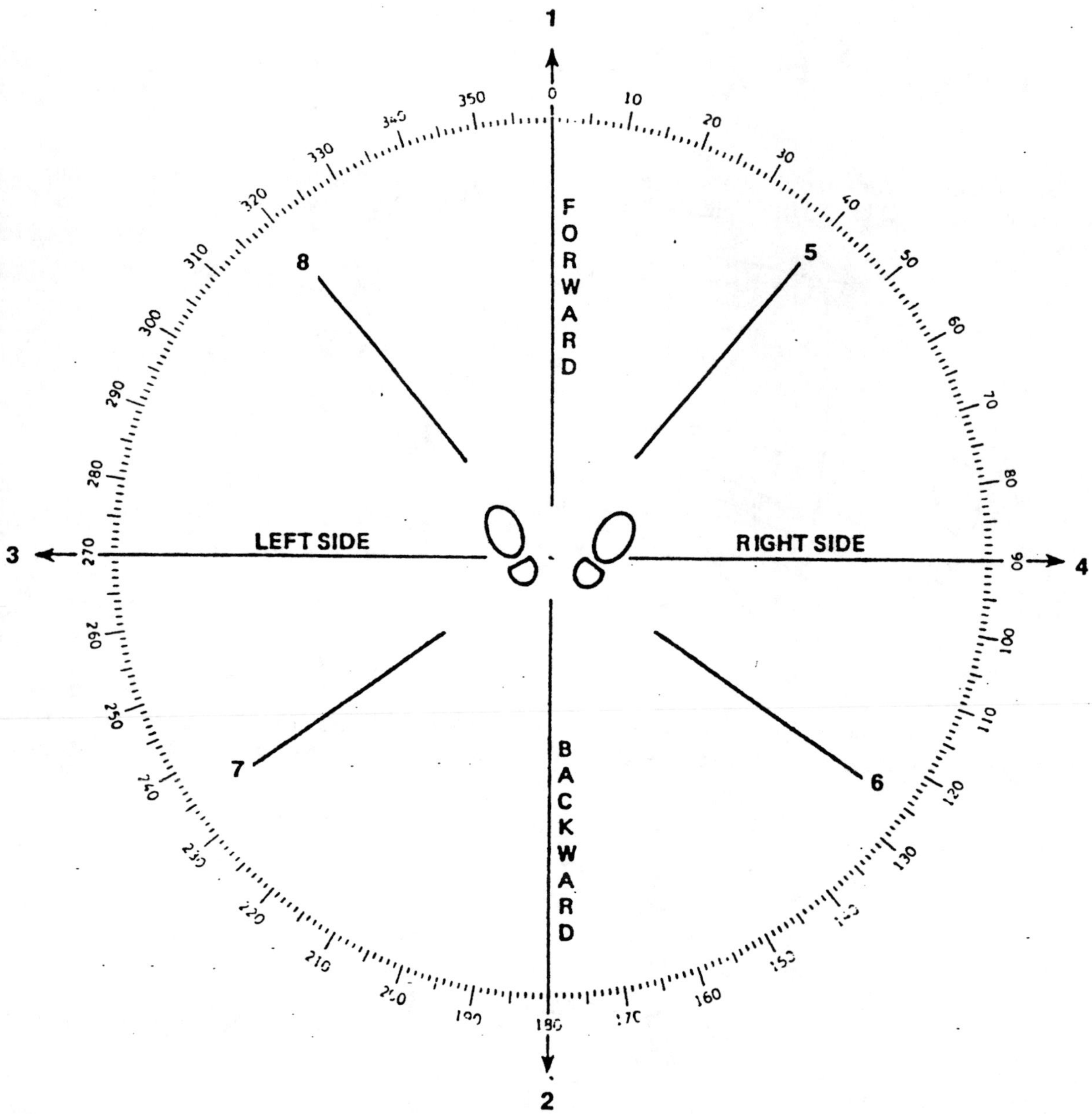

BAL-2

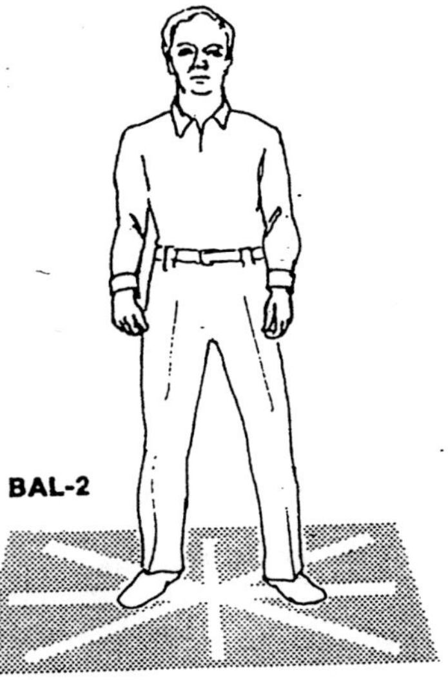

Standing with your feet shoulder width apart gives you good balance to the left and to the right sides.

BAL-3

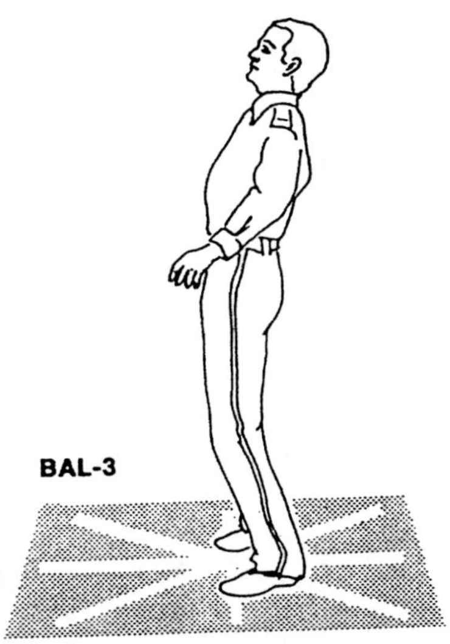

If someone should push on your chest or head, you could be easily moved backward and thus unbalanced.

BAL-4

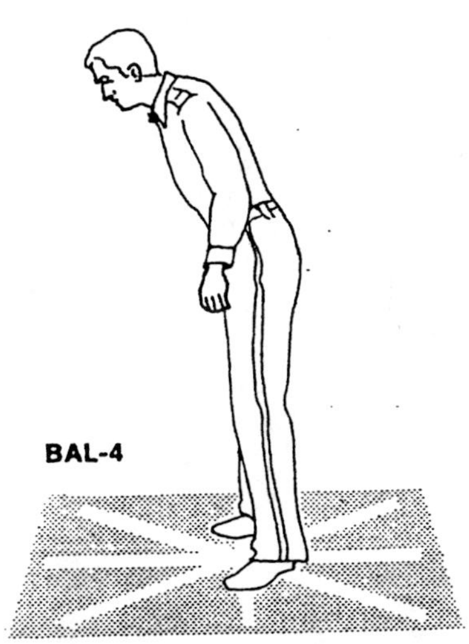

If someone were to push on your back, you could be easily moved forward and thus unbalanced.

BAL-5

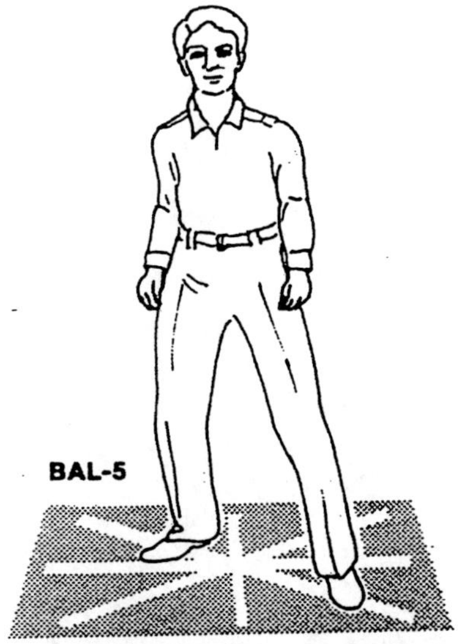

To help remedy the above situations, you could stand so that your right foot is on line 8 and your left foot is on line 6. Commonly called the "interrogation position", you have excellent balance to the right rear and left front should someone push you on your right shoulder or pull you forward by your left hand. This balance position allows you flexibility in movement by bending your left knee if someone pulls you forward, or by straightening your right leg if someone pushes you backward.

BAL-6

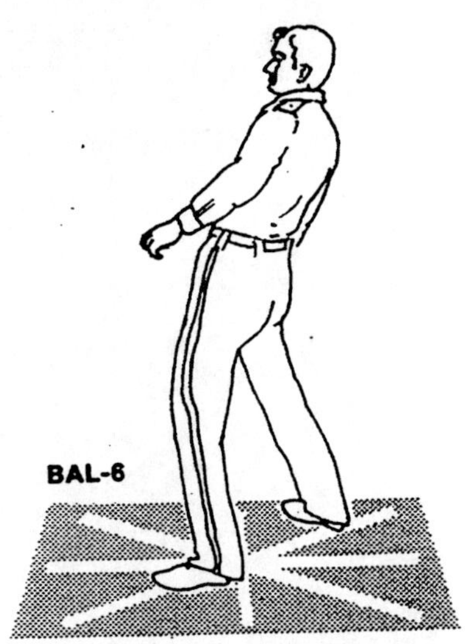

You can easily be unbalanced should someone push you on the left shoulder area in the direction of line 5.

BAL-7

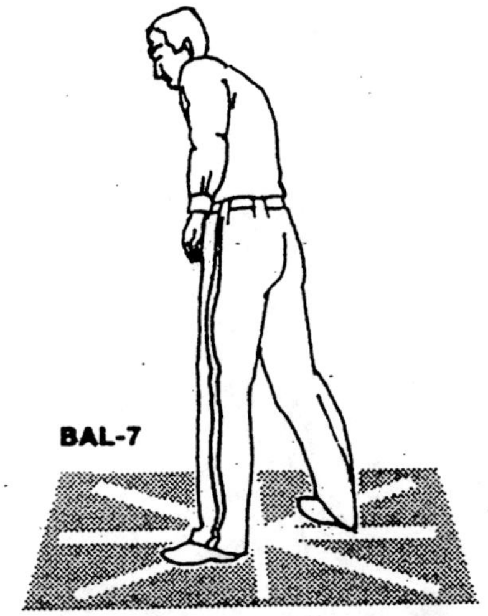

You can easily be unbalanced should someone push you on the left rear shoulder area in the direction of line 7.

BAL-8

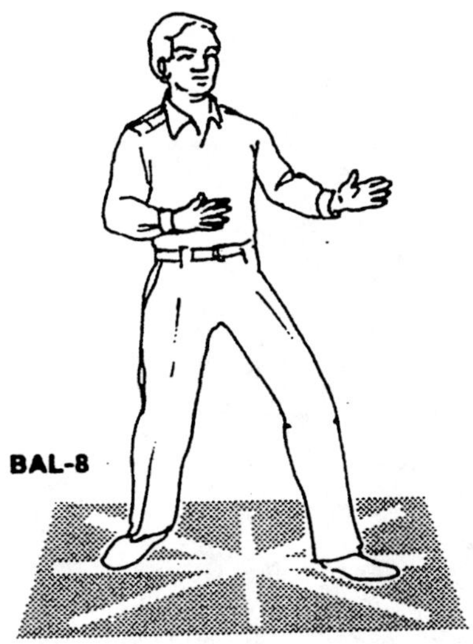

Your balance can be improved by placing your right foot on line 8, and your left foot on line 6. Here you are in a ready stance facing the suspect.

BAL-9

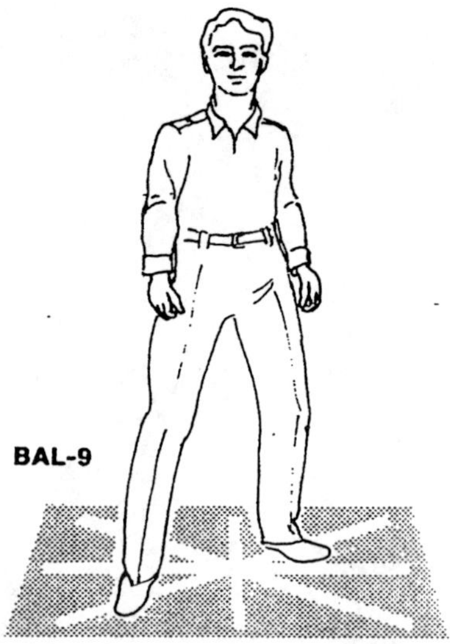

Here is the right-sided stance of BAL-5. Your right foot is on line 7, with your left foot on line 5. You have excellent balance to the left rear and to the right front should someone push you on your left shoulder or pull you forward by your right hand. This balance position allows you flexibility in movement by bending your right knee if someone pulls you forward, or by straightening your left leg if someone pushes you backward.

BAL-10

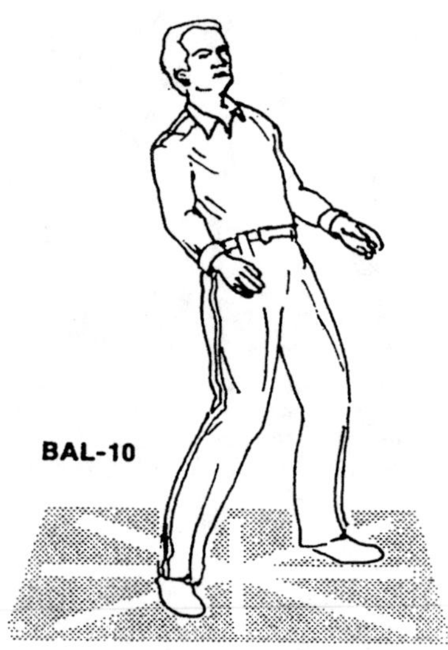

You can easily be unbalanced should someone push you on the right shoulder area in the direction of line 8.

BAL-11

You can easily by unbalanced should someone push you on the right rear shoulder area in the direction of line 6.

BAL-12

Your balance can be improved by placing your left foot on line 5, and your right foot on line 7. Here you are in a ready stance facing the suspect.

# NOMENCLATURE—HANDCUFFS

(1) when putting on or off the cuff never let go.

(2) never move a prisoner by grasping the chain

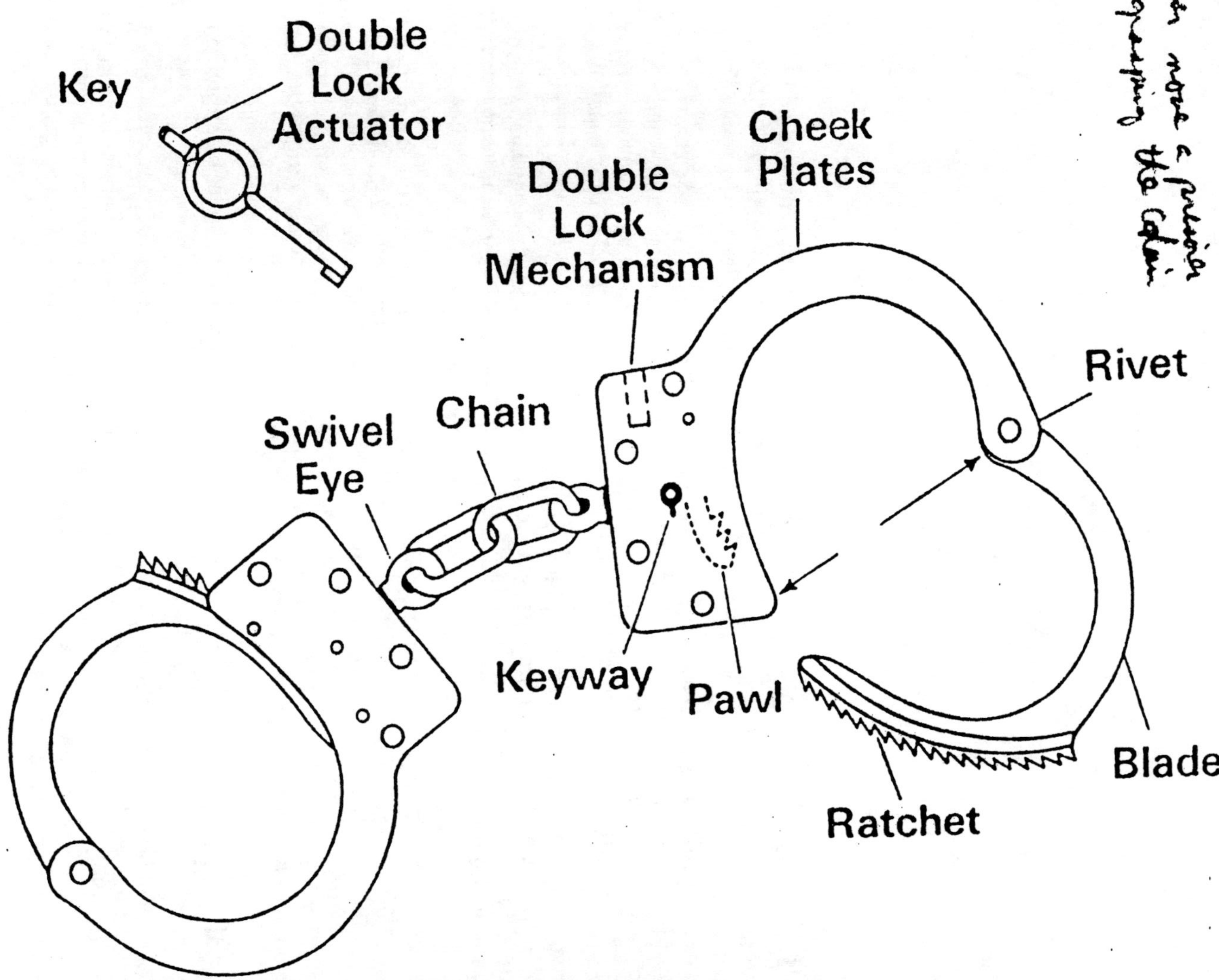

CHAPTER THREE

# HANDCUFFING AND SEARCHING

Immobilize.
Control.
Handcuff.
Search.
Transport.

Remember these five words and the order in which they appear. Some day, these guidelines may save your life. It is hoped, at the very least, that these guidelines will "thaw" your thoughts and behaviour if you are "frozen" into the traditional way of handcuffing and of searching prisoners.

Traditionally, the principle of searching the prisoner FIRST and then HANDCUFFING him/her has been taught to criminal justice, security and military personnel. Now, however, after research and a proactive movement for officer safety and survival, this principle has been discarded by progressive training academies and individuals. The primary reason for rejecting the "traditional" method is officer safety.

Most anyone who has worked in the criminal justice, security or military professions will tell you that the searching of individuals could be dangerous: you could be injured by hidden weapons; you could be attacked by the person; or you could overlook important evidence. Thus, proper handcuffing and searching guidelines are vital, and must be followed.

Immediately following an arrest, the suspect is the most dangerous and you are more prone to bodily harm. The few seconds following an arrest is when the suspect may attempt to flee, may decide to "play-along" until you give him/her an opportunity to escape, may decide to turn and shoot at you with an unseen weapon or may cooperate with you. Therefore, it is important that you quickly and safely immobilize the individual, thus severely restricting his/her mobility. This can be done through the proper positioning of the suspect, keeping him/her unbalanced as shown and described in techniques RCH-1 thru PRK-12.

After the suspect has been immobilized, you may need to control the suspect by applying a wrist lock or other restraint hold as shown in the book.

After the suspect has been immobilized and has been controlled, quickly handcuff the person. The person should be handcuffed with his/her arms behind the back, palms out (unless the person has a deformity or other disability). Handcuffing the suspect's arms behind the back will restrict his/her arm and shoulder mobility. The placement of the hands palms out, will restrict hand movement, making it almost impossible for the suspect to grasp your weapon, open the cuffs, and so forth.

When handcuffing the suspect remember to:

- NEVER let the prisoner remain balanced allowing (s)he to kick you or to move.

- NEVER handcuff the person to yourself, since you are vulnerable to severe injury from the suspect or from an escape attempt.

- NEVER handcuff a prisoner to a fixed object such as a pole or a fence jeopardizing his/her safety should an animal or other peson attack.

- ALWAYS keep your balance so that you can move quickly, and so that you won't lose your balance.
- ALWAYS remain alert for sudden movements the prisoner or other party may make.
- ALWAYS approach the suspect from the rear and at an angle so (s)he can't see you and is less able to defend against your movements. This approach also forces the suspect to "telegraph" any escape or other movements.
- ALWAYS double lock the handcuffs so that they will not become tighter on the person's wrists, and to make them more difficult to "pick."
- ALWAYS check the security of the handcuffs by pushing and by pulling on the handcuff blade.

It must be noted that there are some myths that surround handcuffing: after a prisoner is handcuffed (s)he cannot move; and, after the arrest only handcuff uncooperative persons.

If you believe these myths, forget them. Handcuffs do not immobilize. They are only a temporary restraining tool. A handcuffed person can still strike you by kicking or by swinging his/her arms. And the fact that a suspect is cooperative at the time of arrest doesn't mean that (s)he will not try to fight or to escape.

Occasionally, a prisoner may try to talk you out of handcuffing him/her.(S)he may use their sex, age or race to influence you. A woman will often use her sex as a reason against handcuffing. "Why little ol'me couldn't hurt someone as big as you," she may quip. Age is another factor. A juvenile can be just as deadly as an adult. Finally, race enters the scenario. A minority prisoner will often accuse you of being racist when you handcuff him/her. DON'T BE SWAYED. Handcuff all prisoners.

Only after you have handcuffed the suspect should you attempt to search him/her. The search should be systematic and detailed with its objectives being the location and the removal of evidence of weapons or of anything which could be used as a weapon (e.g., pens, pencils, nail clippers, keys, even band aids, as a razor blade or handcuff key may be hidden under them). You must also remember that there is no one "best" searching procedure because each arrest situation is different.

However there are a few guidelines* you should follow for safely searching an individual:

(1) NEVER permit the prisoner to remain balanced allowing him/her to kick you or to move.

(2) NEVER turn your back on the suspect so (s)he could kick you or run away.

(3) NEVER search the prisoner from the front, since (s)he could kick or knee you in the groin, stomach or leg, bite you or easily unbalance you.

(4) NEVER grasp the chain of the handcuffs to control the prisoner. The reason: See techniques HKL 1-6 pp.

(5) ALWAYS keep your balance so that you can move quickly, and so the suspect can't easily trip you.

(6) ALWAYS remain alert for sudden movements the prisoner may make, or the approach of others.

(7) ALWAYS double lock the handcuffs so that they will not become tighter on the prisoner's wrists, and to make them more difficult to "pick".

(8) ALWAYS check the security of the handcuffs by pushing and pulling on the handcuff blade.

(9) ALWAYS use one hand to conduct the search. Use your other hand to control the prisoner.

(10) ALWAYS grab and squeeze the clothing. Razor blades, knives and so forth, will not be discovered by merely "patting" the prisoner. Crushing the clothing will reduce the chances of missing items. This method may take a little longer, but it may save your life.

Transport the prisoner upon the completion of the search. After placing the prisoner in your police vehicle, tell him/her to "slump" down in the seat so tht his/her hands will be positioned where the vehicle seat and seat back are joined. The prisoner will be able to sit more comfortably with his/her hands in the "V" of the seat.

After the person is in place, fasten the seat belt or shoulder harness around the prisoner to keep him/her firmly in the seat. When you are fastening the belt or harnass be careful as the prisoner could butt you with his/her head or bite you.

If the prisoner has suffered any injuries during the arrest or complains of sickness, you should take him/her to the hospital for medical attention.

The removal of handcuffs can be as dangerous to you as in the application of them. For example, you could be kicked by the suspect, be punched with the suspect's free hand, be struck with an open handcuff or the suspect could attempt to escape while you are attempting to remove the handcuffs. Therefore, it is important for your safety to use those foregoing guidelines when removing handcuffs from a prisoner. In addition, you should request other officers to be present should the prisoner attempt to fight or to escape.

*A more detailed discussion for the handcuffing and searching of individuals can be found in HANDCUFFING TECHNIQUES by Takayuki Kubota and John G. Peters, Jr. This book may be purchased from local supply dealers or from the Defensive Tactics Institute, 15 Cedarcliff Road, Braintree, MA 02184.

Defensive Tactics DTI Institute, Inc.

**ituation:** You position a suspect against the wall so that you can conduct a "traditional" wall search

**ction:**

TWS-1

You position the suspect against a wall using the "traditional" searching position (arms and legs spread).

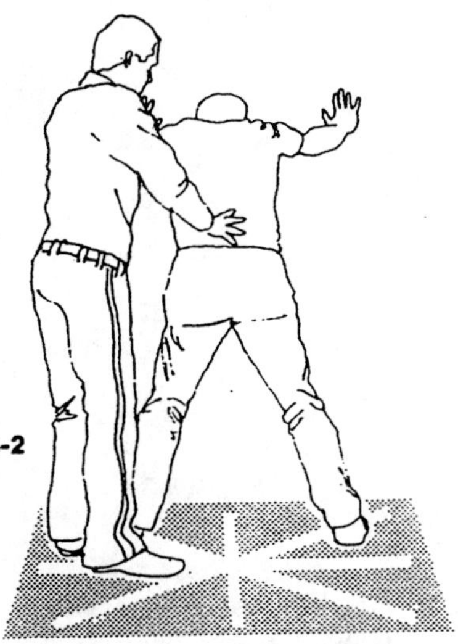

/S-2

You approach from the rear of the suspect and at an angle, placing your right hand on the small of the back. You also place your left foot in front of the suspect's left foot, so that you can "kick-out" his/her leg if necessary. You begin to search the suspect using your left hand.

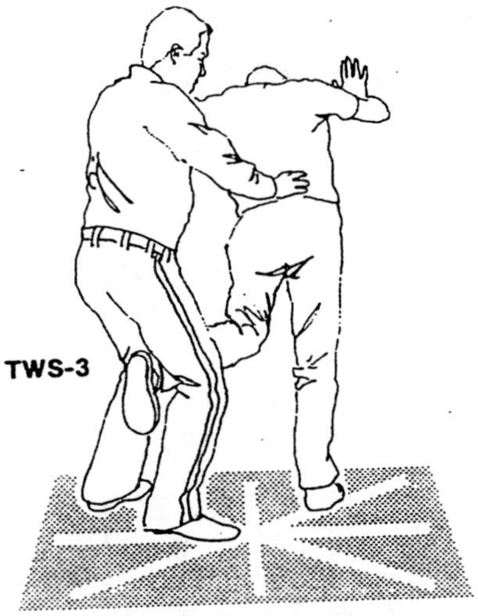

TWS-3

Balancing on his/her hands, the suspect suddenly bends his left leg kicking you in the groin with his/her left foot.

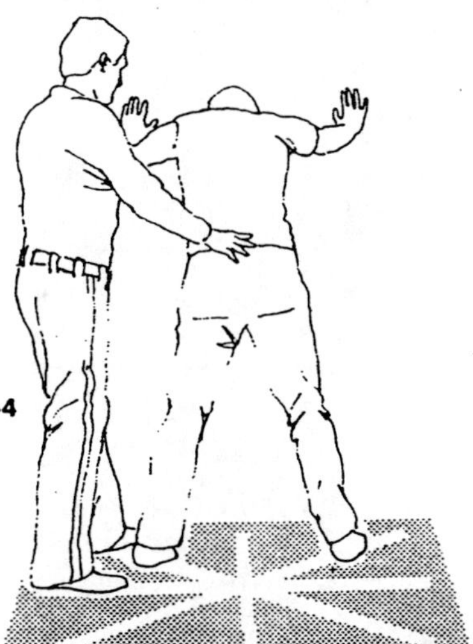

TWS-4

You have positioned the suspect as shown above in TWS-2, only this time you haven't started to search the suspect.

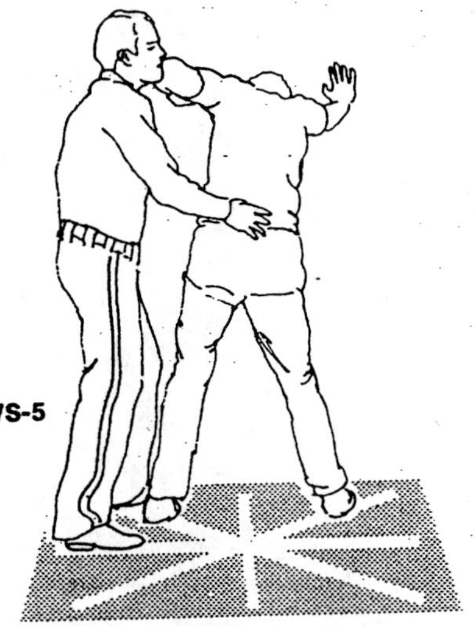

TWS-5

Balancing on his/her right hand, the suspect suddenly bends his/her left arm, striking you in the face.

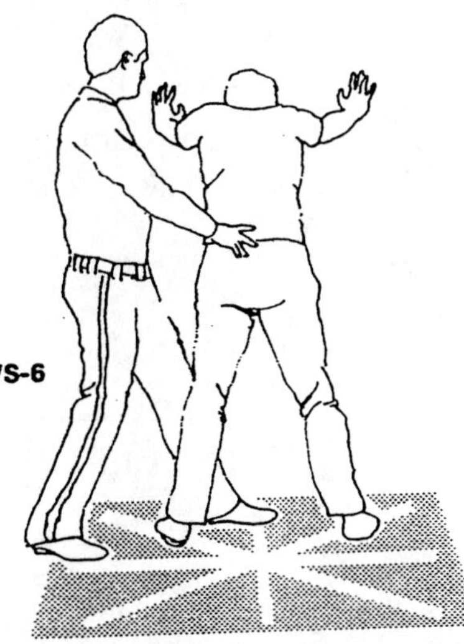

TWS-6

You have positioned the suspect as shown in TWS-4. Once again, you haven't started to search the suspect.

TWS-7

Balancing on his/her right hand, the suspect suddenly swings his/her left arm backward striking you in the face or neck area.

These are only a few of the safety problems you encounter when using the "traditional" wall search. There are few, if any, safe wall searching positions. The one shown in RCH-1 through RCH-8 is a strong technique, but should only be used when you cannot position the suspect on the ground (e.g., broken glass, water, etc.). Also remember the **handcuff first, then search** principle. Handcuffing the person after (s)he is into position will help to minimize your risk of injury.

DTI

**Situation:** You approach a suspect from behind and order him/her to stop. Since a wall is nearby, you plan to handcuff and to search the suspect using the wall as a support.

**Action:**

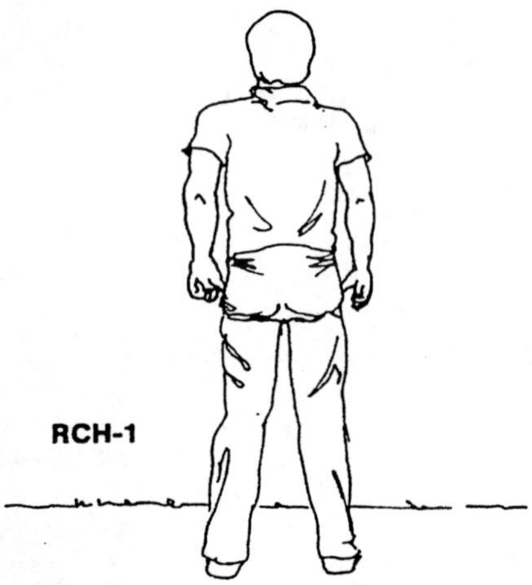

RCH-1

Approaching the suspect from behind, order the suspect to stop. Have him/her face the wall, if not already facing it.

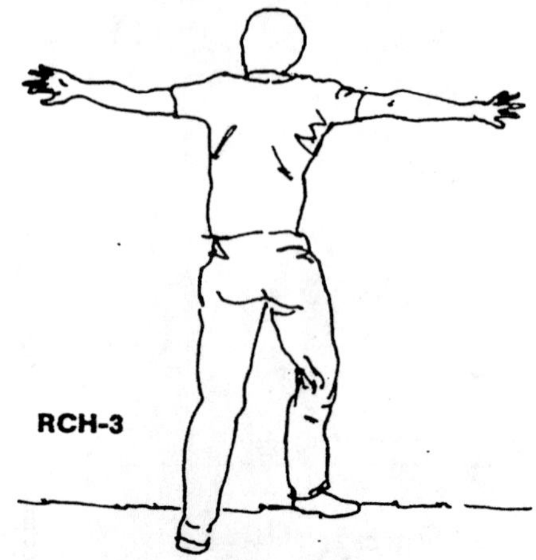

RCH-3

Next, order the suspect to turn his/her right foot to the right, placing it against the wall.

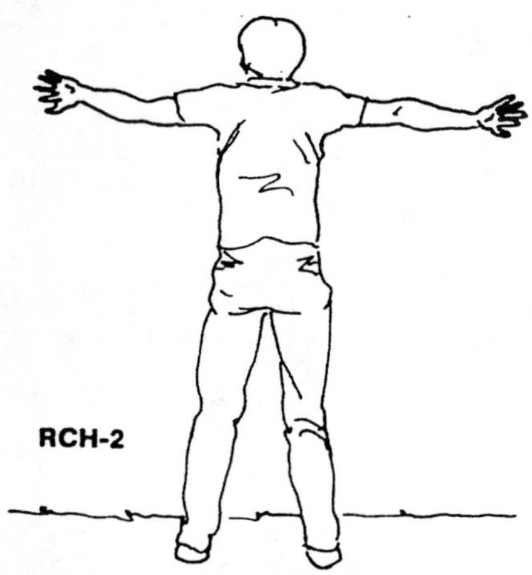

RCH-2

Order the suspect to walk against the wall. Next, order the suspect to outstretch both arms at shoulder height, with his/her hands turned palm out. These movements will "lock" the suspect's arms so that they are less mobile. Also, this position makes it very difficult for the suspect to "spring" off the wall.

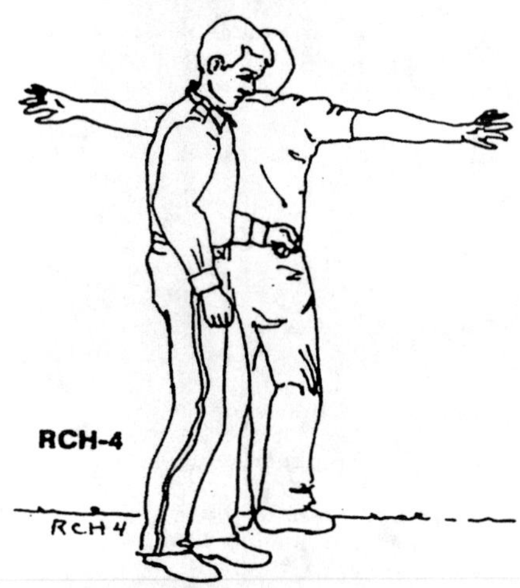


RCH-4

Next, order the suspect to turn his/her left foot to the left, placing it against the wall. Advise the suspect that you are going to place your hand on the small of the back so that (s)he doesn't fall. Next, order the suspect to place his/her heels together. Note: Placing your left hand on the small of the back will allow you to detect any movement the suspect might make.

RCH-5

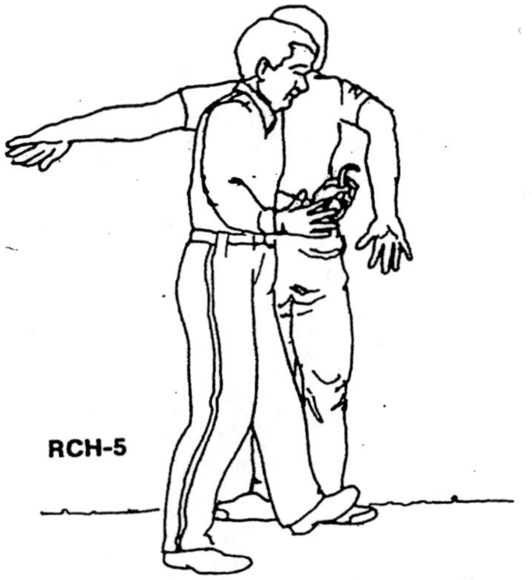

Placing your left elbow against the suspect's back, step on his/her right foot with your right foot. These movements will help to restrict the suspect's mobility. Holding the handcuffs in your left hand, order the suspect to give you his/her right hand.

RCH-6

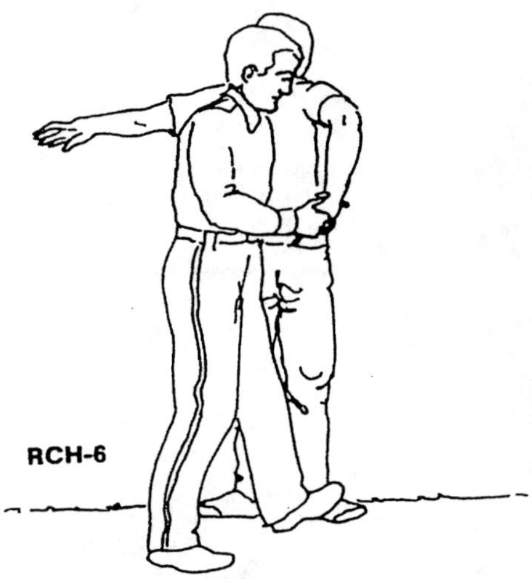

Grasping the suspect's right thumb with your right hand, handcuff his/her right wrist.

RCH-7

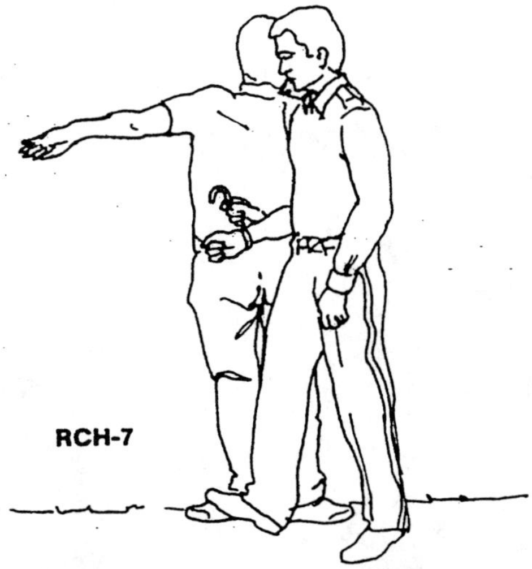

Next, place your right arm between the suspect's right arm and back. Press against the suspect's back with your right arm as you turn to your left. Holding the handcuffs in your right hand, place your right foot on the suspect's left foot. Once again, this will restrict the suspect's mobility. NOTE: You may wish to press your hips against the suspect to help hold him/her against the wall.

RCH-8

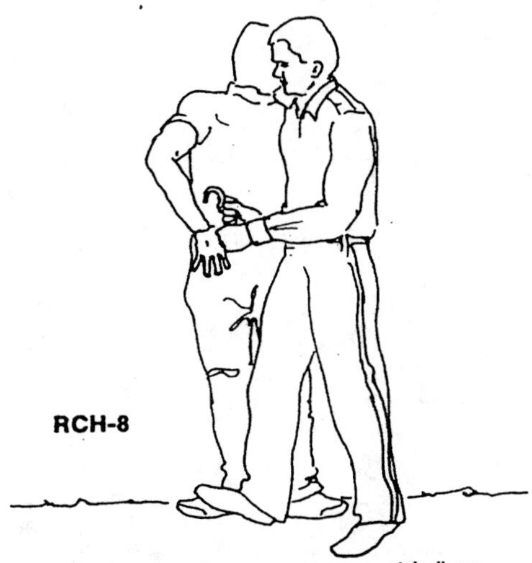

Order the suspect to give you his/her left arm. Grasping the suspect's left thumb with your left hand, handcuff his/her left wrist. You may now search the suspect or use other appropriate follow-up procedures.

NOTE: This technique may be used with a vehicle. Order the suspect to position his/her feet as shown in RCH-4 against the front or rear tire. The suspect will lie face down on the hood of the car; or you can hold him/her against the roof. If you order the person to lie face down on your hood, make sure that it isn't hot, as (s)he could suffer needless injury. This technique may be modified, too. Rather than have the suspect stand as shown in RCH-2, have him/her drop to both knees and cross both ankles. Stepping on the top ankle with your foot, continue with technique as shown.

**Situation:** You direct a suspect into a prone position so that you can handcuff and then search him/her.

**Action:**

PRL-1

Position the suspect in a prone position as shown and described in PRK-1 through PRK-5.

PRL-2

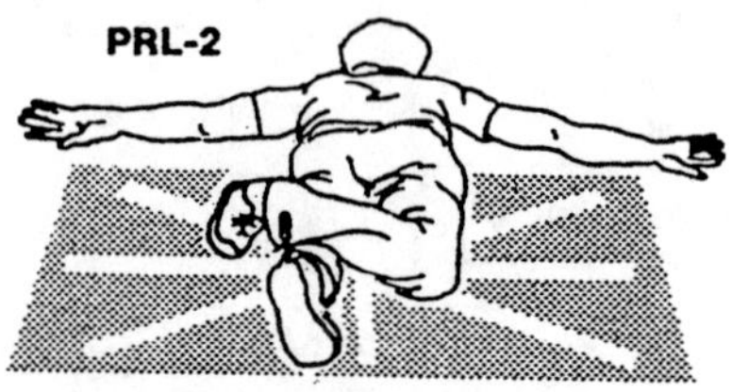

Tell the suspect to bend his/her right leg, placing the right ankle over the left knee.

PRL-3

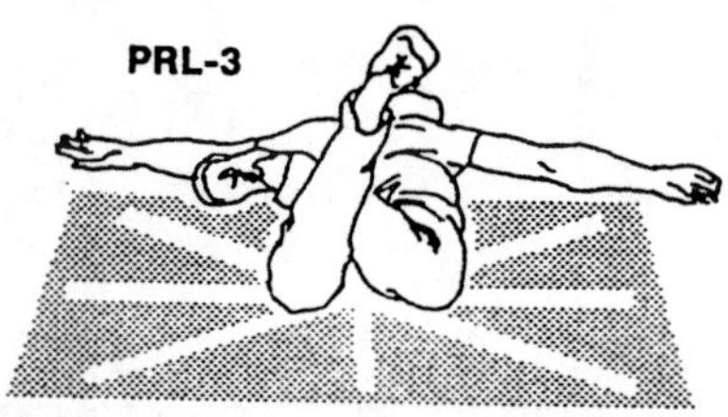

Next, tell the suspect to raise his/her left leg, bending it at the knee.

PRL-4

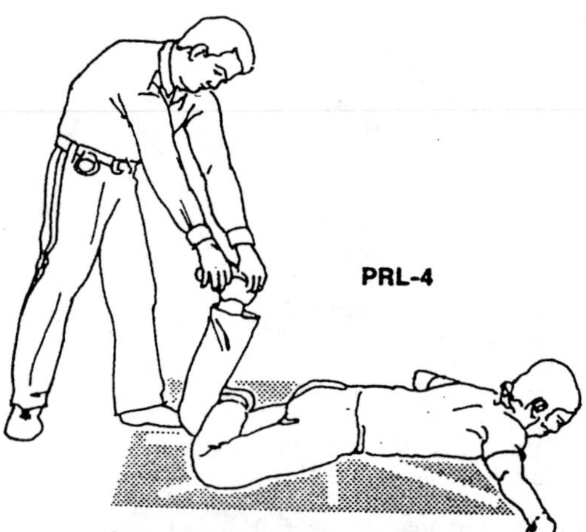

Approaching the suspect from the rear, grasp the suspect's left foot with both of your hands. This will help to control the suspect's foot so (s)he doesn't kick you.

PRL-5

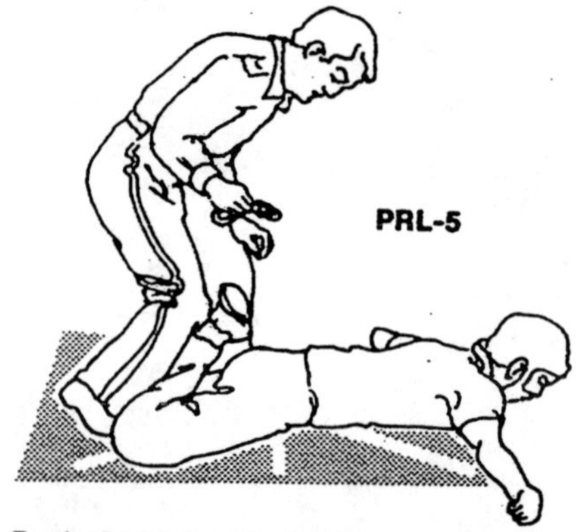

Push the suspect's foot forward with your hands until you can hold the person's left leg with your right leg. For better balance, place your left leg alongside the person's waist. Prepare to handcuff.

PRL-6

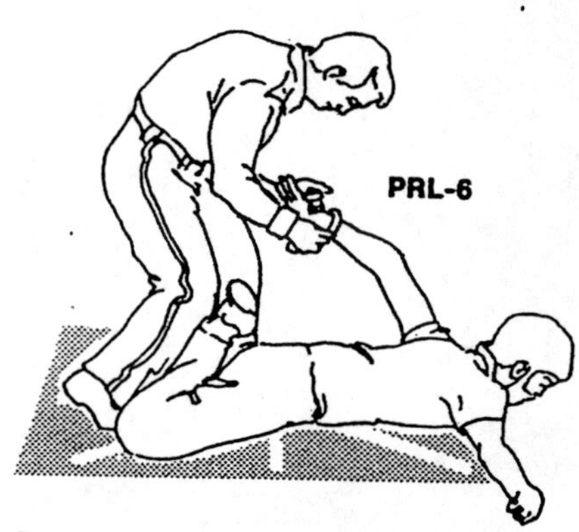

Order the suspect to give you his/her left hand. Grasping his/her left thumb with your left hand, handcuff the left wrist.

PRL-7

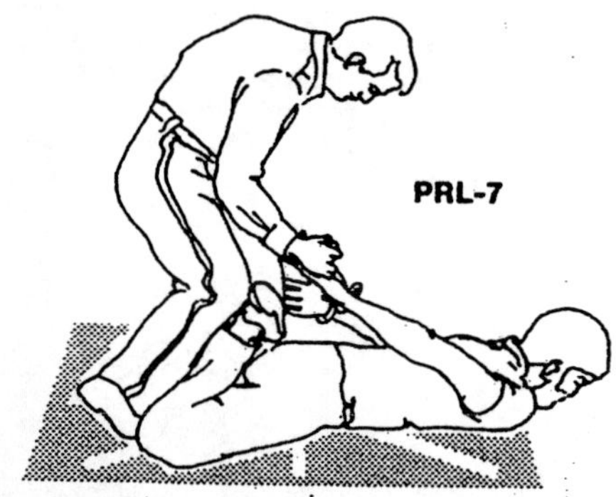

Holding onto the handcuffs with your left hand, order the suspect to give you his/her right hand. Grasping the person's right thumb with your right hand, handcuff the right wrist.

PRL-8

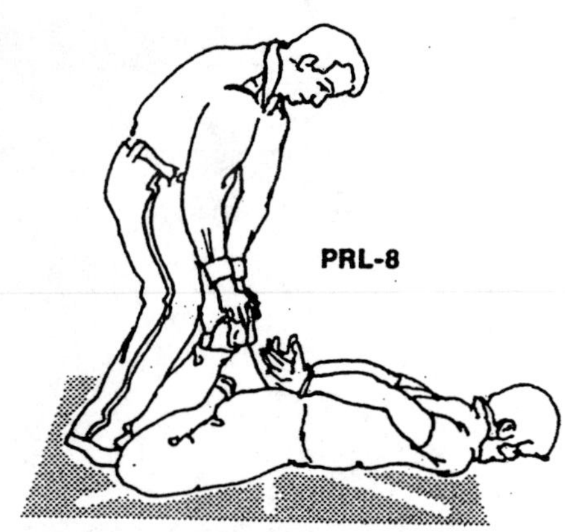

After handcuffing the suspect, once again grasp his/her left foot with both of your hands. The reason: so (s)he doesn't kick you as you release the left leg. Search the suspect or use appropriate follow-up procedures, after releasing the suspect's left leg.

## ituation:

You confront a suspect in a field, parking lot or similar situation and are forced to handcuff and to search him/her before moving them. Since there are no walls or cars nearby, you direct the suspect into a prone position.

## \ction:

PRW-1

'osition the suspect in a prone oosition as shown and described in 'RK-1 through PRK-5.

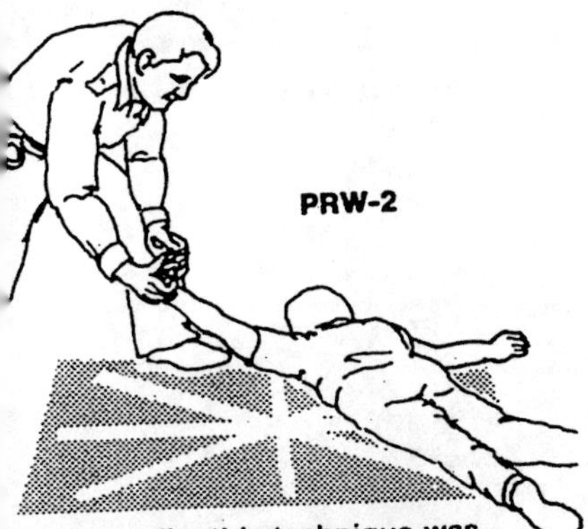

PRW-2

Traditionally, this technique was shown as follows. You would approach the suspect from an angle, grasping his/her hand with both of your hands. Next, you would slightly lift the suspect's arm and hand upward.

PRW-3

As you attempted to lift the suspect's arm upward in an effort to fold it behind him/her, many times, the suspect could roll into you, striking you in the face with his/her fist. To help remedy this problem, use the techniques as shown in PRW-4 through PRW-8.

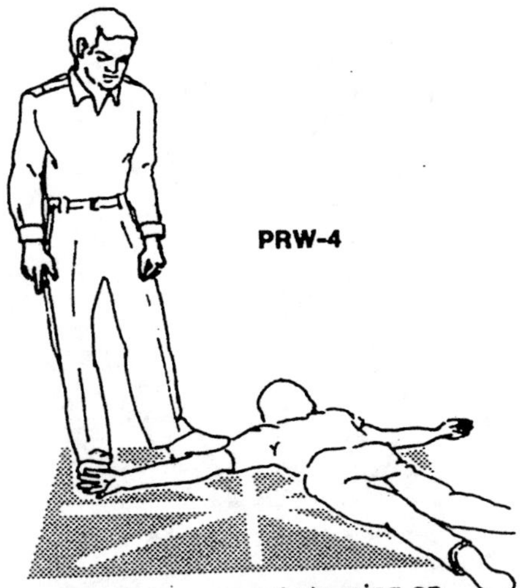

PRW-4

Approach the suspect stepping on his/her tricep area with your left foot. This action will help to keep him/her from rolling into you.

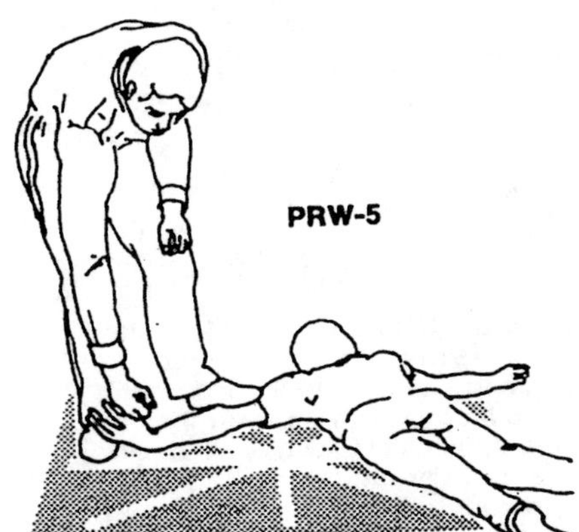

PRW-5

Bending forward at the waist, grasp the suspect's thumb using your right hand.

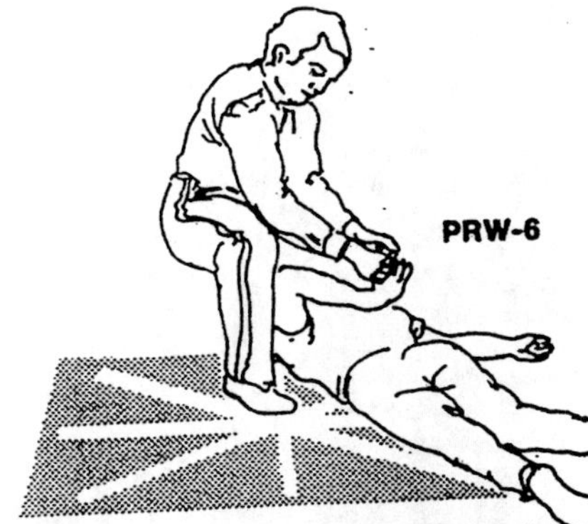

PRW-6

Having grasped the suspect's thumb, quickly fold his/her arm behind the back. NOTE: As you begin to fold the person's arm, remove your left foot from the tricep area. The reasons: to let the arm move, and to prevent injury to the suspect.

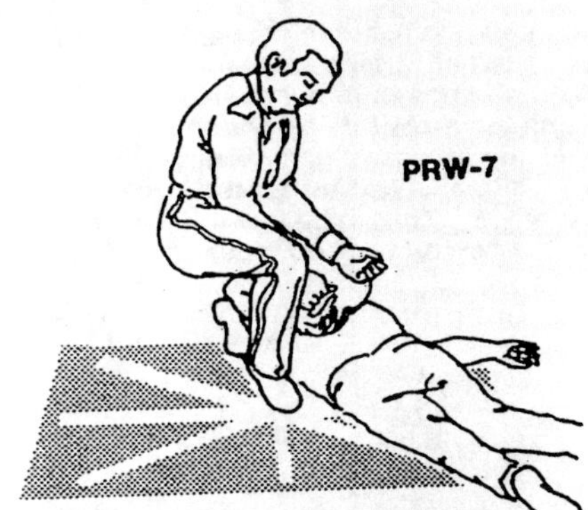

PRW-7

After the person's arm is folded behind the back, place your left knee on the suspect's left shoulder blade. This action will help to control the suspect's movement. Also, position your right leg to the outside of the suspect's left arm for better control.

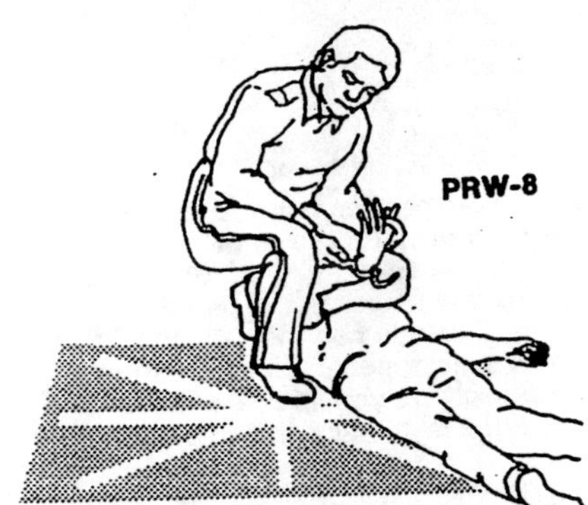

PRW-8

Lifting the suspect's left hand upward, handcuff that wrist. Next, tell the suspect to give you his right hand; handcuff that wrist. Search the suspect or use appropriate follow-up procedures.

**Situation:** You confront a suspect in a field, parking lot or similar location and are forced to handcuff and search him/her before moving them. Since there are no walls or cars nearby, you direct the suspect into a prone position.

**Action:**

PRK-1

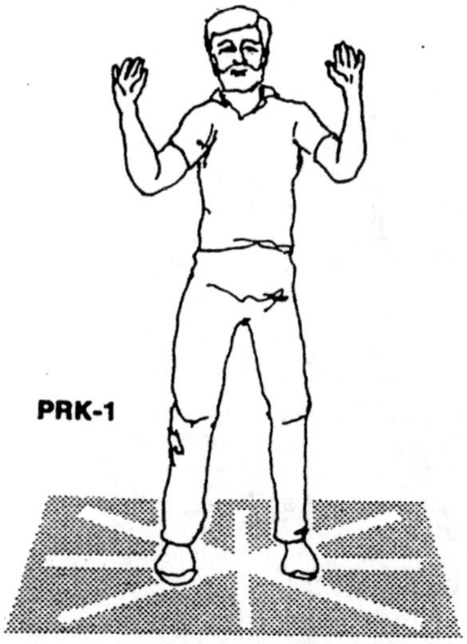

When you confront the suspect, order him/her to face you and to raise both arms high overhead. Raising the arms this height should reveal any bulges (e.g., a weapon) in the waistband. Next, order the person to turn 360°. This will allow you to view the person from all sides.

PRK-2

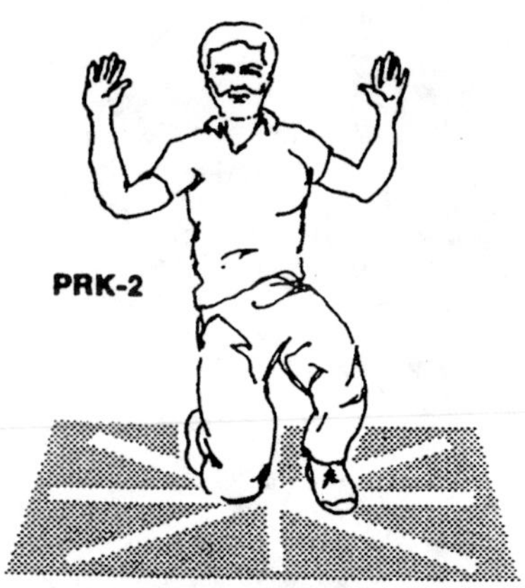

With the suspect facing you, order him/her to drop on the right knee. Having the suspect drop on one knee at a time will place you in better control. Also you can monitor the suspect's movements. Finally, should the suspect fall, you will be able to see if (s)he is actually falling or is pulling a firearm.

PRK-3

Next, order the suspect to place his/her left knee on the ground.

PRK-4

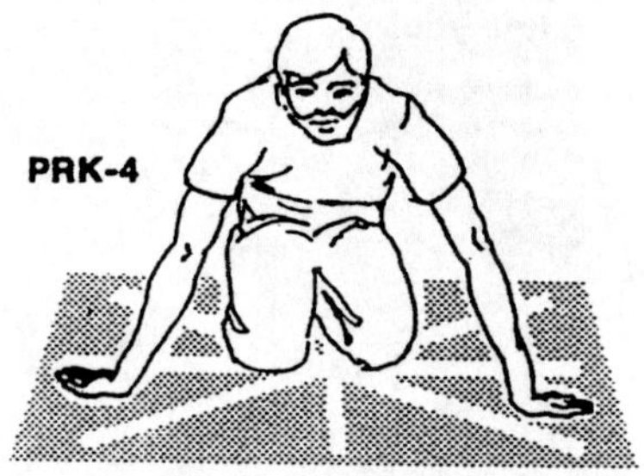

Next, order the suspect to place the tops of his/her hands on the ground. Placing the tops of the hands on the ground minimizes the use of the hands. After the suspect's hands are in place, order him/her to lie down on the ground.

PRK-5

Order the suspect to place both arms away from his/her body, palms upward. Both arms should be at shoulder height. These movements will "lock" the suspect's elbow and wrist restricting their mobility. After the suspect is in position, walk to the rear of the suspect.

PRK-6

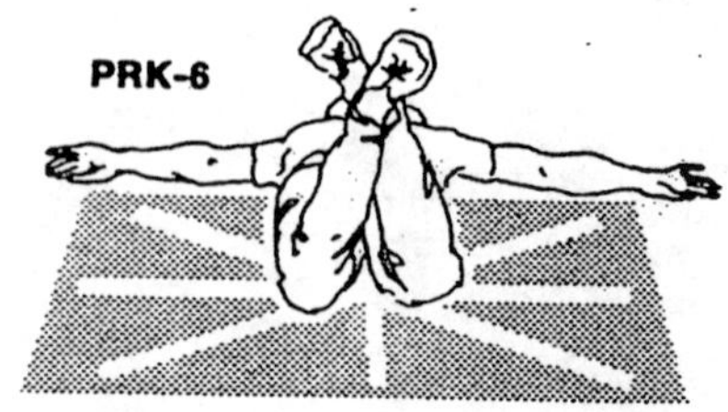

Order the suspect to bend his/her legs at the knee, crossing both ankles.

PRK-7

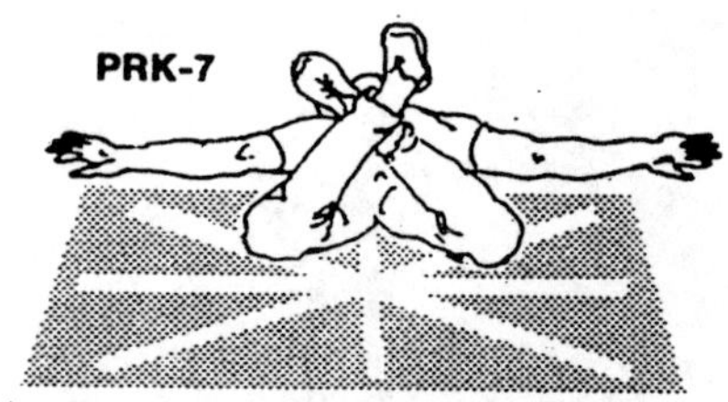

Next, order the suspect to spread both knees. This action will reduce the strength in the person's legs.

PRK-8

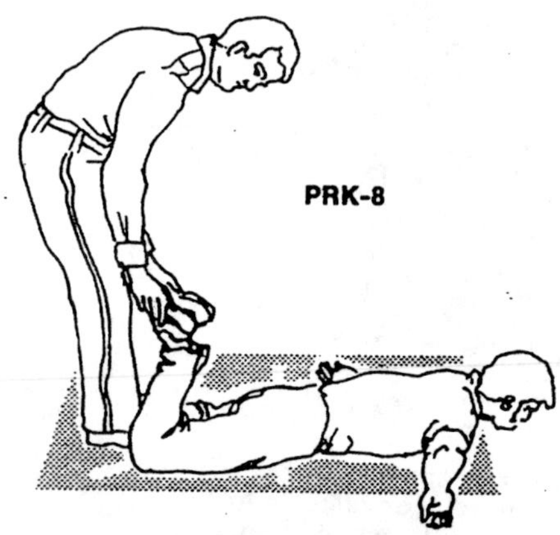

Approaching the suspect from the rear, grasp a foot with each hand. This will allow you to detect any sudden movements, and to also minimize being kicked. Push both feet toward the person's buttocks.

**PRK-9**

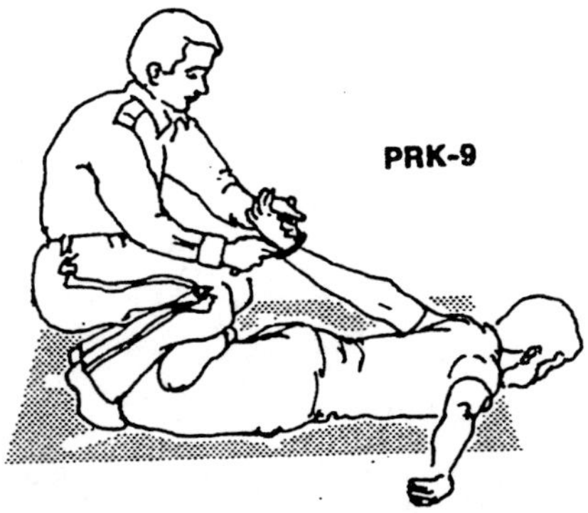

Kneel on the suspect's feet with your knees. For more support, you may grasp the suspect's belt with one of your hands.

**PRK-10**

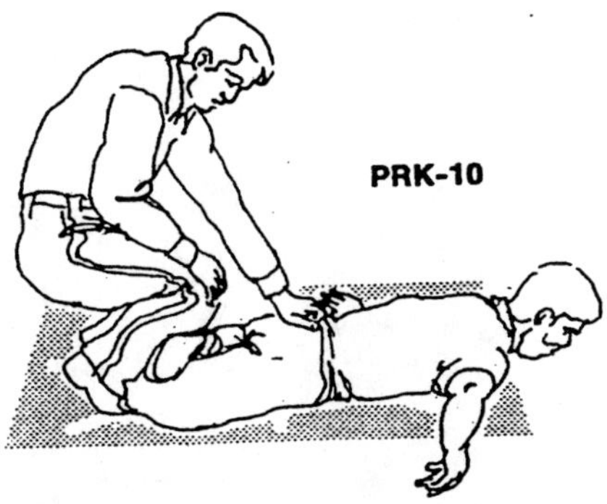

Order the suspect to give you his/her left arm. Grasping the suspect's left thumb with your left hand, handcuff the left wrist.

**PRK-11**

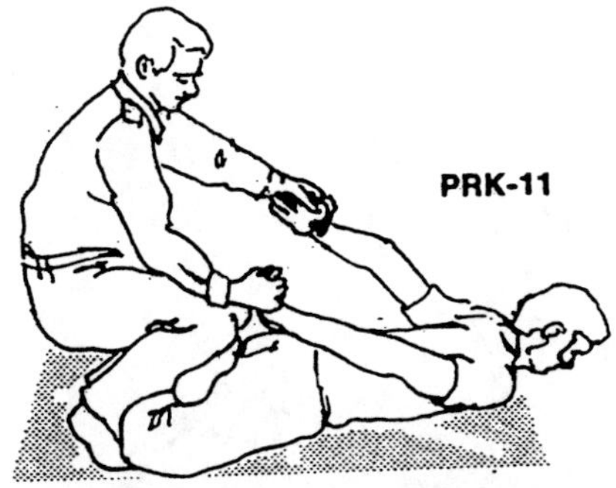

Holding onto the handcuffs with your left hand, order the suspect to give you his/her right hand. Grasping the person's right thumb with your right hand, handcuff the right wrist.

**PRK-12**

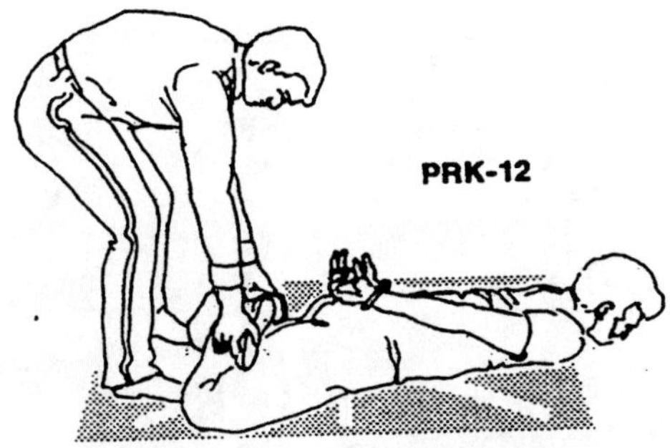

After handcuffing the suspect, once again grasp his/her feet with your hands. The reason: so (s)he doesn't kick you as you release the legs. Search the suspect or use appropriate follow-up procedures, after releasing the suspect's legs.

**Situation:** You attempt to move a handcuffed prisoner by grasping the handcuff chain.

**Action:**

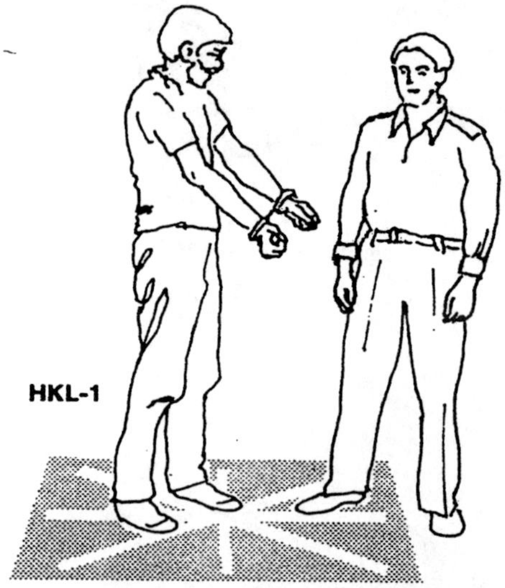

HKL-1

You approach a handcuffed prisoner in preparation of moving him/her to another place.

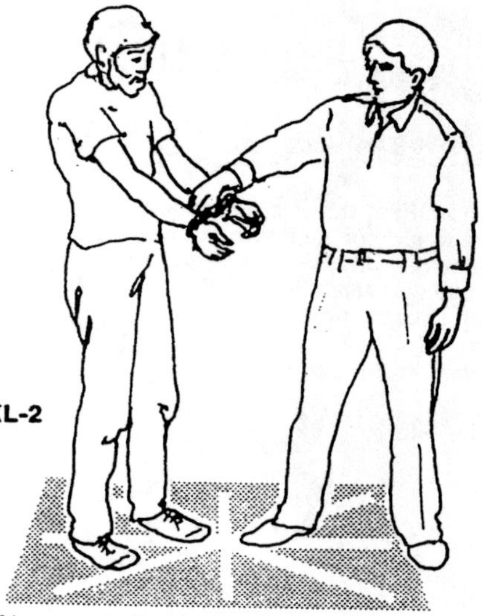

HKL-2

You reach for the handcuff chain so that you can both lead and control the prisoner.

HKL-3

As you reach out with your right hand, the prisoner suddenly wraps the handcuff chain around your right wrist.

HKL-4

Using a scissors-type motion, the prisoner applies pain to your wirst by squeezing and rotating the handcuffs. (S)he also lifts your arm upward, in preparation for a takedown.

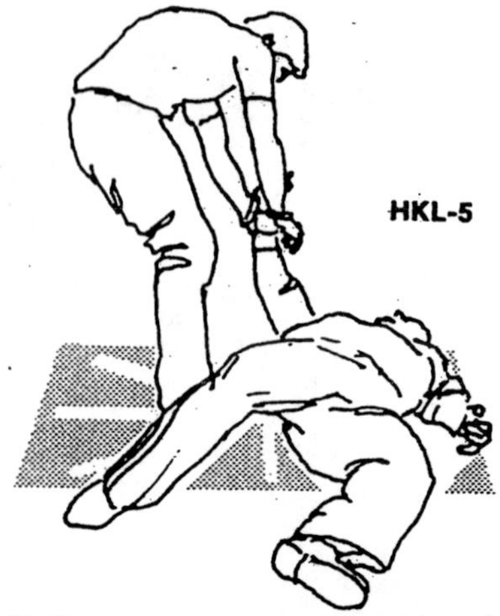

HKL-5

Pulling your arm backward (past your head) and to the outside, (s)he forces you to the ground.

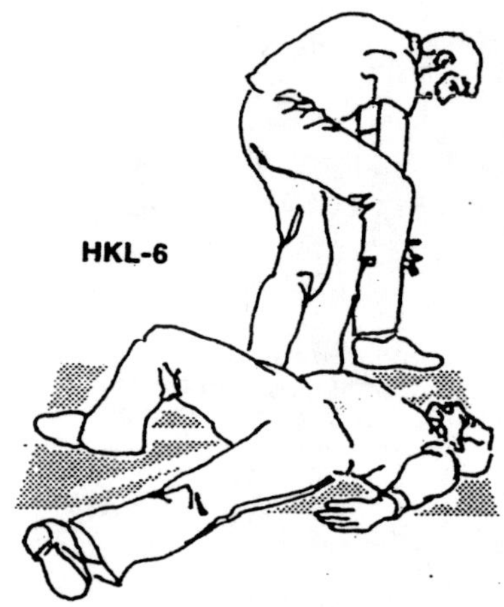

HKL-6

After you are lying on the ground, the prisoner may kick you in the throat or remove your firearm. NOTE: This technique illustrates the reason why you should never attempt to lead a person who is handcuffed by the handcuff chain. A handcuffed person can apply this technique on you whether (s)he is handcuffed in front or back, palms facing in or out.

DTI

# CHAPTER FOUR: CHOKE DEFENSES

This section contains numerous escape and restraining techniques should you be choked by another person. Since a choke can quickly render you unconscious allowing the person to virtually do anything to you, your defensive technique must be promptly executed.

We have offered you a selection of various defensive techniques which you can use in many different situations. Select and practice the ones you like best. After all, you never know when you may need to use them.

## Situation:

You are being choked from the front by a person who has grasped you around the neck and the throat with his/her hands. You have decided to use the "V" wedge technique which was shown to you in recruit school.

## Action:

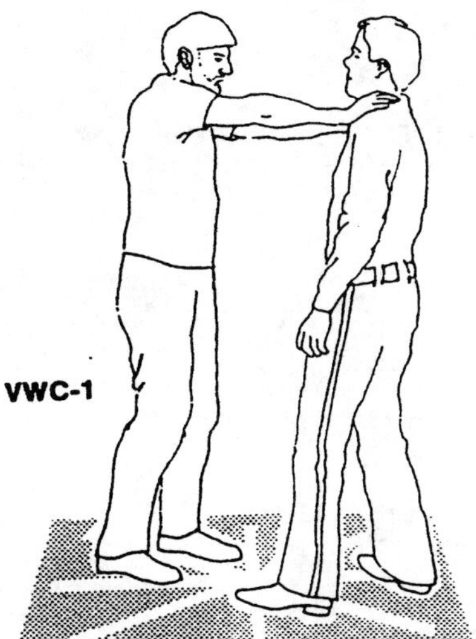

VWC-1

A person begins to choke you from the front by placing his/her hands around your throat and neck.

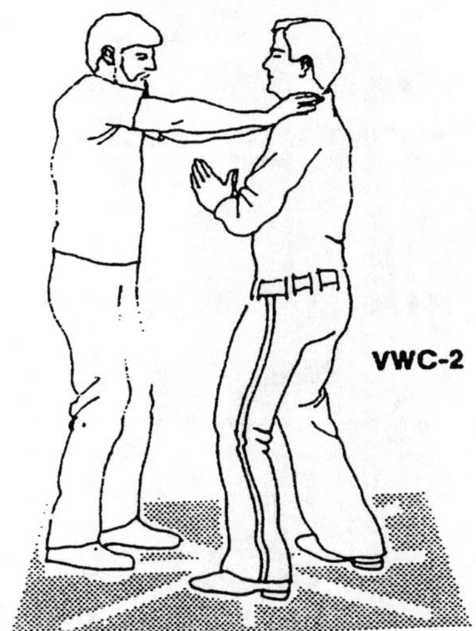

VWC-2

Remembering the "V" wedge technique which was shown to you in recruit school, you put the palms of your hands together in preparation to separate the attacker's arms by thrusting your arms between his/her arms.

VWC-3

Thrusting your arms upward your forearms stop when they strike the attacker's forearms. Repeated tries also fail. Why?

This is one of the most overrated techniques. It will generally work in the classroom where your partner isn't choking you very hard. However, when the attacker's forearms are tight because (s)he is squeezing your throat, seldom will you be able to separate his/her arms using the "V" wedge. This is especially true if you are of small stature.

Unlike the "V" wedge, the following choke defenses will work, if properly applied. They have been street-proven and will work regardless of your physical size.

**Situation:** You are being choked from the front by a person who has grasped you around the neck and the throat with his/her hands.

**Action:**

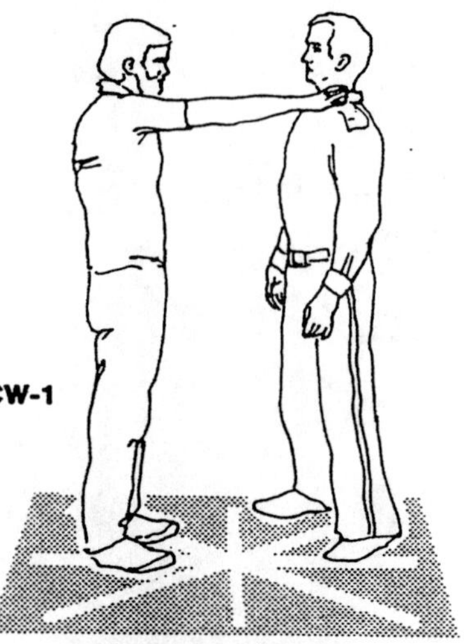

FCW-1

A person begins to choke you from the front by placing his/her hands around your neck and throat.

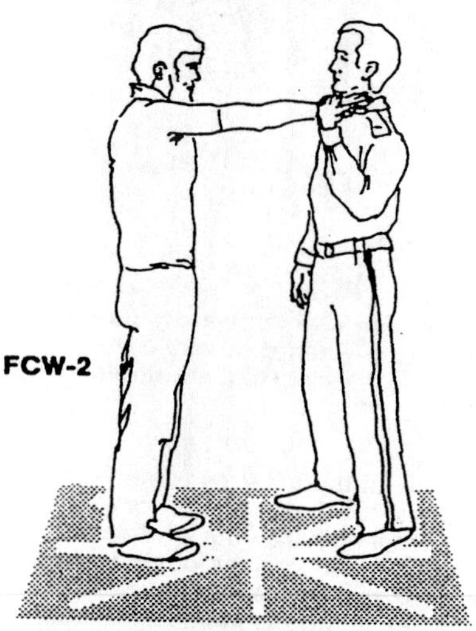

FCW-2

Grasp the attacker's left wrist using your left hand. NOTE: Grasping the wrist is not intended to produce pain, only to control it.

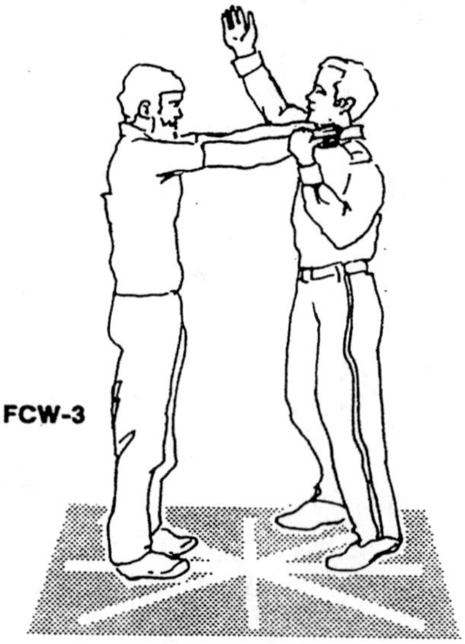

FCW-3

Raise your right arm so that your hand is over your head.

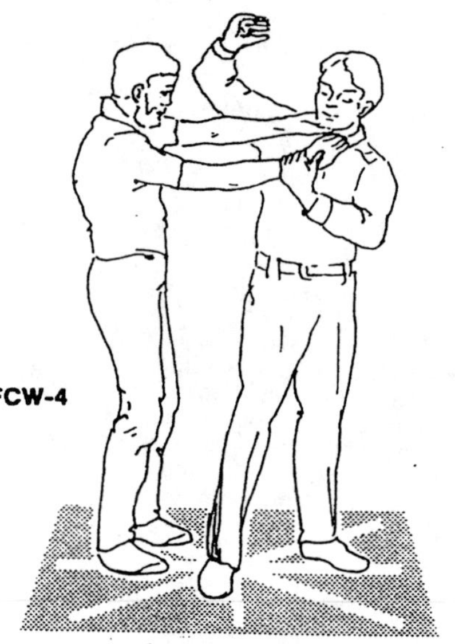

FCW-4

Holding the person's left wrist with your left hand, bring your right arm over the person' arms. Simultaneously, turn to the left, placing your right foot in front of his/her right foot.

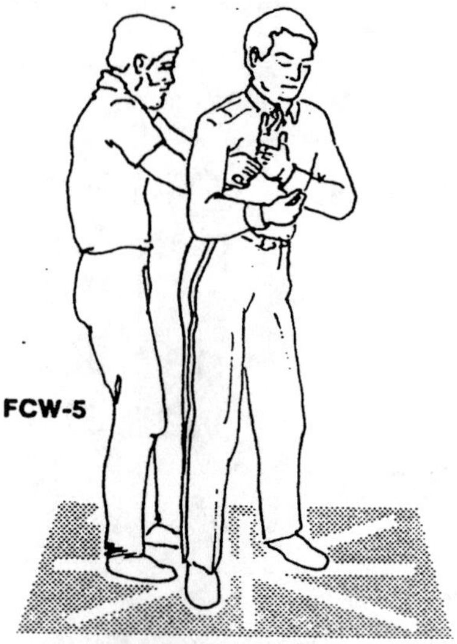

FCW-5

While maintaining good balance, pin the person's arms against your body by clamping your right arm over his/her two arms.

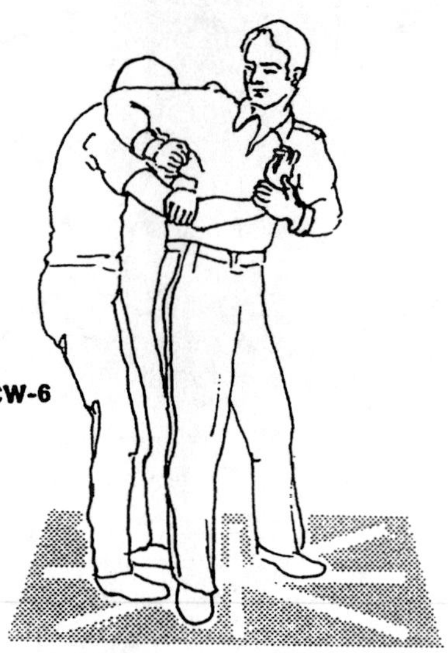

FCW-6

Forcefully deliver an elbow strike into the person's facial area. Use appropriate follow-up procedures.

DTI

**Situation:** You are being choked from the front by a person who has grasped you around the neck and the throat with his/her hands.

**Action:**

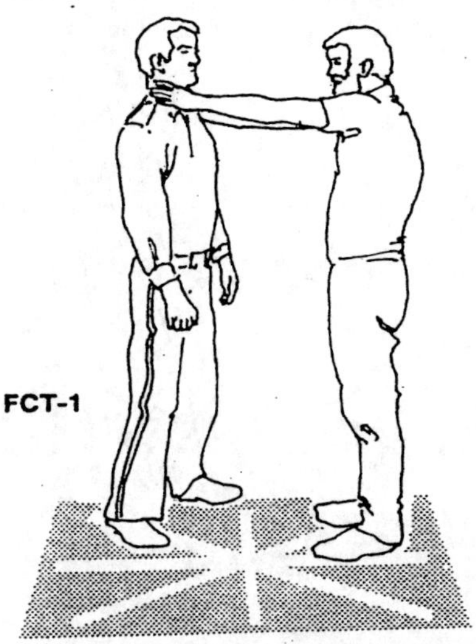

FCT-1

A person begins to choke you from the front by placing his/her hands around your throat and neck.

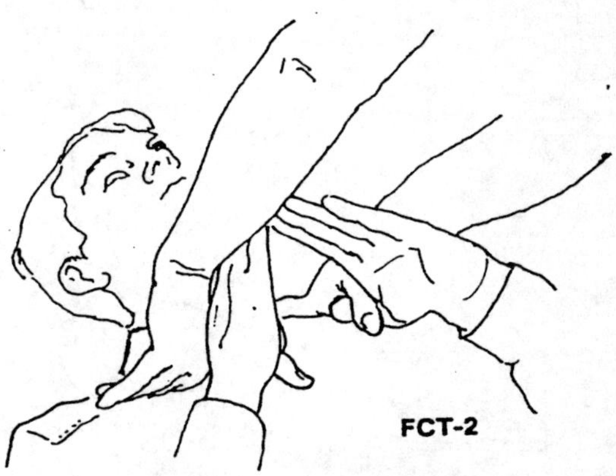

FCT-2

Quickly, grasp the person's thumbs with your hands. Bending slightly forward at the waist will force the person's hands away from your throat, making the thumbs easier to grasp.

FCT-3

Forcefully, pull the person's thumbs and arms downward, causing the person's knees to bend.

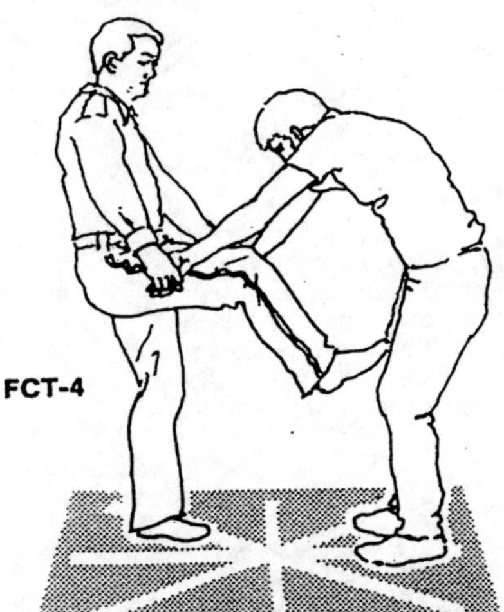

FCT-4

If necessary, kick the person in the lower abdominal area with your right foot. Use appropriate follow-up procedures.

**Situation:** You are being choked from the front by a person who has grasped you around the neck and the throat with his/her hands.

**Action:**

FCD-1

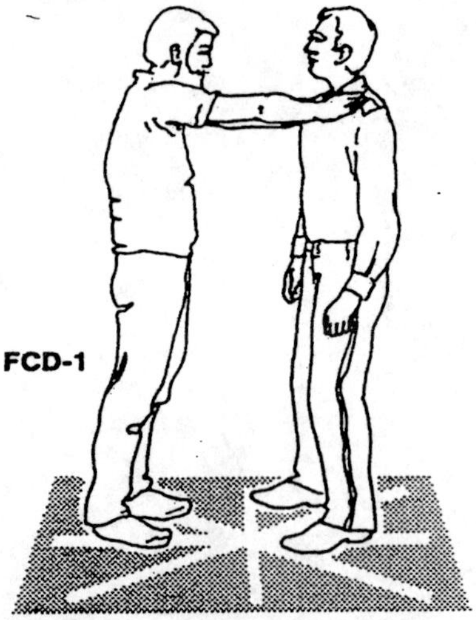

A person begins to choke you from the front by placing his/her hands around your throat and neck.

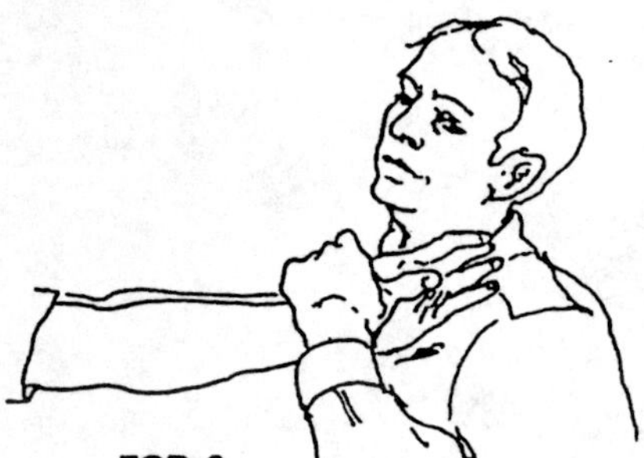

FCD-2

Immediately, grasp the person's right thumb and hand using your left hand. Your fingers should grasp the "drumstick" of the thumb while your left thumb is placed on the top of the hand, just below the middle knuckle.

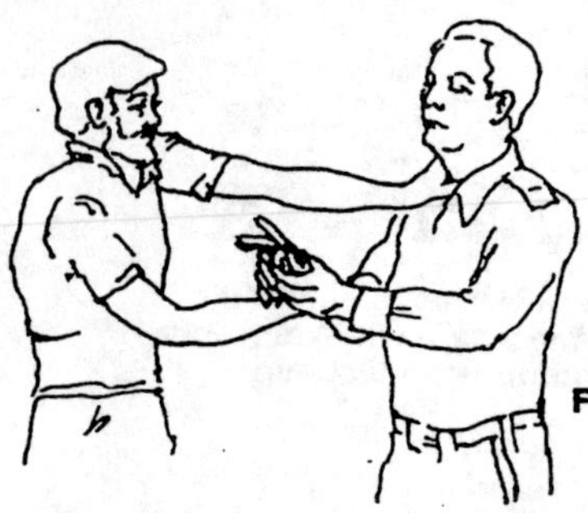

FCD-3

Stepping back with your left leg, peel the attacker's right hand from your neck. Quickly, grasp the attacker's right hand with your right hand, and begin to apply pressure to the wrist.

FCD-4

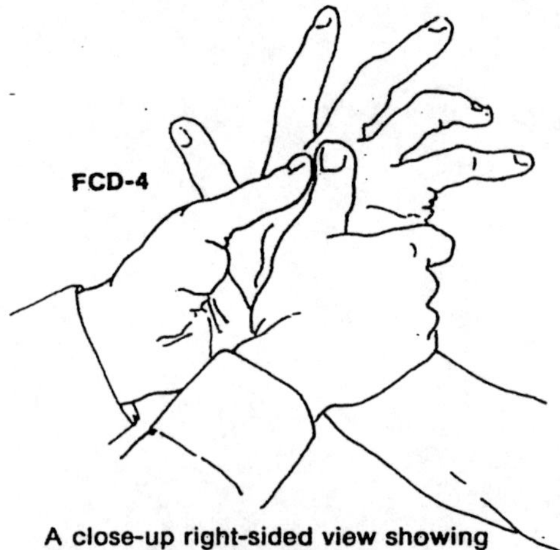

A close-up right-sided view showing the proper position of your right hand. Your right fingers are grasping the fleshy side of the person's right-hand, with your thumb positioned at the center knuckle.

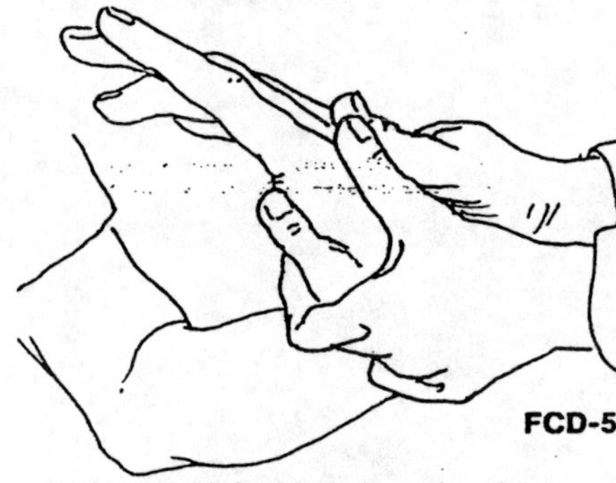

FCD-5

A close-up left-sided view showing the proper position of your left hand. Your left fingers are grasping the "drumstick" of the thumb, with your left thumb positioned at the center knuckle.

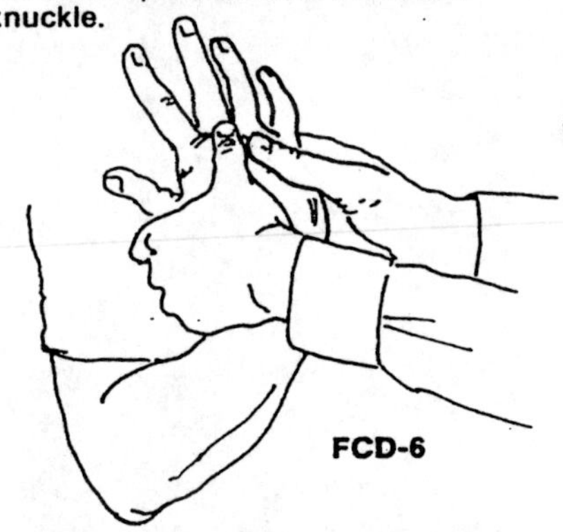

FCD-6

A close-up frontal view showing the proper positioning of your thumbs. Both thumbs are positioned together on the top of the person's right hand, just below the third knuckle. This position will let you exert maximum leverage to the person's hand. Apply pressure to the person's hand by pushing the hand backward and to the outside. Continue the pressure until the person falls to the ground. Remember to keep the attacker's right hand and wrist turned outward and to the left. The reasons: to create pain; to off-balance the person, and to prevent him/her from placing the right fingers against the shoulder area, thus voiding the technique.

FCD-7

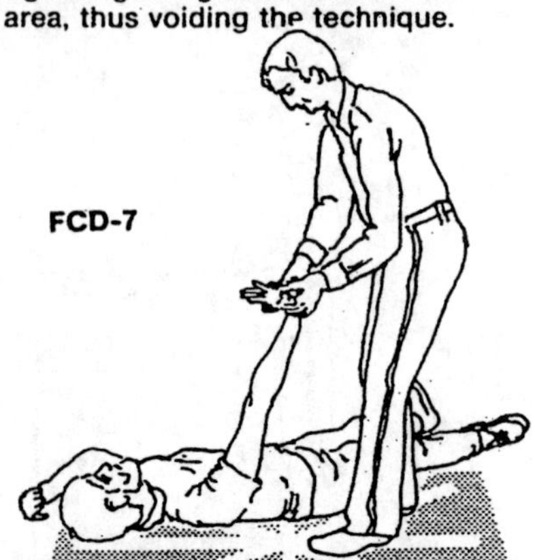

Continue to exert pressure until the person falls onto the ground. After (s)he is on the ground, keep the person's arm straight by pulling up on the right hand. Keeping the arm straight will aid you in positioning the person for handcuffing.

FCD-8

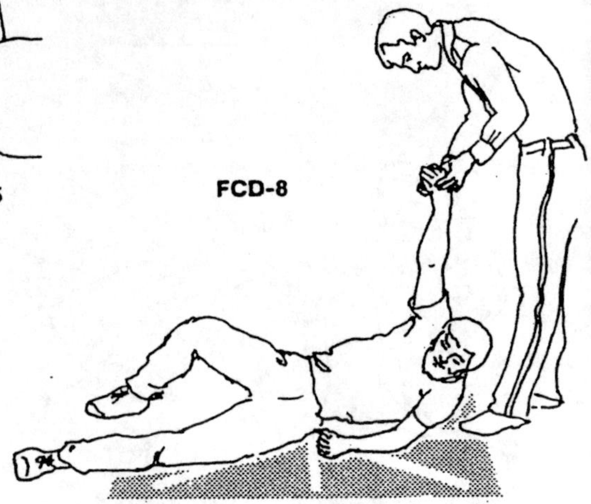

Quickly, walk to your left which will begin to roll the person onto his/her stomach. Keep his/her right arm straight as you walk.

FCD-9

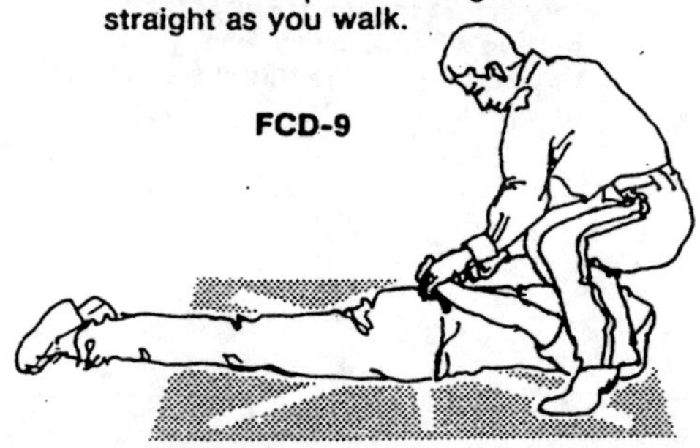

Having rolled the person onto his/her stomach, kneel on the right shoulderblade area with your right knee. This will help to keep the person's chest and shoulder area restrained. Bend the person's arm--at the elbow--so that you can handcuff the right wrist, then the left wrist. Use appropriate follow-up procedures.

**Situation:** You are being choked from the front by a person who has grasped you around the neck and throat with his/her hands.

**Action:**

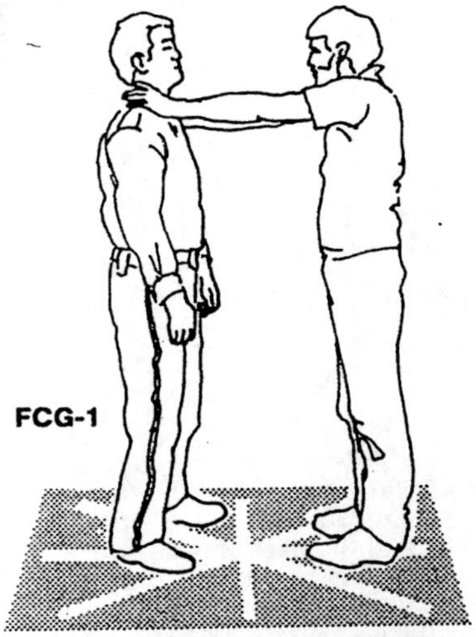

FCG-1

A person begins to choke you from the front by placing his/her hands around your throat and neck.

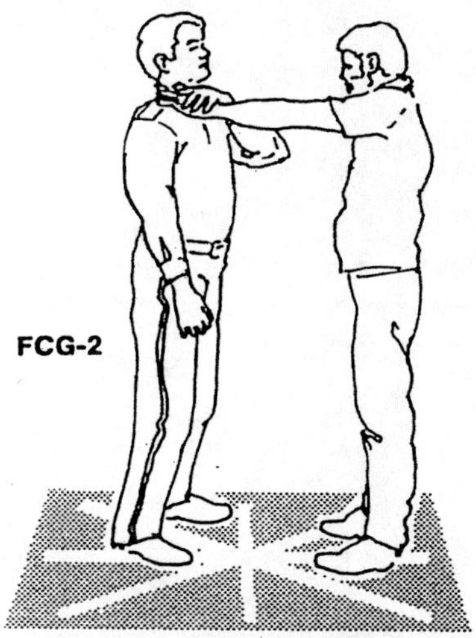

FCG-2

Quickly, grasp the person's left hand with your left hand, by reaching under the person's right arm.

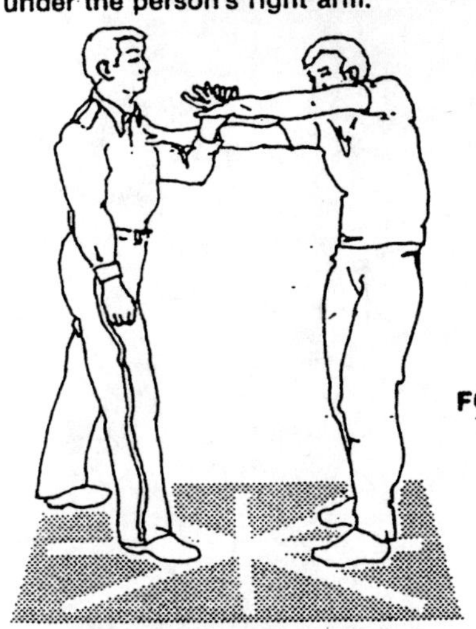

FCG-3

Stepping backward with your left foot, peel the person's left hand from your neck by twisting it counterclockwise. Turn the person's hand until you can see the palm.

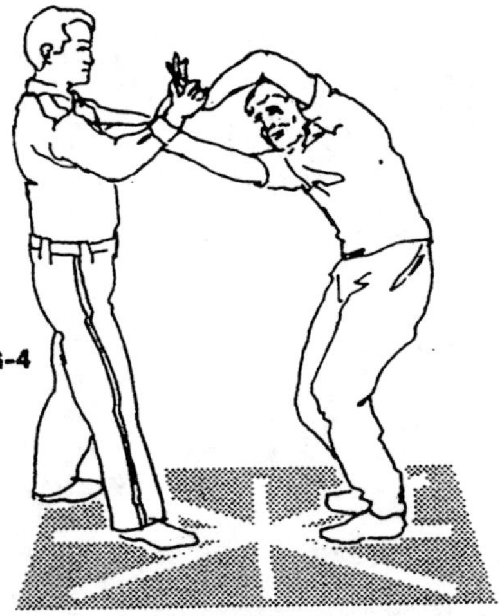

FCG-4

Quickly, grasp the person's left thumb—"microphone style"—with your right hand.

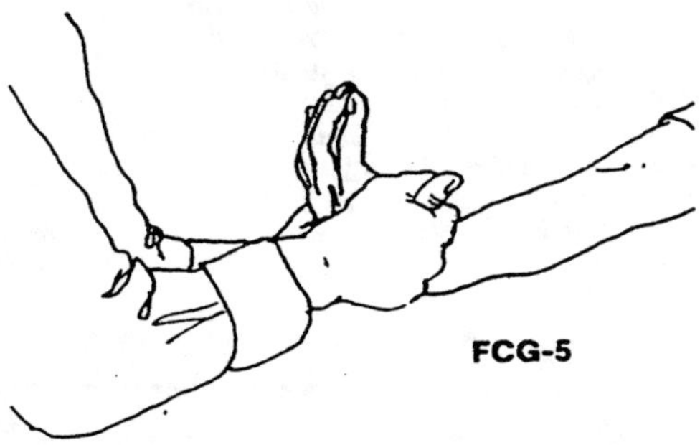

FCG-5

A close-up showing the proper grasp of the person's thumb with your right hand.

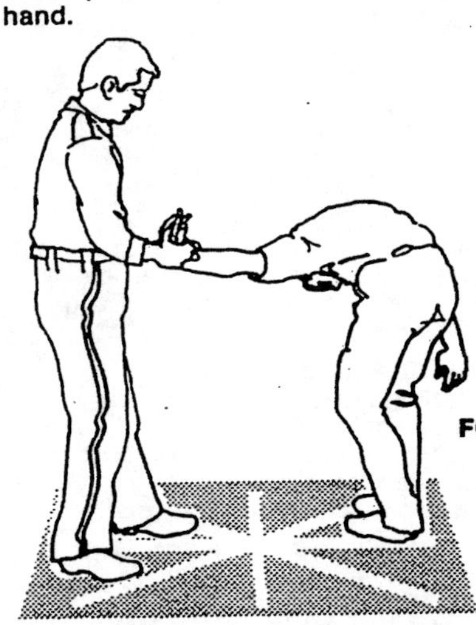

FCG-6

Stepping backward with your right leg, apply pressure against the person's hand forcing him/her to bend forward at the waist. Notice that the person's left arm is straight, elbow flat.

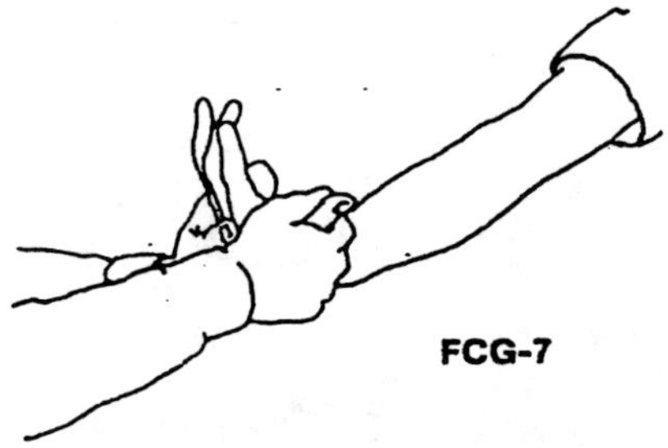

FCG-7

A close-up showing the proper grasp of the person's hand so maximum pressure can be applied. Note that your left thumb is placed on the top of the person's hand, just below the third knuckle. The fingers of your left hand grasp the edge of the person's hand.

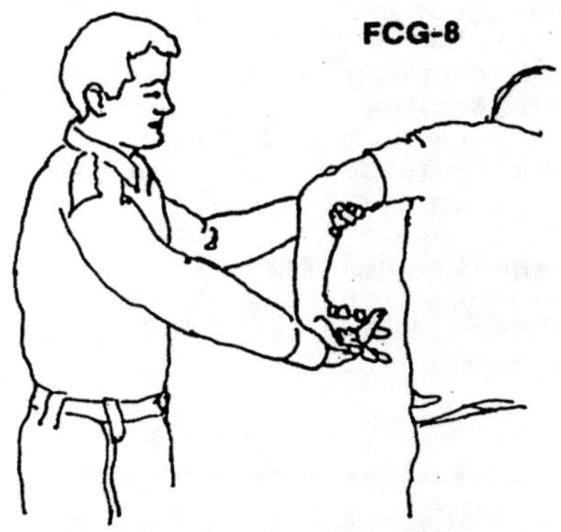

FCG-8

Stepping into the person with your left leg, point his/her right thumb toward his/her ribs. Simultaneously, turn the person's wrist and hand so that his/her fingers are also pointing toward the ribs. Turning the hand toward the ribs will cause the person to bend his/her elbow. Grasp the elbow with your left hand.

FCG-9

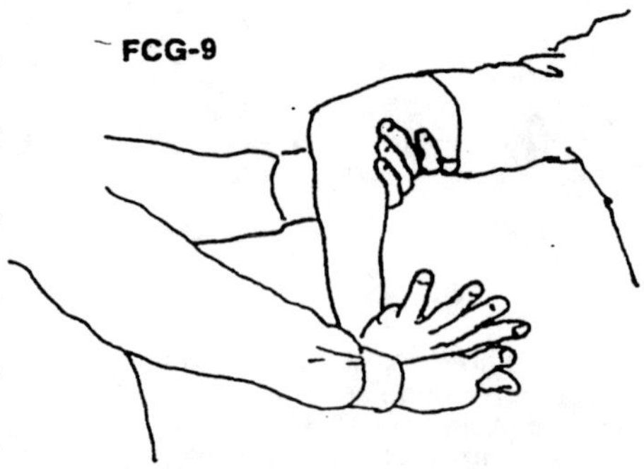

A close-up showing the person's hand and fingers being turned toward the ribs. NOTE: To effectively control the attacker, you must keep the top of his/her left hand against the bottom of your right wrist. (The bottom of your wrist will be facing you.) After the left thumb, fingers and hand are pointed toward the ribs, grasp the crook of the person's left arm with your left hand. Keeping the person's left arm bent at the elbow, pull the elbow toward you while simultaneously pushing his/her left hand away from you. For best results, as you push the person's left hand forward, keep it level with his/her waist.

CG-10

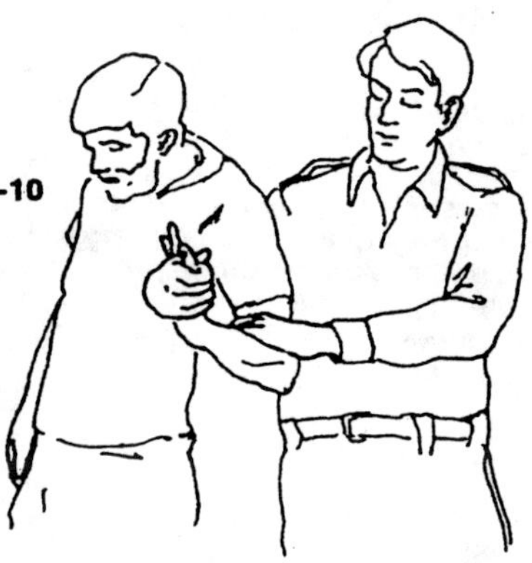

As you push the person's left hand away from you, move closer to the attacker by taking a partial step with your right foot. Pull his/her elbow toward your armpit area, while beginning to apply pressure against the attacker's left wrist. Notice that the attacker's left arm is parallel to the ground, with your right arm between the person's left rib and left forearm areas.

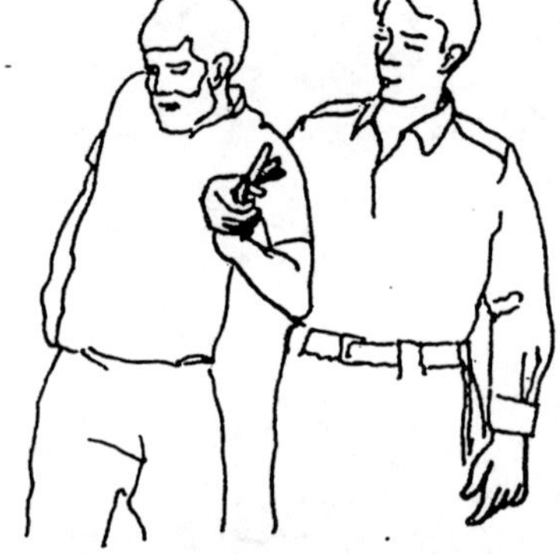

FCG-11

After the person's elbow is in place, remove your left hand. Apply pressure to the person's wrist by twisting it slightly to the left. This should cause the attacker to shift his/her weight to the left leg in an attempt to ease the pain. Remember to keep the attacker's left hand and wrist turned outward and to the right. The reasons: to maintain compliance through pain, and to prevent him/her from placing the left fingers against the shoulder area, thus voiding the technique.

FCG-12

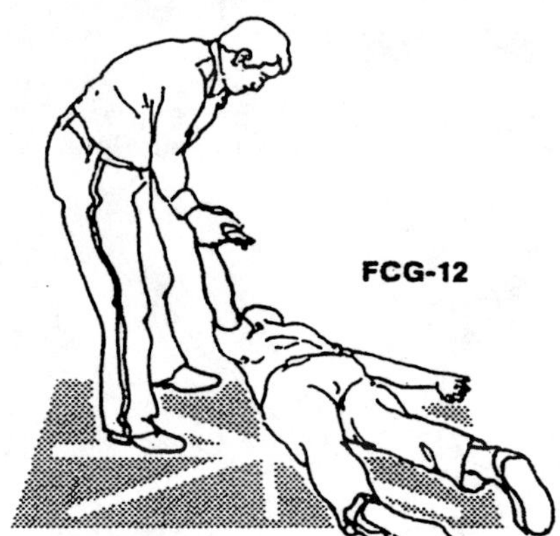

To place the person into a handcuffing position, pull downward on the person's wrist and arm. Through pain, force the person onto his/her stomach. Keep a firm wristlock on the person's left wrist.

FCG-13

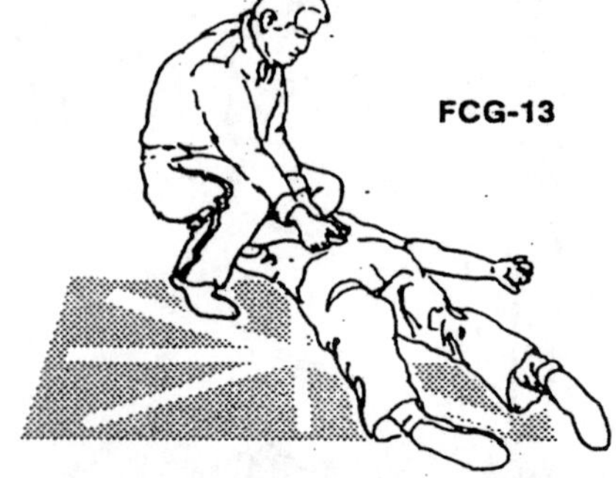

After the person is upon the ground, bend his/her arm so that the left wrist is in the small of the back. Place your left knee across the person's shoulderblade area, pinning the upper chest and shoulder areas to the ground. Handcuff the person's left wrist first, then the right wrist. Use appropriate follow-up procedures.

**Situation:** You are being choked from the front by a person who has grasped you around the neck and the throat with his/her hands.

**Action:**

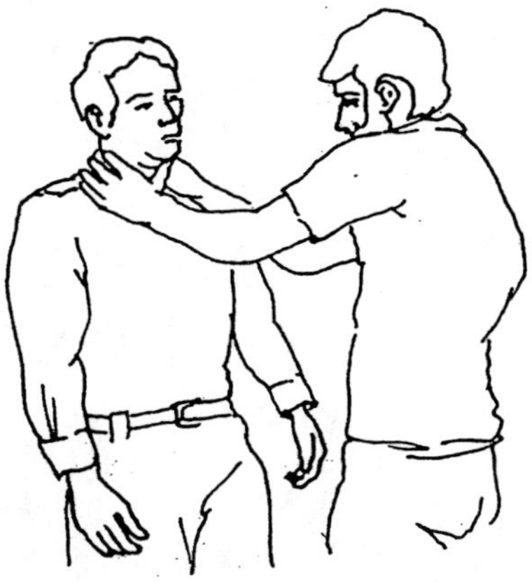

FCH-1

A person begins to choke you from the front by placing his/her hands around your throat and neck.

FCH-2

Immediately, reach between the person's arms with your right hand and grasp his/her chin. Simultaneously, with your left hand, grasp the attacker's hair or ear. Keep your left hand to the outside of the person's right arm, so that you can reach the head area.

FCH-3

Forcefully, twist the attacker's head in a counterclockwise direction. This is done by pushing the chin upward and to the right with your right hand, while simultaneously pulling the head (really the hair or the ear) downward and to the inside with your left hand.

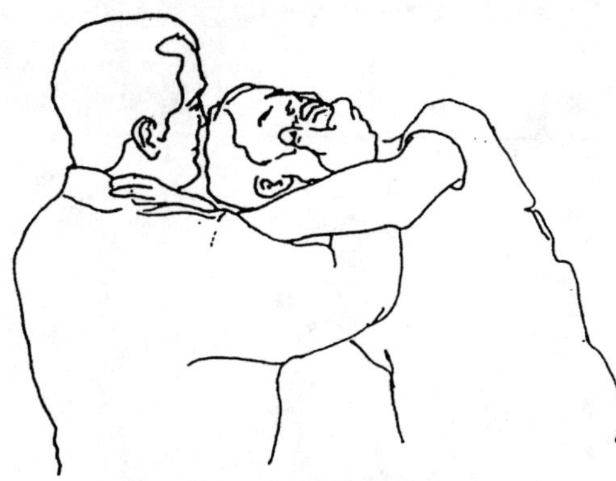

FCH-4

Close-up view showing the proper position of your right hand. Continue twisting the attacker's head until (s)he loses balance and begins to fall to your left.

FCH-5

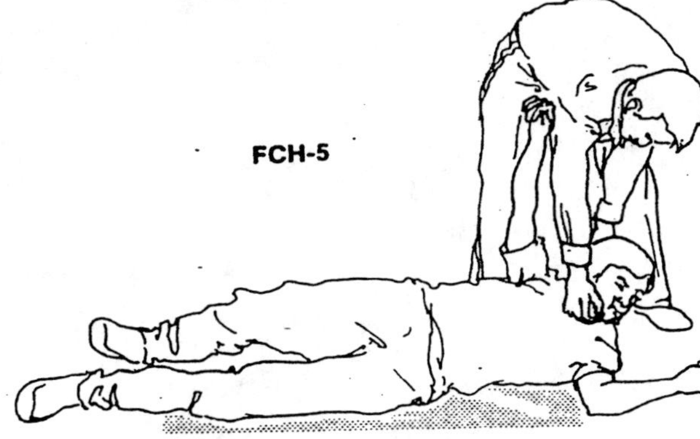

After you have "twisted" the attacker onto the ground, use appropriate follow-up procedures.

**Situation:** You are being choked from the front by a person who has grasped you around the neck and the throat with his/her hands.

**Action:**

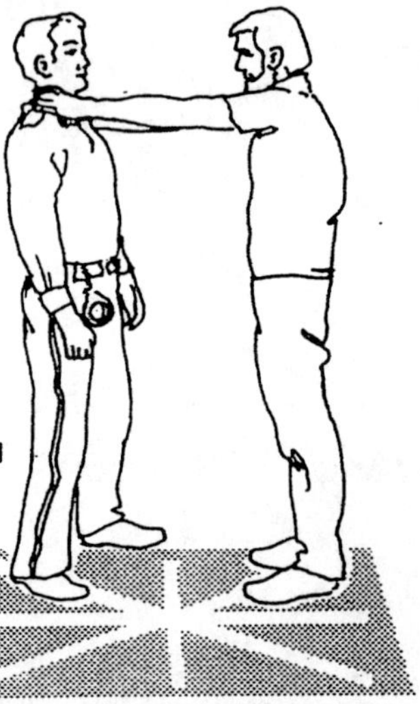

FCB-1

A person begins to choke you from the front by placing his/her hands around your throat and neck.

FCB-2

Immediately, remove your handcuffs and prepare to "snap" one cuff over the attacker's wrist.

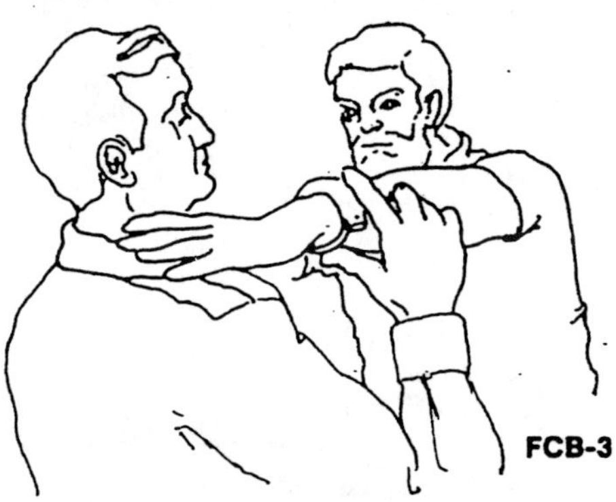

FCB-3

The handcuff on the wrist, place your right thumb on the underside of the single bar. Your right index finger is placed over the key hole.

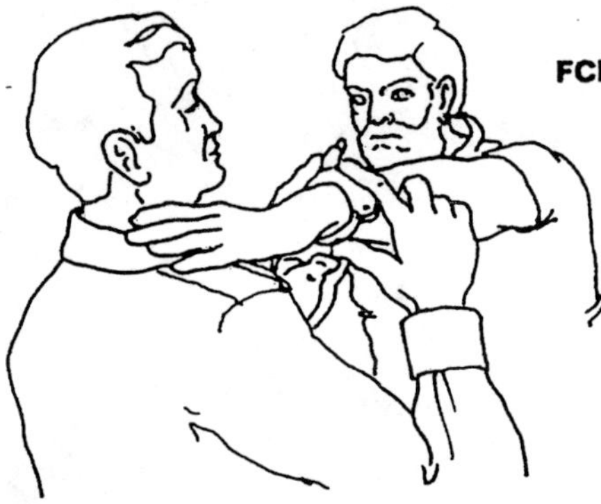

FCB-4

Next, insert your left hand between the attacker's arms, grasping the handcuff in the same manner.

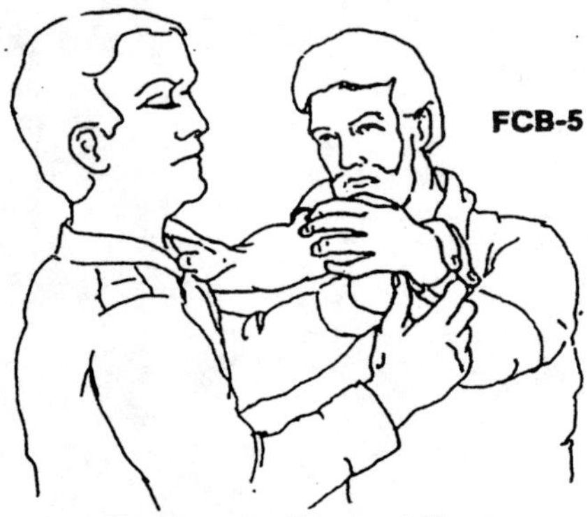

FCB-5

Twist the handcuff toward the attacker's elbow. The pain should cause the person to remove his/her left hand from your neck, and also to fall upon the ground.

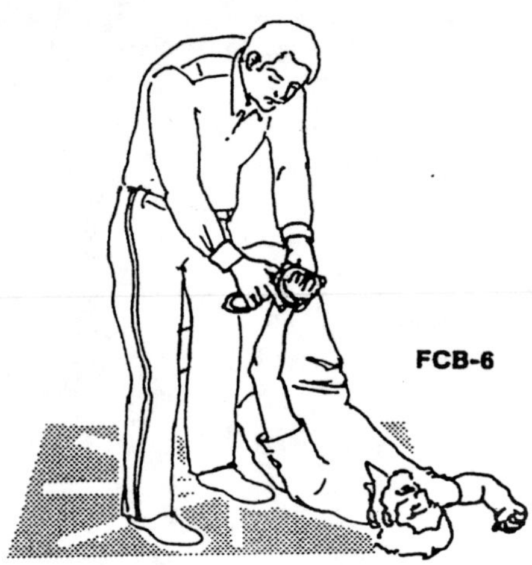

FCB-6

Keeping pressure applied to the person's wrist, pull his/her arm upward.

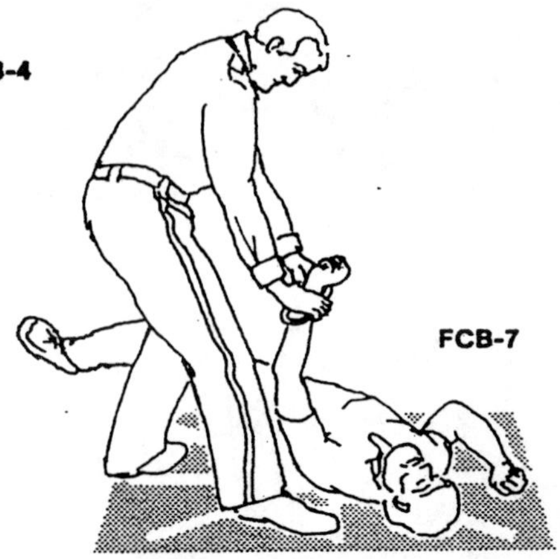

FCB-7

To roll the person onto his/her stomach, quickly walk around the person's head.

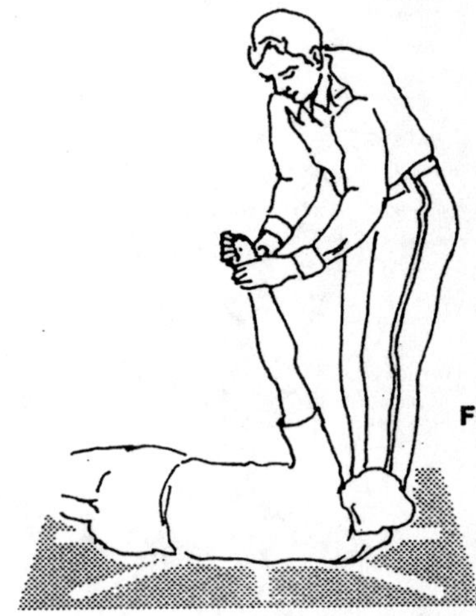

FCB-8

As you walk, keep the person's arm straight which will make it easier to roll him/her over.

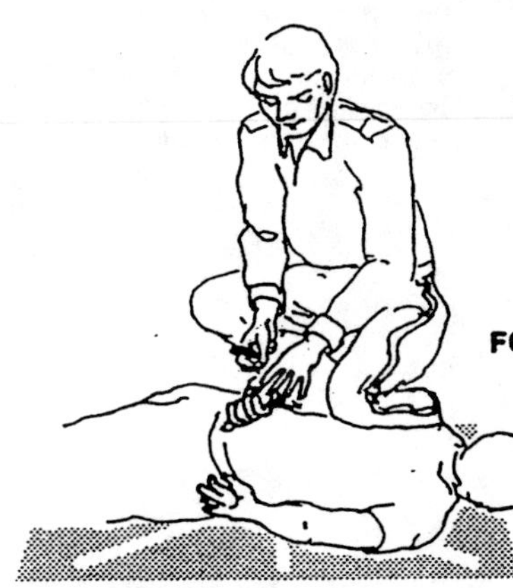

FCB-9

After the person is on his/her stomach, kneel on the suspect with you left knee. Your left knee should be placed diagonally across the person's shoulder blade. Handcuff the person's right wrist. Use appropriate follow-up procedures.

**Situation:** You are being choked from behind by a person who has grasped you by the neck with his/her hands.

**Action:**

RHC-1

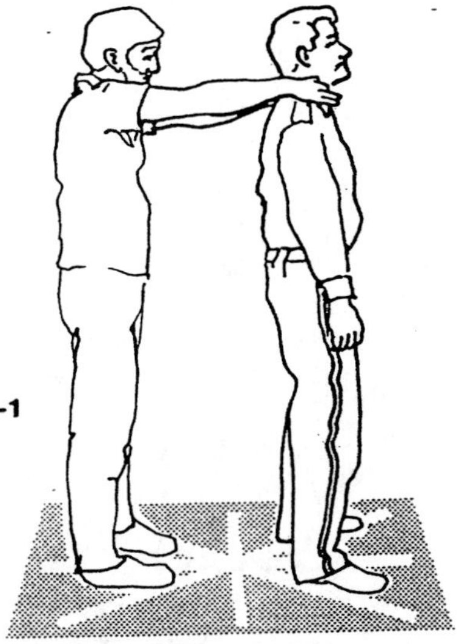

A person begins to choke you from behind by wrapping his/her hands around your neck and throat.

RHC-2

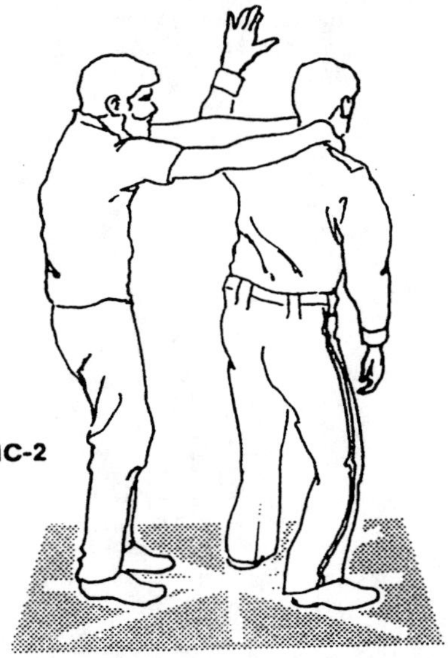

Raising your left arm so that your hand is above your head and your elbow is neck height, prepare to turn into the person by stepping back with your left foot (two quarter turns). Your weight has shifted to your right leg.

RHC-3

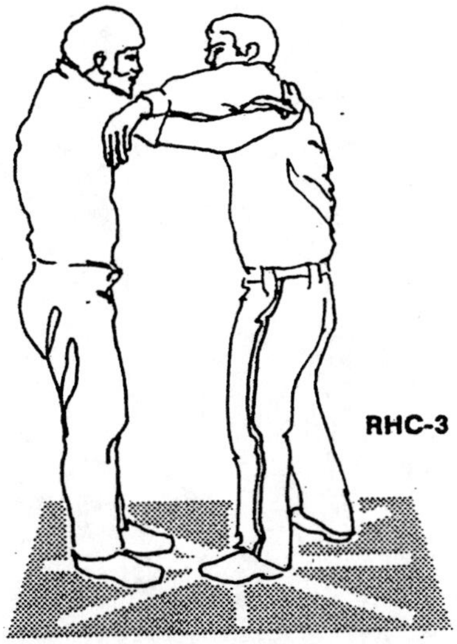

Pivoting on your right foot, turn 180° to your left, bringing your left arm over the attacker's arms.

RHC-4

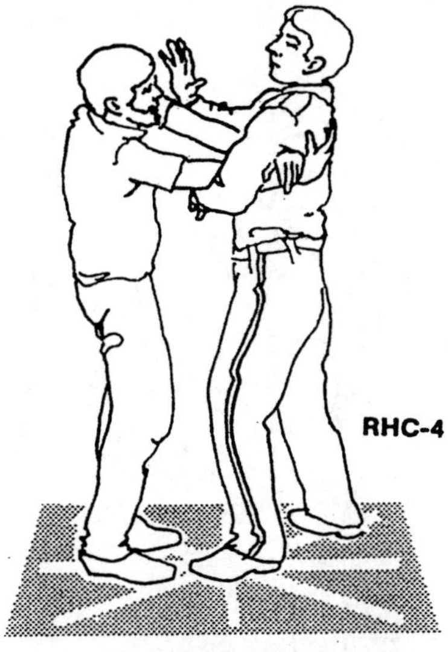

Trapping the attacker's wrists under your armpit, wrap your left arm around the attacker's arms; deliver a palm strike to the attacker's facial area.

**Situation:** You are being choked from behind by a person who has grasped you around the neck and throat areas with his/her arm.

**Action:**

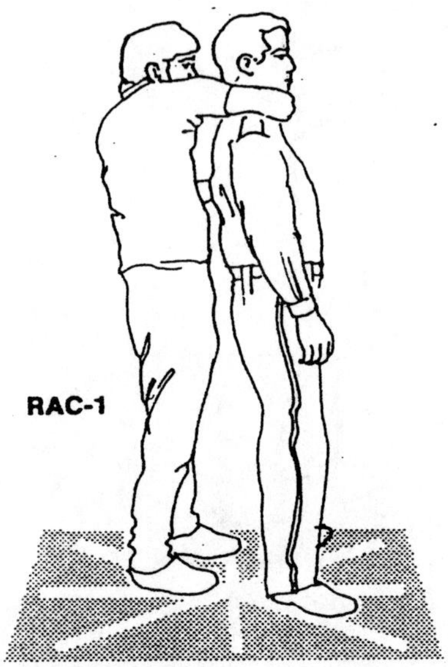

RAC-1

A person begins to choke you from behind by placing his/her forearm across your throat.

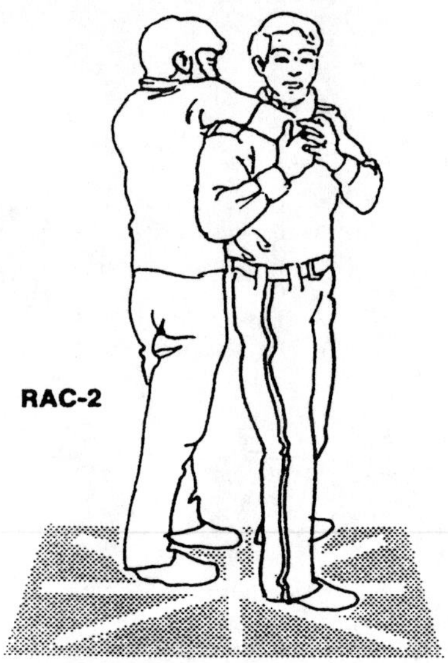

RAC-2

Immediately, turn your head and throat into the "V" (crook of the arm) of the attacker's arm. The reason: so that you can breathe. Also, grasp the attacker's elbow area with both of your hands, pushing it onto your chest. This will help ease pressure on your throat.

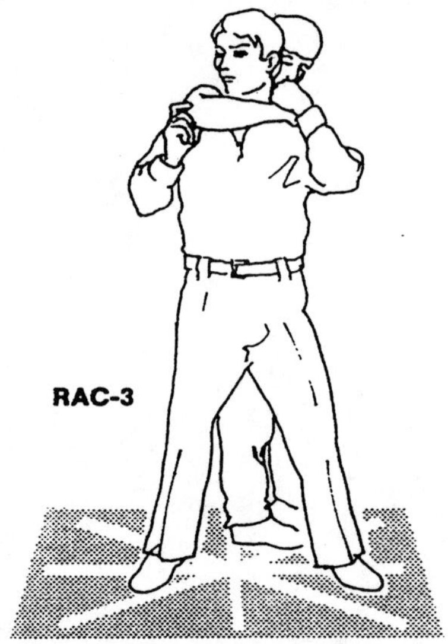

RAC-3

With your right hand and index finger, grasp a small amount of skin on the underside of the attacker's bicep. Also, grab the attacker's wrist with your left hand.

RAC-4

Simultaneously, pinch the attacker's bicep (twist and pinch the skin) while pulling his/her wrist downward, toward the ground. Prepare to make a quarter turn movement with your left foot.

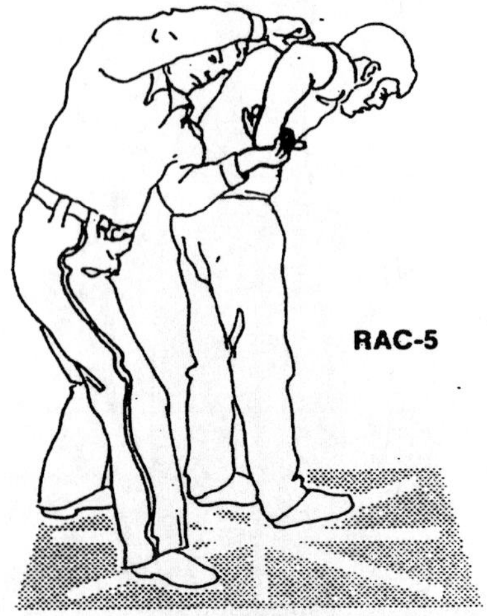

RAC-5

Push up on the attacker's bicep while pinching it; simultaneously, step back and to the right with your left foot while pulling the attacker's arm downward. Freeing your head and neck area, step behind the attacker. Use appropriate follow-up methods.

**Situation:** You are being choked from behind by a person who has grabbed you around the neck and throat areas with his/her arm.

**Action:**

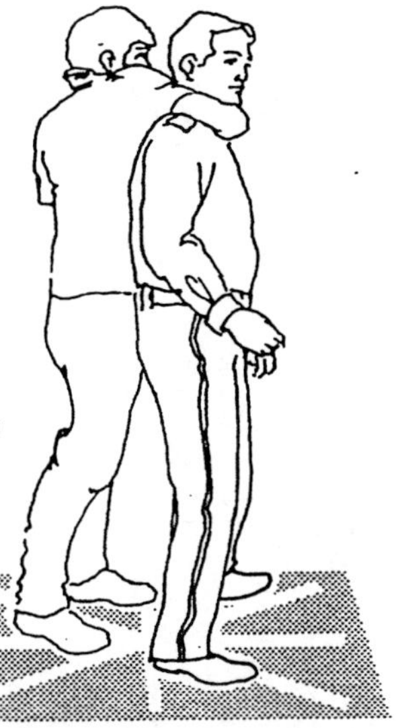

RAC-6

A person begins to choke you from behind by placing his/her forearm across your throat.

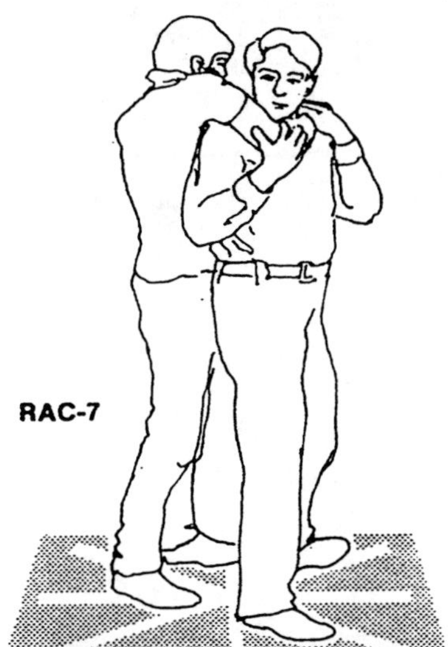

RAC-7

Immediately turn your head and throat into the "V" (crook of the arm) of the attacker's arm. The reason: so that you can breathe. Also, grasp the attacker's elbow area with your right hand, pushing it onto your chest. This will help ease pressure on your throat. Grasp his/her right wrist with your left hand.

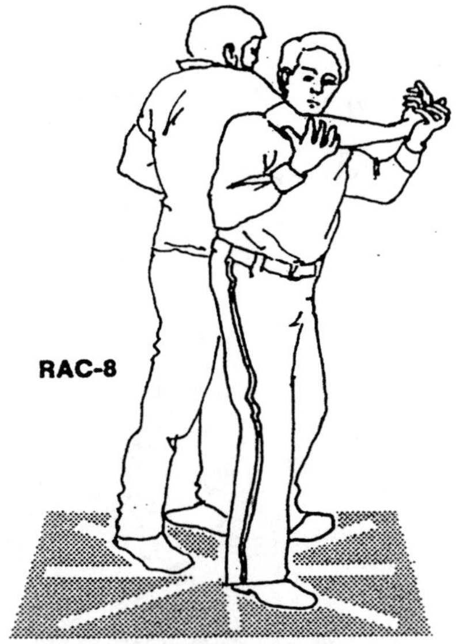

RAC-8

Pulling his/her elbow into your chest, maintain your balance by slightly flexing your knees. Simultaneously, with your left hand, pull your attacker's wrist forward, forcing his/her arm to straighten.

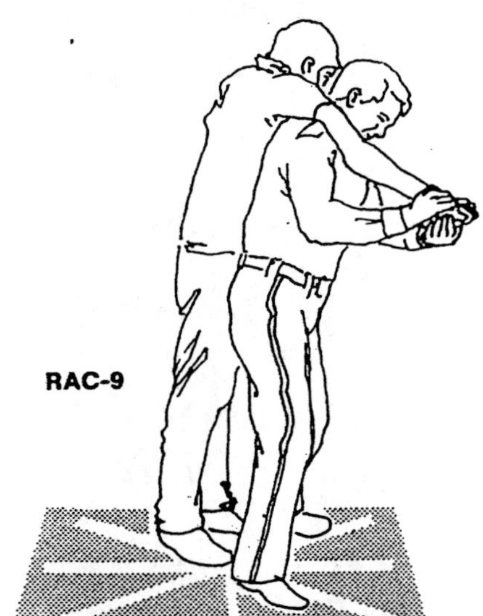

RAC-9

After the attacker's arm is straight, grasp his/her wrist with both of your hands. Pull the attacker into you, so that his/her bicep is on top of your shoulder, elbow pointed toward the ground. If the attacker is shorter than you, bend your knees to compensate for the height difference.

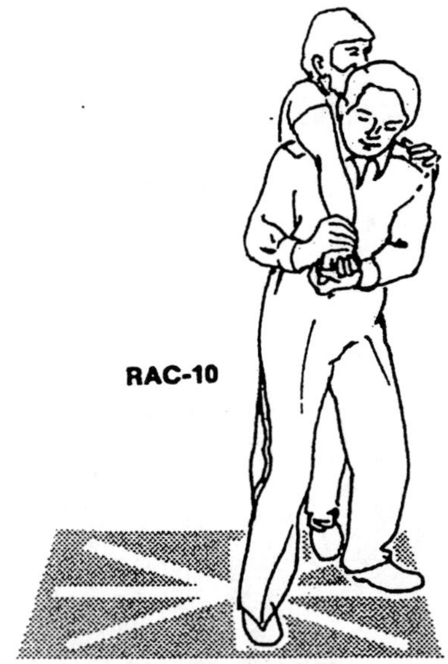

RAC-10

Forcefully, pull down on the attacker's wrist, while simultaneously straightening your legs. This should result in the breaking of the attacker's elbow. CAUTION: If the attacker is a lot taller than you, this technique may not work as well.

## CHAPTER FIVE: BREAKAWAYS

This section is the largest one in the book. We have selected over twenty escape techniques which you can use, if suddenly grabbed by an attacker.

Once again, there are many escape techniques offered; select the ones you like best. In making your selection, pick the ones that best fit your physical size and agility. After your selection, practice them. They work.

**Situation:** A person grabs you by the right wrist using his/her right hand.

**Action:**

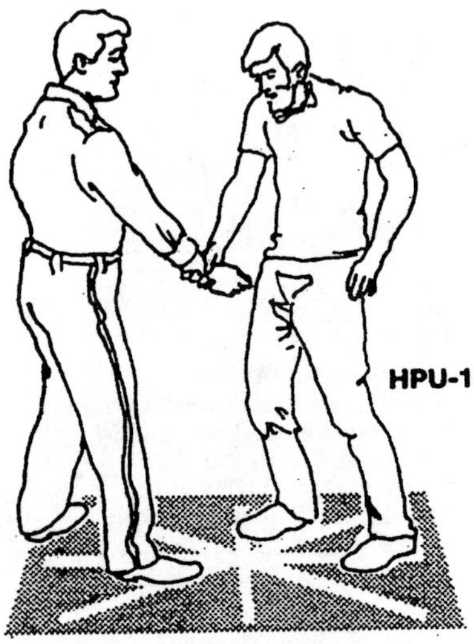

HPU-1

A person grasps your right wrist using his/her right hand.

HPU-2

Make a fist with your right hand and begin to apply upward pressure against the person's thumb, by bending your arm at the elbow. Don't lift your arm, since this is ineffective.

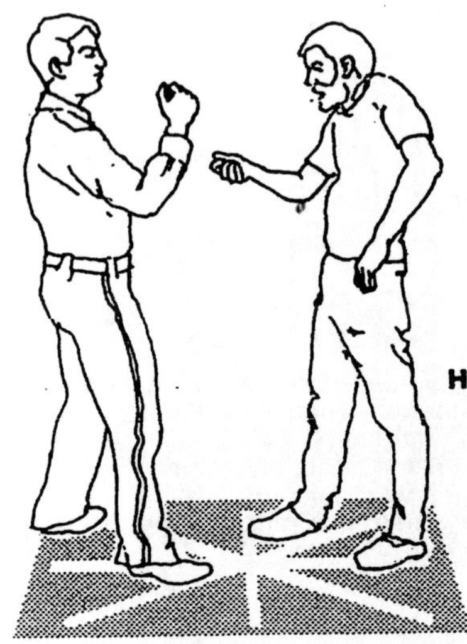

HPU-3

Apply upward pressure against the person's thumb with your right wrist until you're free.

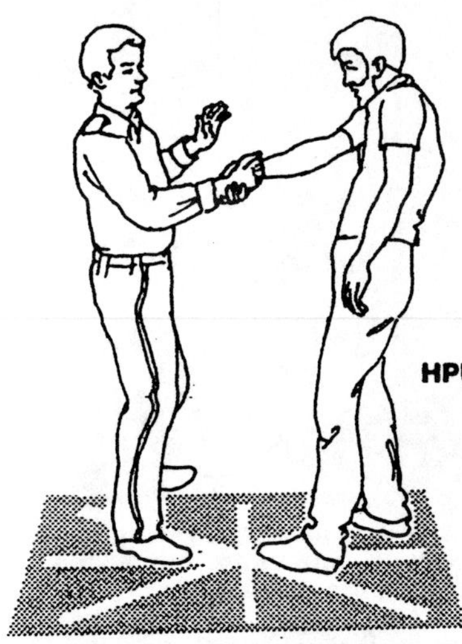

HPU-4

To develop more power as you bend your arm, step backward with your right leg. This action will also straighten the person's arm, pulling him/her slightly forward.

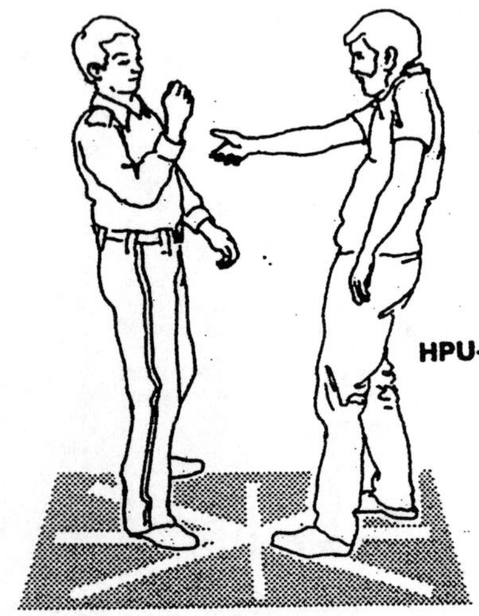

HPU-5

Keep upward pressure against the person's thumb with your right wrist as you step backward with your right leg. This will free your wrist. Use appropriate follow-up procedures.

**Situation:** A person grabs your right wrist using both his/her hands.

**Action:**

HPU-6

A person grasps your right wrist using both his/her hands.

HPU-7

Make a fist with your right hand. Grab the fist with your left hand by reaching between the person's arms.

HPU-8

Pull your fist upward—against the person's thumb—while bending your right arm at the elbow.

HPU-9

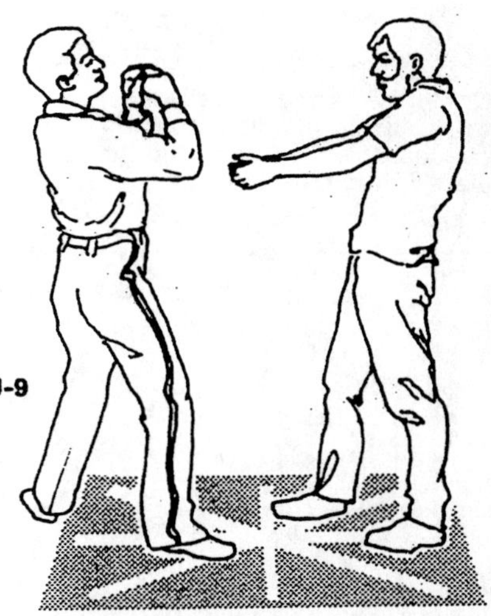

Continue the upward pressure until you're free. NOTE: For more power, step backward with your right foot as you bend your arm. Use appropriate follow-up procedures.

**Situation:** A person grabs your right wrist using both his/her hands. One of the person's hands is thumb down; the other with the thumb on top, making it appear difficult to escape. In reality, this technique would be more likely applied using two people who would grab your wrist.

**Action:**

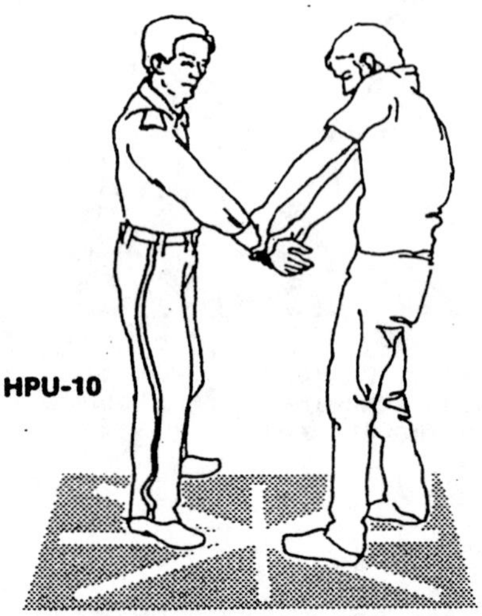

HPU-10

One or two people grab your right wrist placing one hand thumb pointed down with the other hand placed thumb on top.

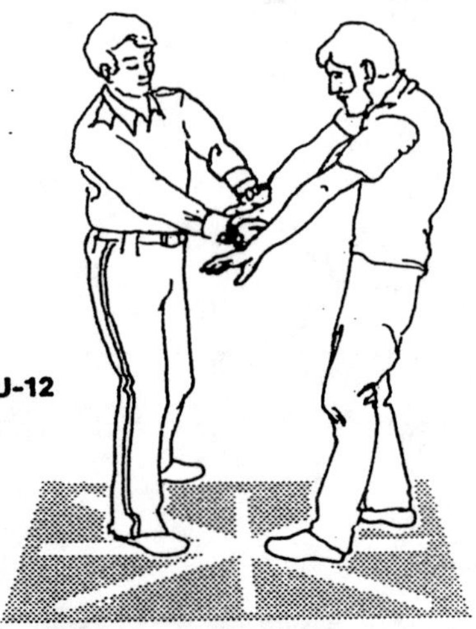

HPU-12

Deliver a forceful palm strike to the person's outside arm, just above the wrist. This action will remove one hand from your wrist.

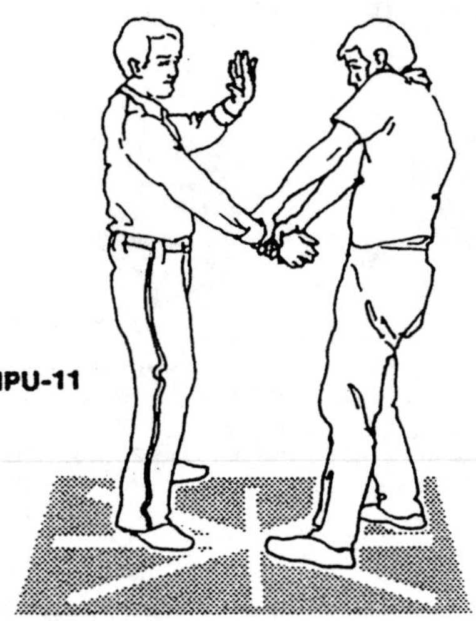

HPU-11

Raise your left hand preparing to deliver a palm strike.

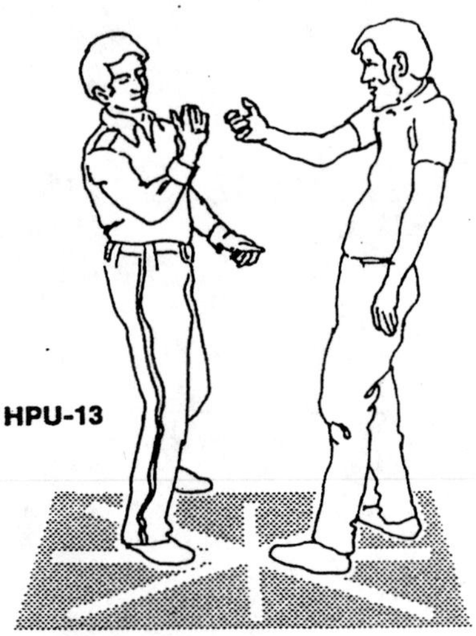

HPU-13

Now, bend your right arm at the elbow while applying upward pressure against the person's thumb with your right wrist. Use appropriate follow-up procedures.

**Situation:** A person using his/her right hand, grasps you by the right wrist.

**Action:**

RWG-1

A person grasps your wrist with his/her right hand.

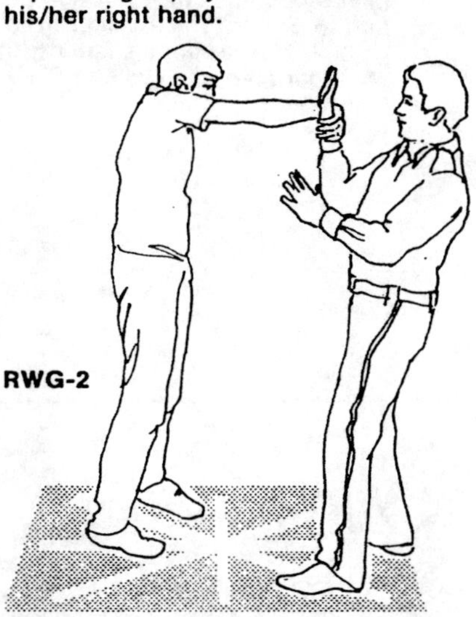

RWG-2

Keeping your right hand open, rotate your hand and wrist in a small semi-circular clockwise motion. Stop the motion when the palm of the right hand is facing you. Simultaneously, step back with your right foot (quarter turn), pivoting on your left foot.

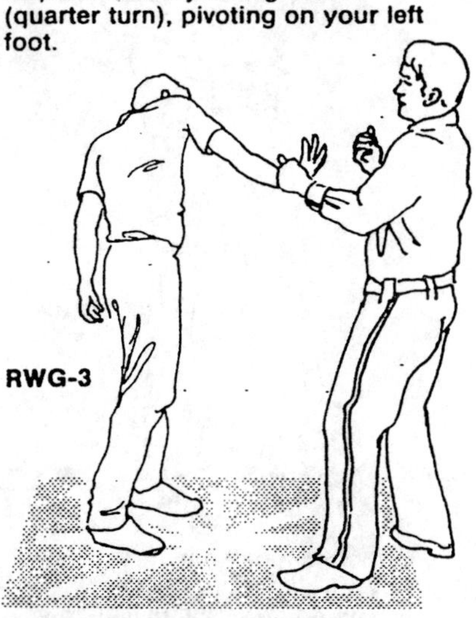

RWG-3

Quickly grasp your attacker's thumb—"microphone style"—with your left hand. Pull your right wrist from the attacker's hand.

RWG-4

Keeping the attacker's right arm bent toward the elbow, pull the elbow toward you while simultaneously pushing his/her right hand away from you. For best results, as you push the attacker's right hand forward, keep it level with his/her waist.

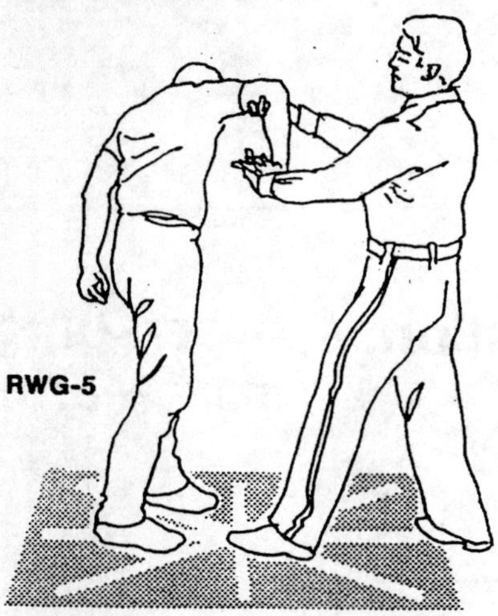

RWG-5

Stepping into the attacker with your left leg, point his/her right thumb toward his/her ribs. Simultaneously, turn the attacker's wrist and hand so that his/her fingers are also pointing toward the ribs. NOTE: To effectively control the attacker, you must keep the top of his/her right hand against the bottom of your left wrist. (The bottom of the wrist will be facing you.) After the right thumb, fingers and hand are pointed toward the ribs, grasp the crook of the attacker's right arm with your right hand.

RWG-6

As you push the attacker's right hand away from you, move closer to the attacker by taking a partial step with your left foot. Pull his/her elbow toward your armpit area, while beginning to apply pressure against the attacker's right wrist. Notice that the attacker's right arm is parallel to the ground, with your left arm between the attacker's right rib and right forearm areas.

RWG-7

Push the attacker's right elbow between your left bicep and left rib cage. Apply pressure to the attacker's wrist by twisting it slightly to the right. This should cause the attacker to shift his/her weight to the right leg in attempt to ease the pain.

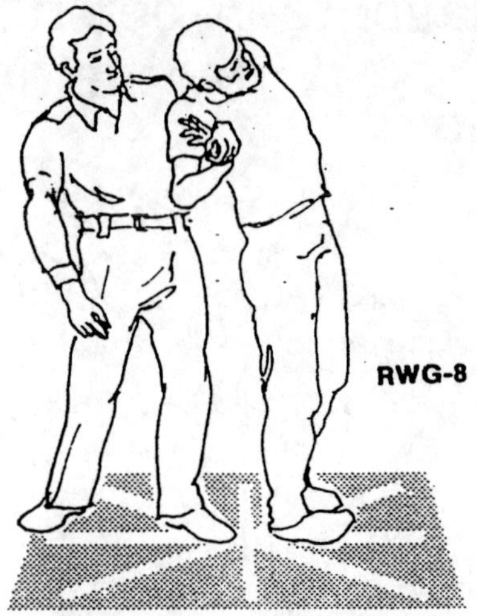

RWG-8

After the attacker's elbow is in place, release your right hand. Maintain constant pressure on the attacker's wrist. Remember to keep the attacker's right hand and wrist turned outward to the right. The reasons: to maintain compliance through pain and to prevent the attacker from placing his/her fingers against the shoulder area, thus voiding the technique.

## Situation: A person grabs you around the waist from the front—arms unpinned.

## Action:

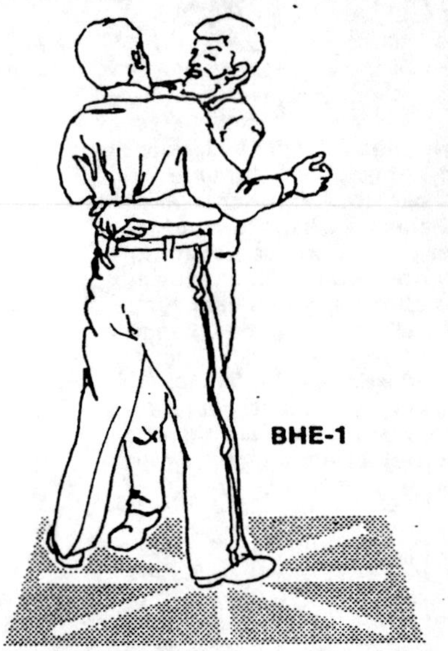

BHE-1

You are grabbed around the waist—arms free—by a person who is facing you.

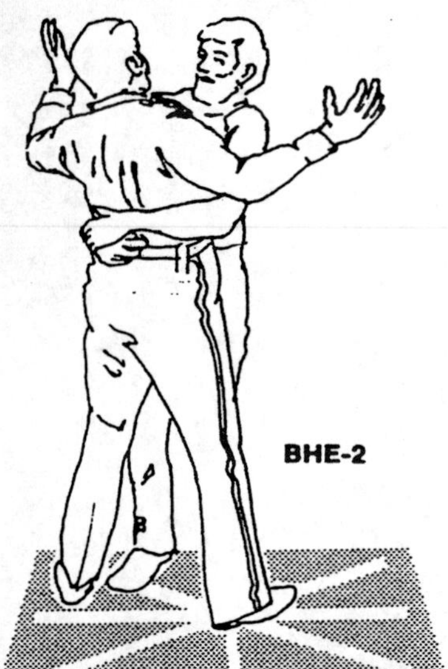

BHE-2

Quickly raise both of your arms and open your hands.

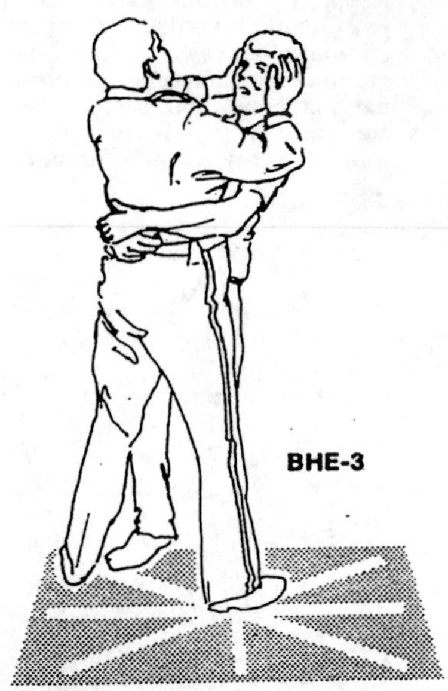

BHE-3

With cupped hands, deliver a slap to both of the person's ears. This action should make the person release his/her grasp. Use appropriate follow-up procedures.

**Situation:** An attacker places you in a front bearhug, arms pinned by your side.

**Action:**

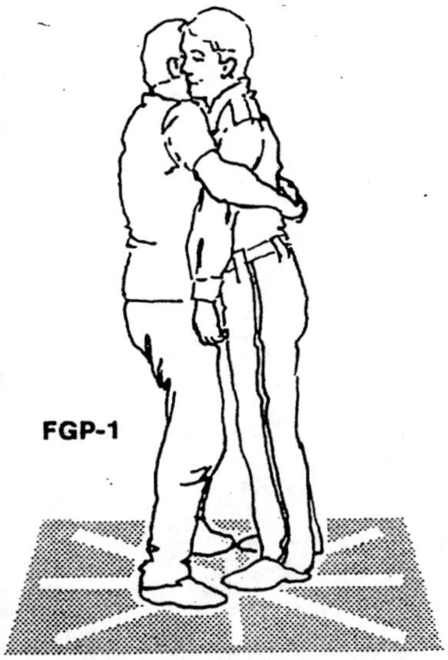

FGP-1

An attacker places you in a front bearhug, arms pinned by your side.

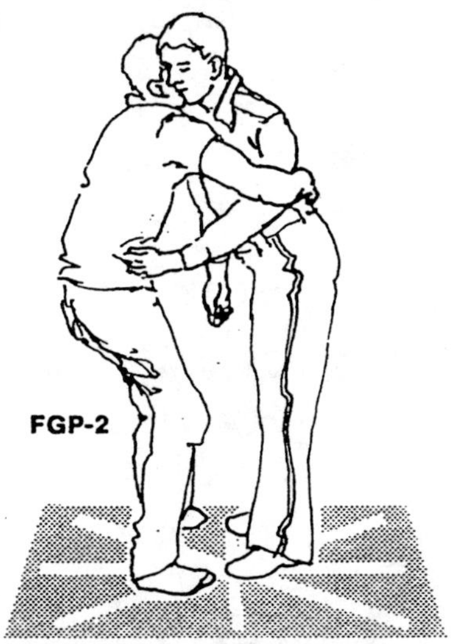

FGP-2

To move the attacker away from you, pinch the skin at his/her waist using your thumb and index finger.

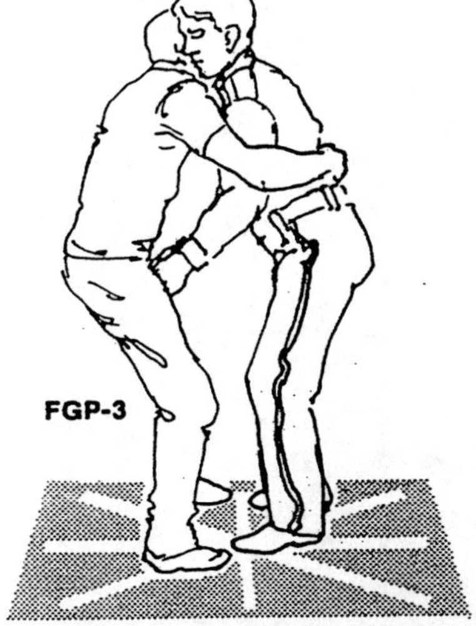

FGP-3

You can also move the attacker away from you by making a fist with both hands. Placing your thumbs over your index fingers, forcefully push them into the attacker's lower abdominal area (just above the groin).

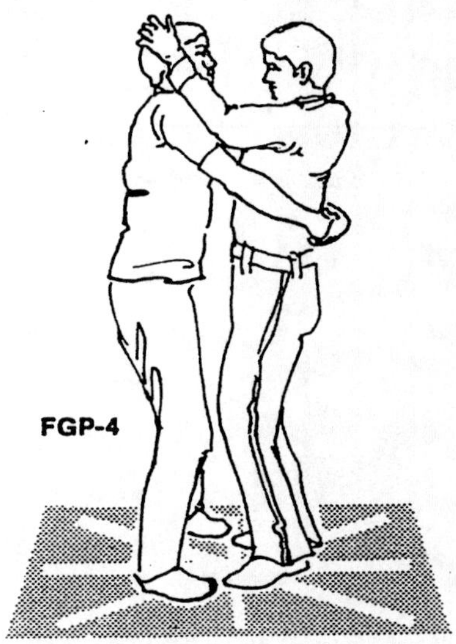

FGP-4

As the attacker's body moves away from you, quickly bring both of your arms upward between the two of you. Grasp the attacker's hair or ear with your left hand.

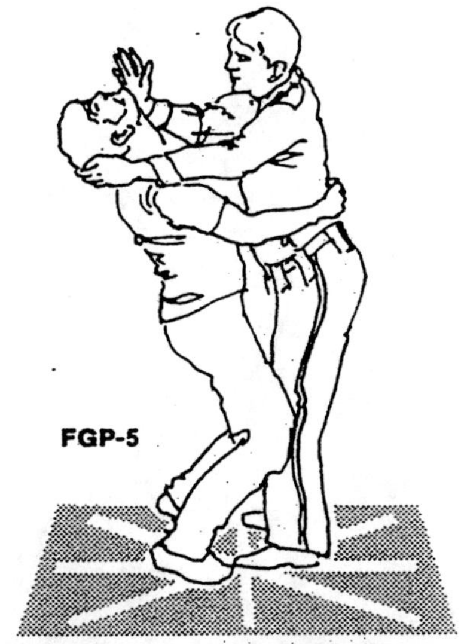

FGP-5

Forcefully pull the attacker's hair or ear backward and downward, bending him/her at the waist and knees. Then, forcefully strike the person in the chin with the heel of your hand. This action should cause the person to fall backward. Use appropriate follow-up procedures.

**Situation:** You are placed in a front bearhug by an attacker.

**Action:**

FBH-1

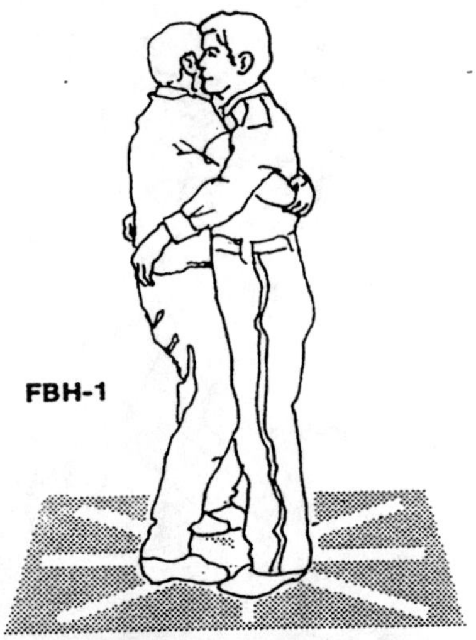

An attacker places you in a front bearhug, arms unpinned.

FBH-2

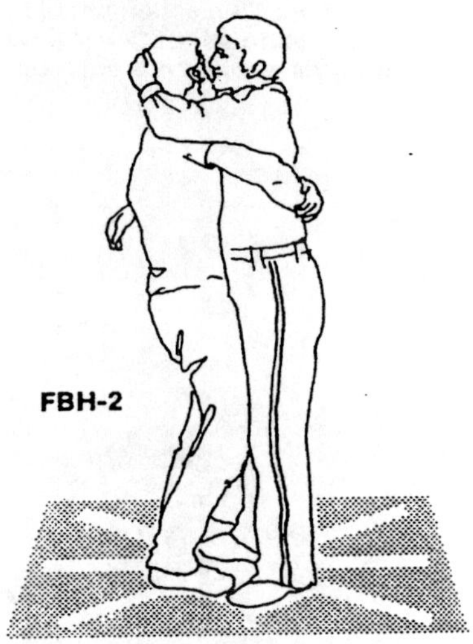

Immediately, grasp the hair on the back of the attacker's head with your left hand. If the attacker is bald, is wearing a hat or wig, grasp the collar of the shirt or coat. Better still, grasp the attacker's ear.

FBH-3

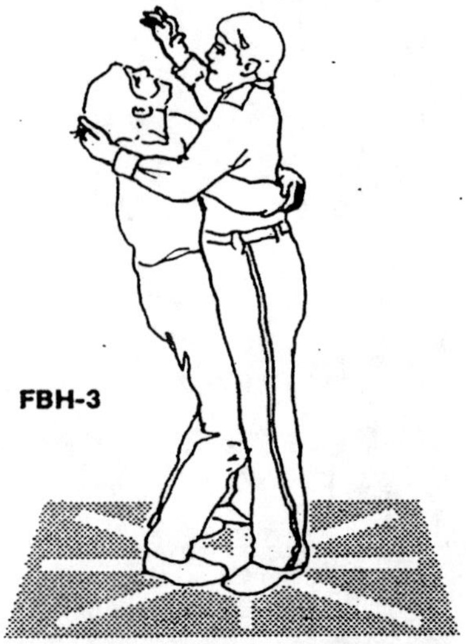

Forcefully, pull the hair backward and downward, causing the attacker's head to go back and his/her body to arc. Raise your right hand in preparation to deliver a palm strike or finger flick to the attacker's face.

FBH-4

While continuing to pull the attacker's hair, if necessary, deliver a palm strike to the face or a finger flick to the eyes of the attacker. Use appropriate follow-up procedures.

**Situation:** You are placed in a front bearhug by an attacker.
**Action:**

FBH-5

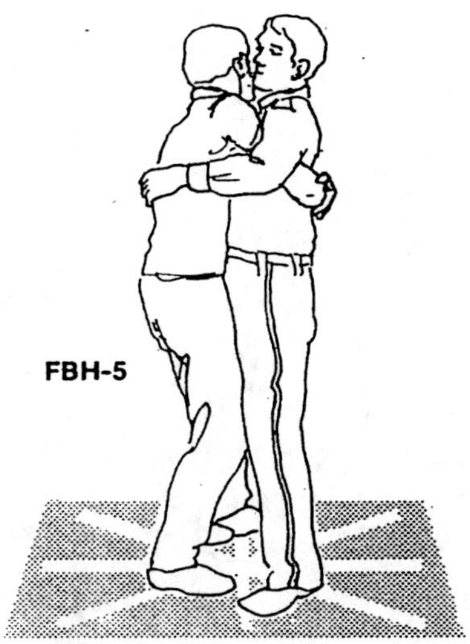

An attacker places you in a front bearhug, arms unpinned.

FBH-6

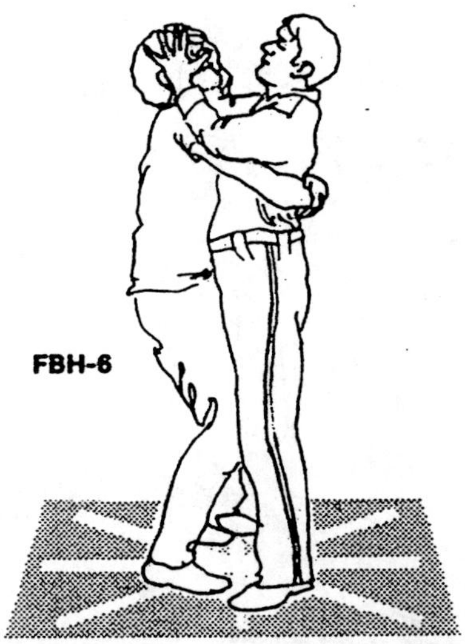

Quickly, place your hands on the attacker's face, so that your thumbs are under his/her nose, and your fingers are on the forehead. Forcefully, snap the attacker's head backward by applying pressure under the nose with your thumbs and on the forehead with your fingers. Use appropriate follow-up procedures.

**Situation:** An attacker has grasped you around the neck, placing you in a headlock.

**Action:**

SHL-1

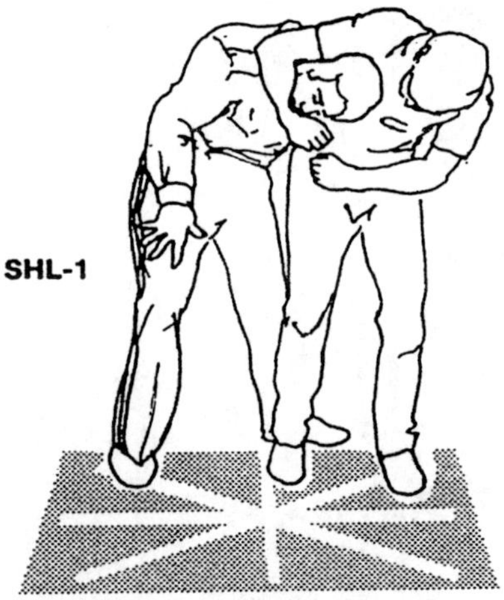

As soon as the attacker has placed a headlock on you, step behind him/her with your left leg.

SHL-2

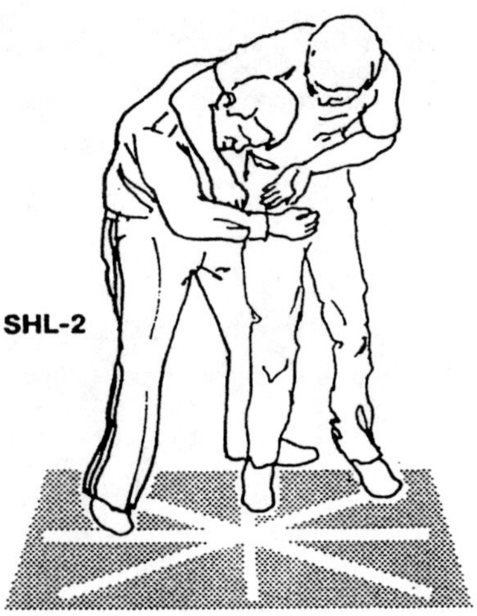

With your left leg behind the attacker for both balance and positioning, forcefully strike the attacker's groin area with your right hand.

SHL-3

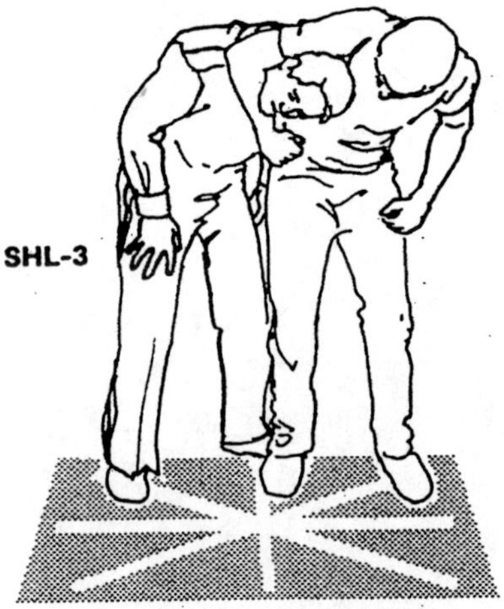

The groin strike should have "softened" the attacker, forcing him/her to release the two-handed headlock and to bend forward. Begin to reach for the attacker's head area using your left hand (follow the person's back).

SHL-4

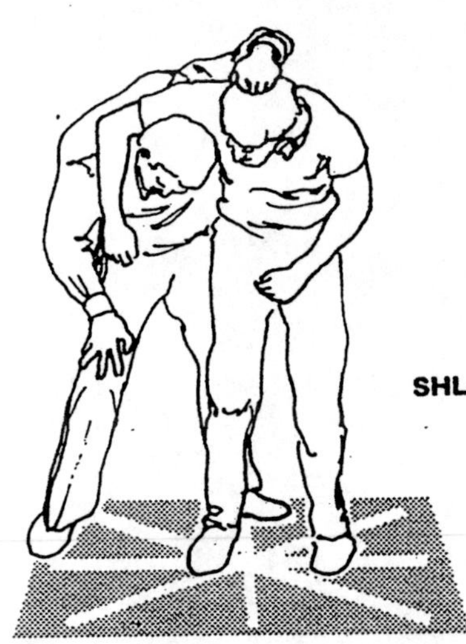

Grasp the attacker's hair with your left hand. If (s)he is wearing a hat, wig or is bald, grasp the collar of his/her coat or shirt. You may also grasp either ear.

SHL-5

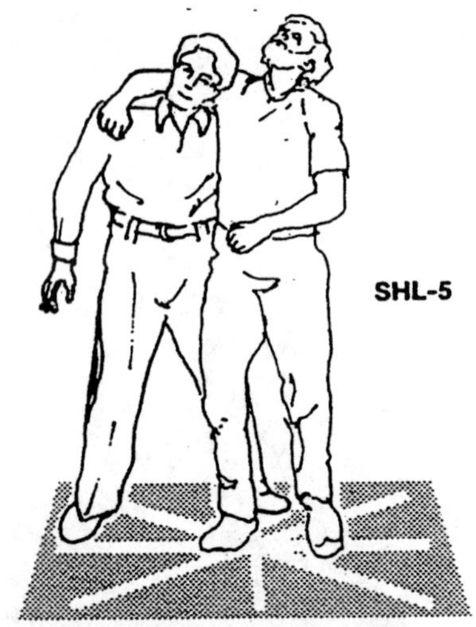

Forcefully pull the attacker's hair, using a downward and backward motion, while simultaneously standing erect. Use appropriate follow-up procedures.

**Situation:** From behind, a person grabs you around the waist.

**Action:**

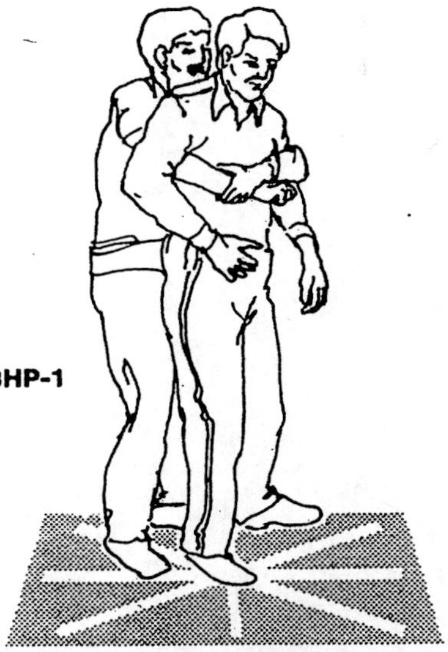

BHP-1

From behind, a person grabs you around the waist, arms unpinned.

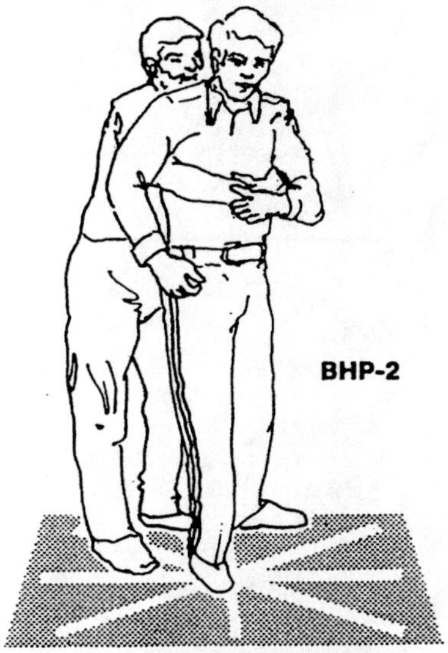

BHP-2

Look at the person's hands to determine which one is on the top and thus exposed. In this case, it's the person's left hand. Using your left hand, grasp the fingers which are on the person's left hand.

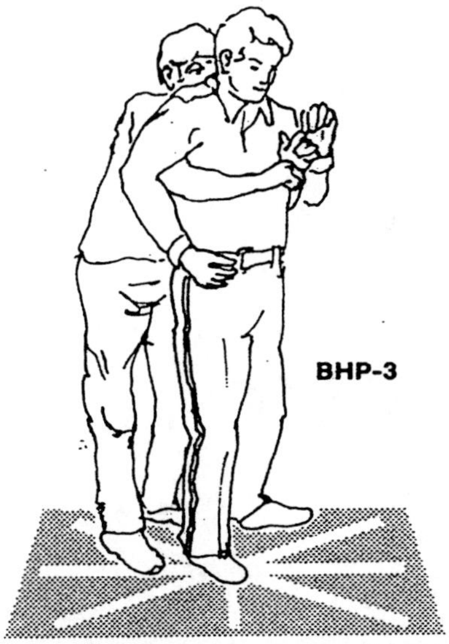

BHP-3

Having grasped one or more fingers, begin to bend them backward (counterjoint movement).

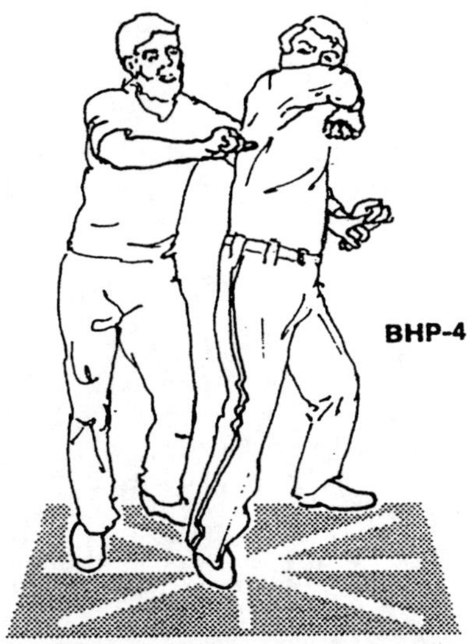

BHP-4

Applying counterjoint pressure, peel the person's left hand away from your waist. Keeping a strong grasp on the person's left fingers, take one step forward with your right foot. Then, raise and "cock" your right arm to head level.

BHP-5

Forcefully strike the person in the face with your right elbow. Use appropriate follow-up procedures.

**Situation:** From behind, a person grabs you around the waist pinning your arms.

**Action:**

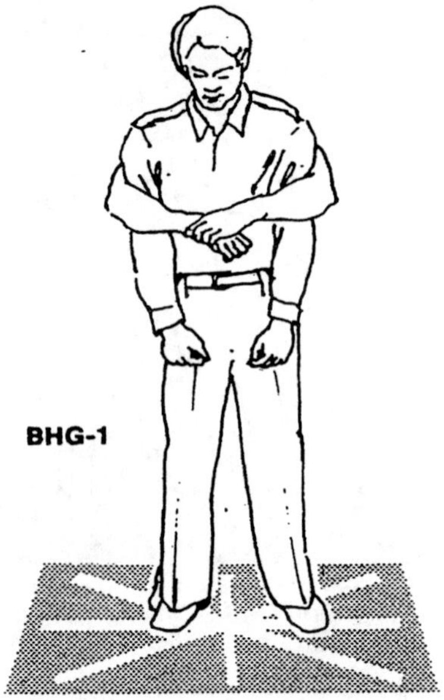

BHG-1

From behind, a person grabs you around the waist pinning your arms against your side.

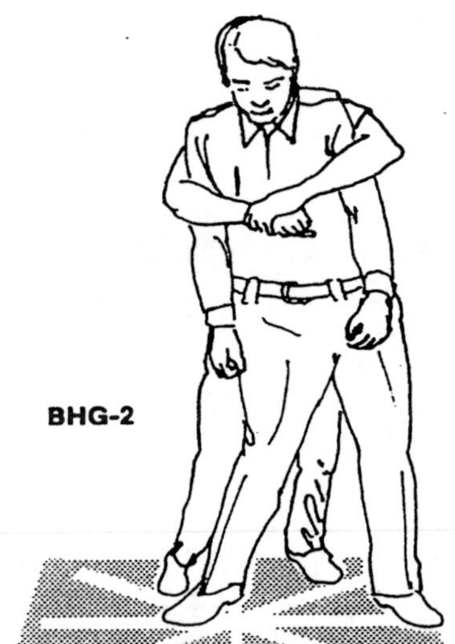

BHG-2

Immediately, shift your hips to the left.

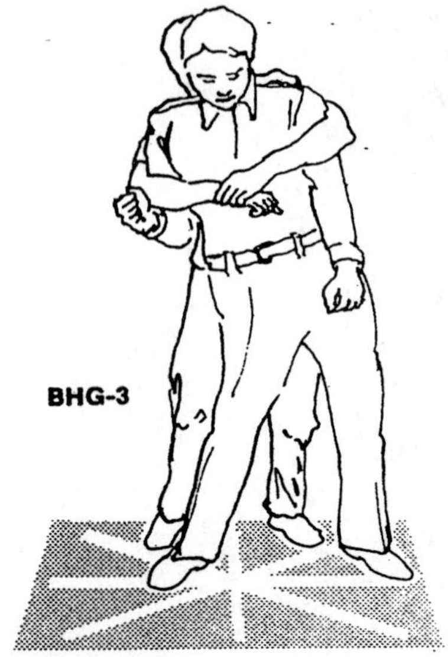

BHG-3

Raise your right arm by bending it at the elbow.

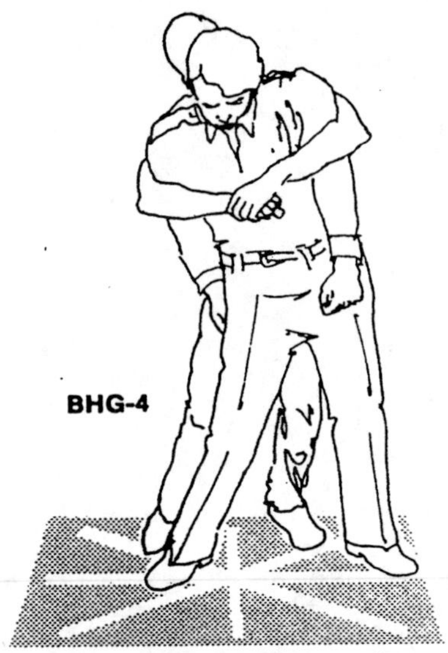

BHG-4

Forcefully deliver a strike to the person's groin area. This action should make the person release his/her grasp. Use appropriate follow-up procedures. NOTE: This technique may not be effective if the attacker is wearing a long coat.

**Situation:** From behind, a person grabs you around the waist pinning your arms against your side.

**Action:**

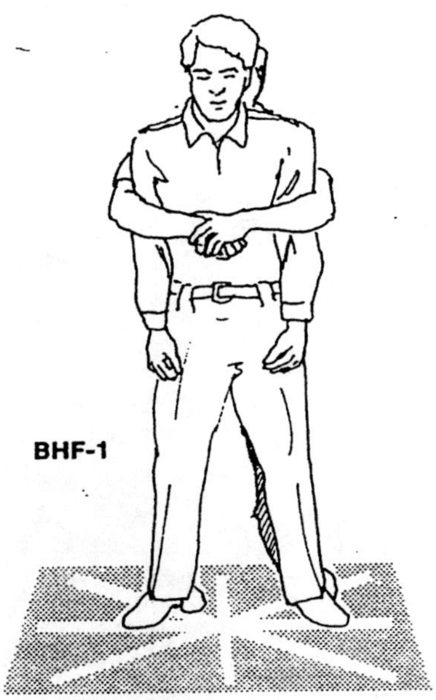

BHF-1

From behind, a person grabs you around the waist pinning your arms against your side.

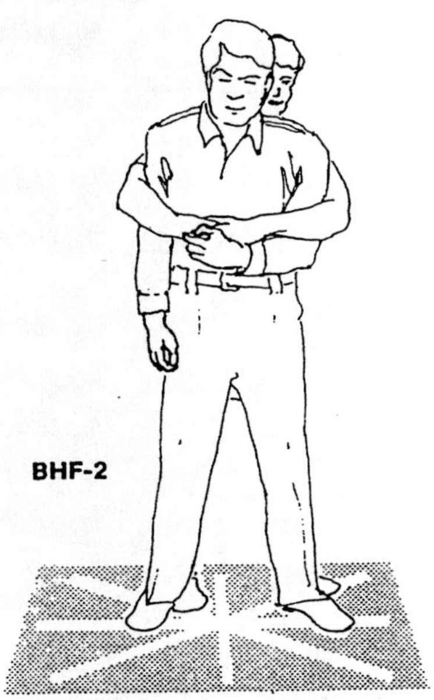

BHF-2

Look at the person's hands to determine which one is on the top and thus exposed. In this case, it is the person's left hand. Using your left hand, grasp the fingers which are on the person's left hand.

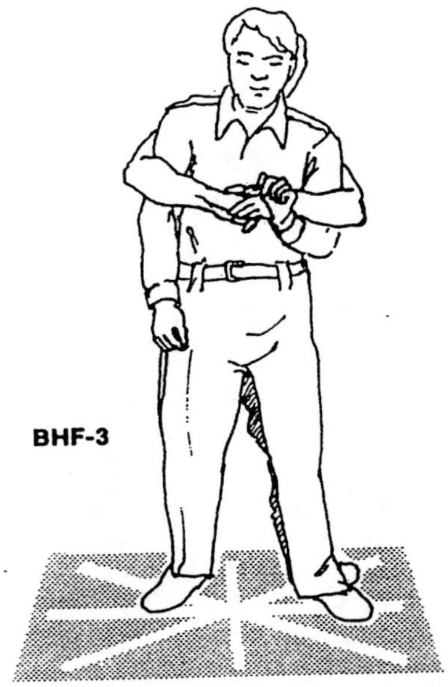

BHF-3

Having grasped one or more fingers, begin to bend them backward (counterjoint movement).

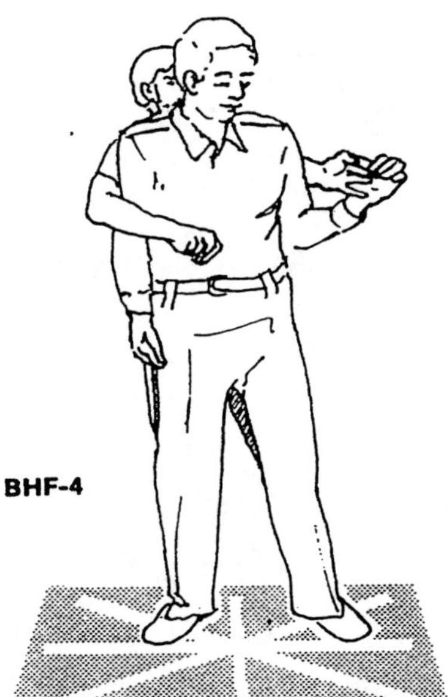

BHF-4

Applying counterjoint pressure, peel the person's left hand away from your waist.

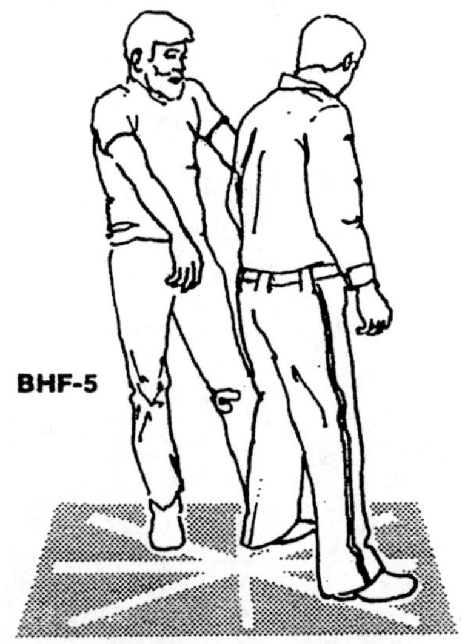

BHF-5

Maintaining a strong grasp on the person's left fingers, step away from the person using your right foot. Use appropriate follow-up procedures.

**Situation:** From behind, a person grabs you around the waist pinning your arms against your side.

**Action:**

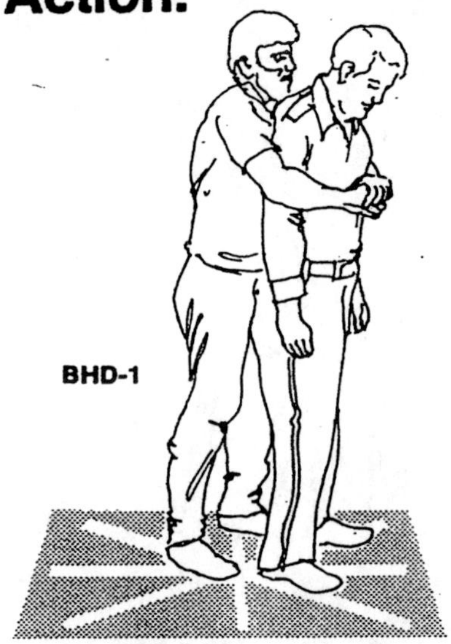

BHD-1

From behind, a person grabs you around the waist pinning your arms against your side.

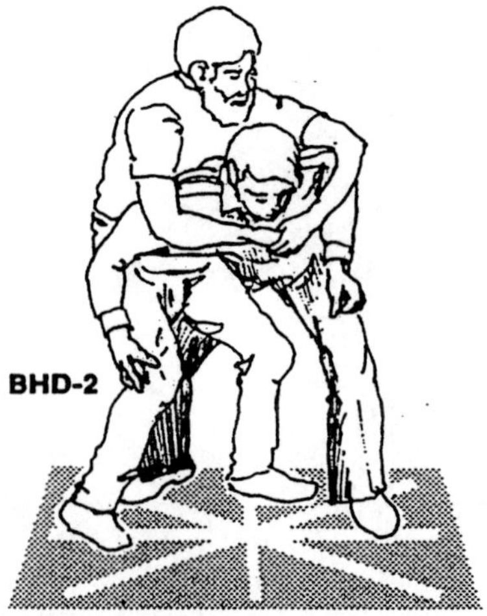

BHD-2

Quickly, move your left foot to the left so that you can place your right leg behind the attacker.

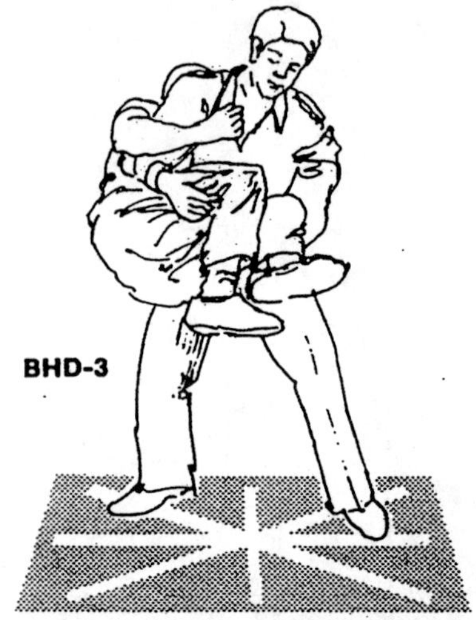

BHD-3

After your right leg is in place, grasp the person by both legs and lift him/her off the ground. As you lift, stand erect. This action should make the person release his/her grip, and thus drop to the ground. Use appropriate follow-up procedures.

**Situation:** An attacker applies a full nelson hold on you.

**Action:**

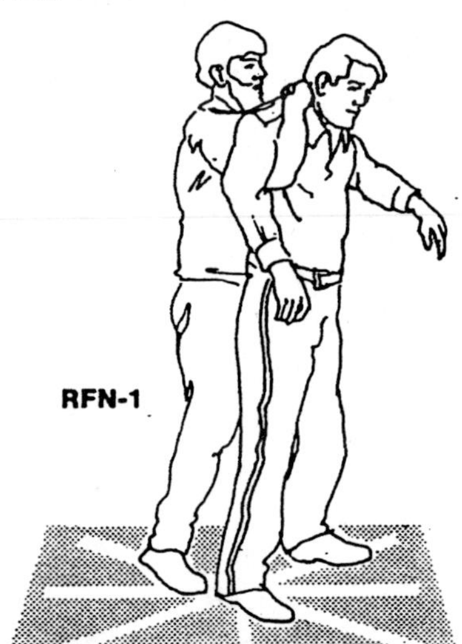

RFN-1

An attacker applies a full nelson hold on you.

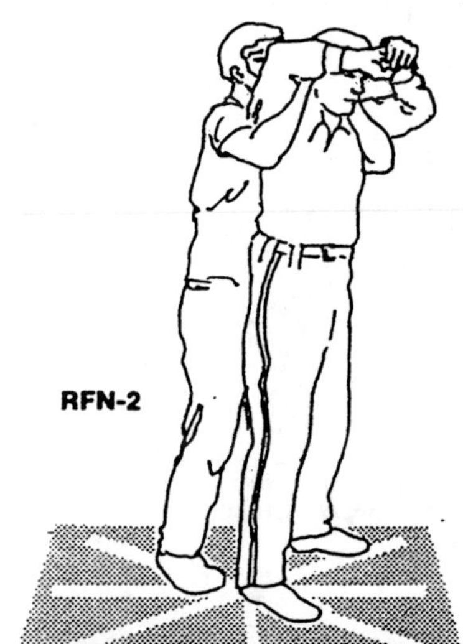

RFN-2

Immediately, lift both of your arms and place your clasped hands against your forehead--palms out. Press your hands against your forehead, preventing the attacker from moving your head forward. Hold this position until you can escape.

**Situation:** An attacker applies a full nelson hold on you.

**Action:**

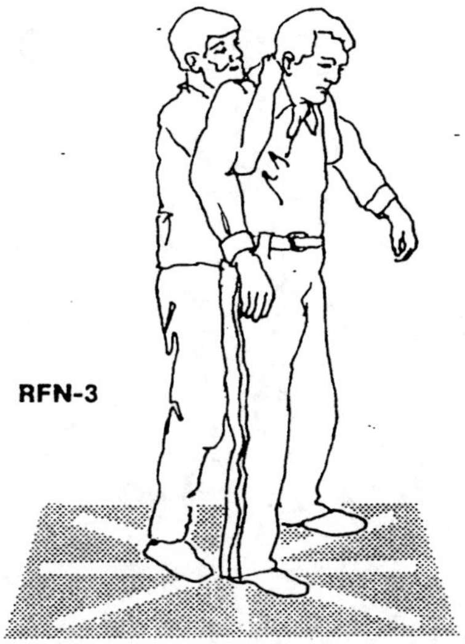

RFN-3

An attacker applies a full nelson hold on you.

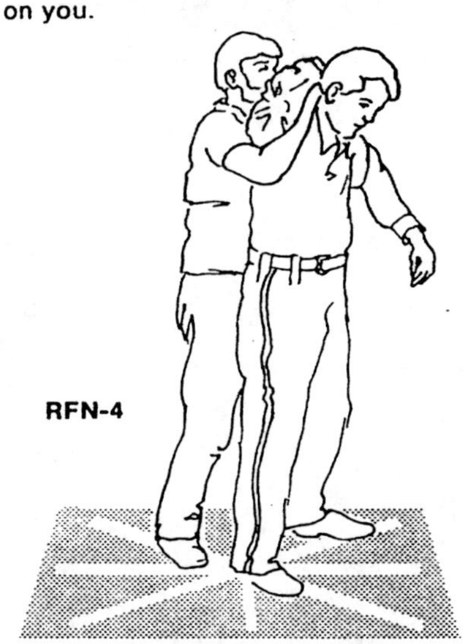

RFN-4

Lift your right arm, grasping the attacker's fingers with your right hand.

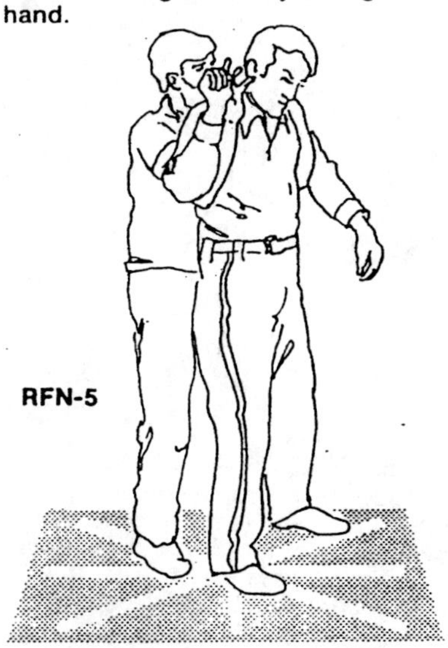

RFN-5

After grasping the attacker's fingers, bend them backward (counterjoint movement), "peeling" his/her hand from your neck.

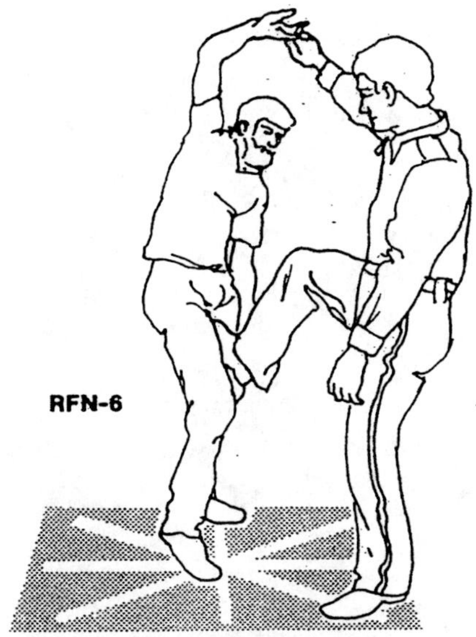

RFN-6

As the attacker's hand is forced from your neck, simultaneously step and turn forward in a 180° arc so that you will be facing the attacker. Continue your fingerlock on the person, keeping his/her hand and arm head-level. This will help to keep him/her unbalanced.

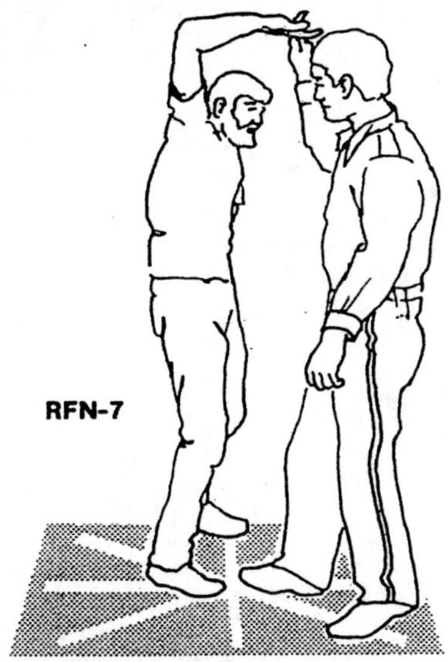

RFN-7

While maintaining your balance, swiftly kick the attacker in the lower abdominal area. Use appropriate follow-up measures.

**Situation:** An attacker applies a full nelson hold on you.

**Action:**

RFN-8

An attacker applies a full nelson hold on you.

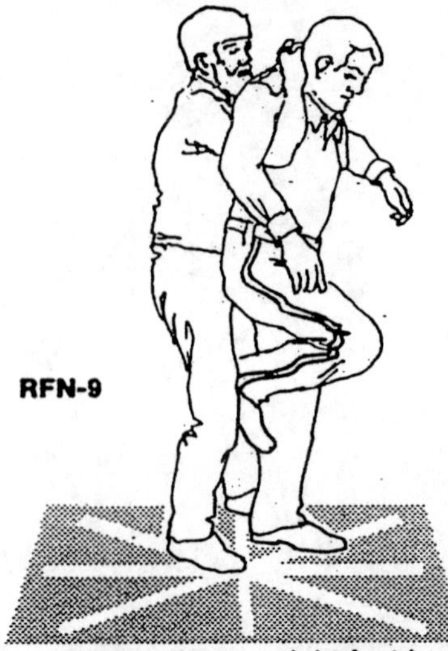

RFN-9

Immediately, lift your right foot by bending at the knee, striking the attacker in the groin. Use appropriate follow-up measures. CAUTION: If the attacker is a lot taller than you,this technique may not work as well.

**Action:** An attacker applies a full nelson hold on you.

**Situation:**

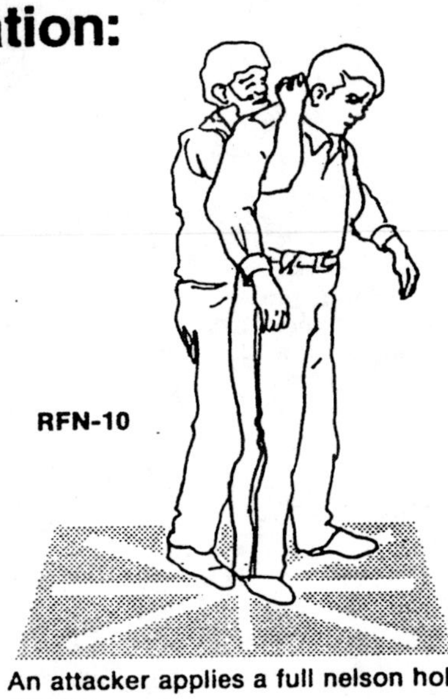

RFN-10

An attacker applies a full nelson hold on you.

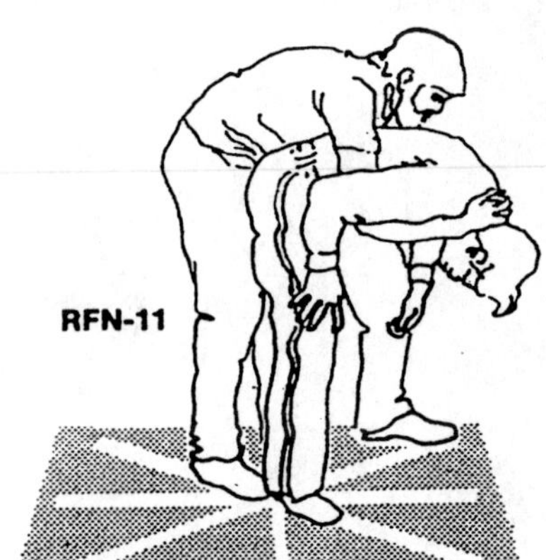

RFN-11

Without giving you chance to react, (s)he forces you to bend forward, by applying pressure on you neck. Keep your feet shoulder-width apart to keep good balance.

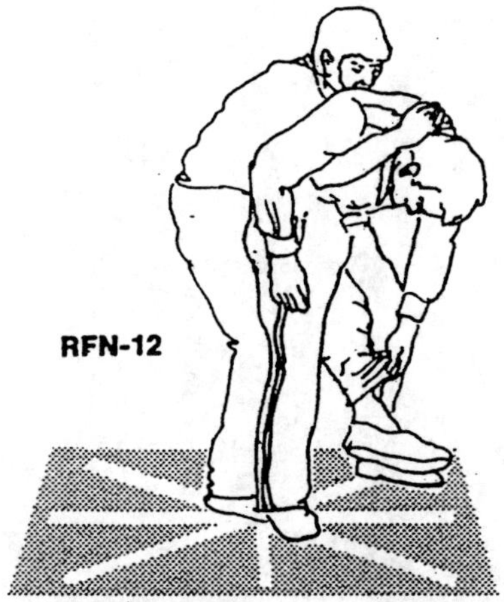

RFN-12

Reaching between your legs, grasp the ankle or the trouser leg of the attacker, and begin to pull it upward and through your legs.

RFN-13

Pulling upward will cause the attacker's leg to straighten, and cause him/her to lose balance. As the attacker loses balance, his/her hands will release the grip on your neck. As you feel the grip loosen, forcefully pull up on the attacker's leg, while simultaneously squatting on the upper leg (above the knee). This action should cause the knee to break. Use appropriate follow-up procedures.

**Situation:** An attacker applies a full nelson hold on you.
**Action:**

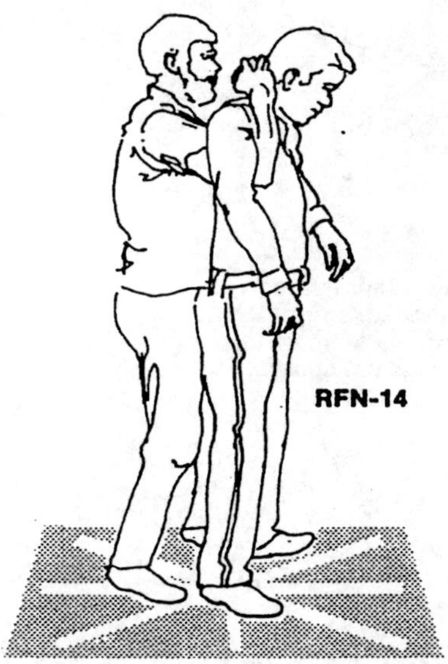

RFN-14

An attacker applies a full nelson hold on you.

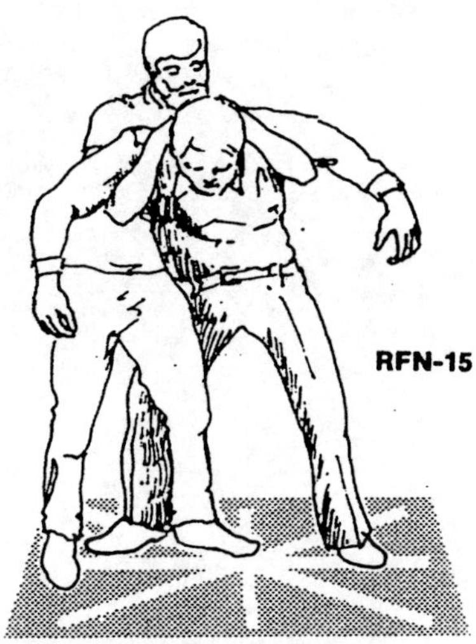

RFN-15

Quickly, move your left foot to the left so that you can place your right leg behind the attacker.

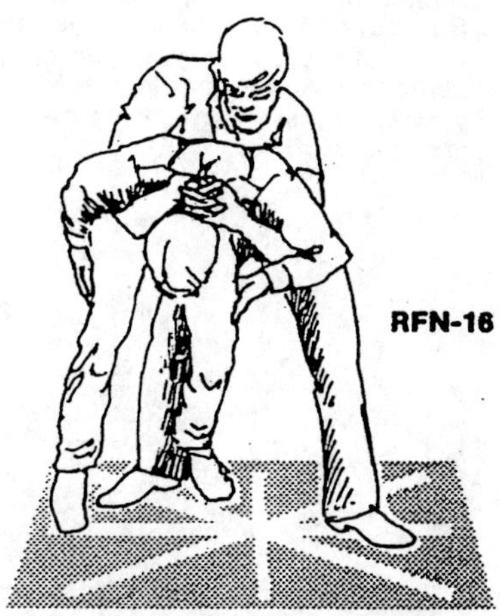

RFN-16

After your right leg is in place, bend forward grasping the person by both legs and lift him/her off the ground. As you lift, stand erect. This action should make the person release his/her hold, and thus drop to the ground. Use appropriate follow-up procedures.

**Situation:** An attacker holds you on your back by sitting upon your stomach while pinning down your arms by grasping your wrists.

**Action:**

POB-1

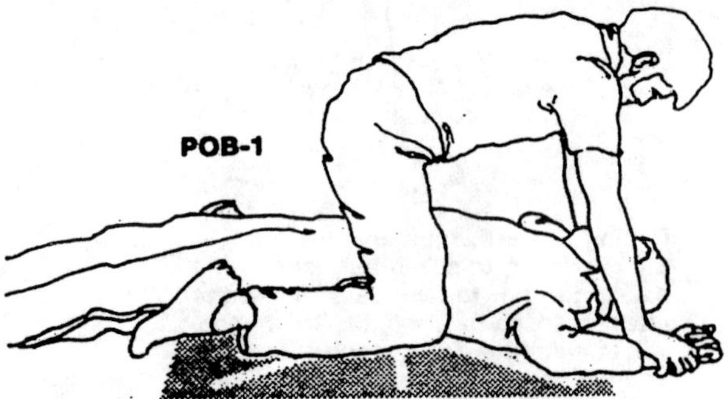

You are pinned on your back by an attacker who is sitting on your stomach, and who is also firmly holding onto your wrists.

POB-2

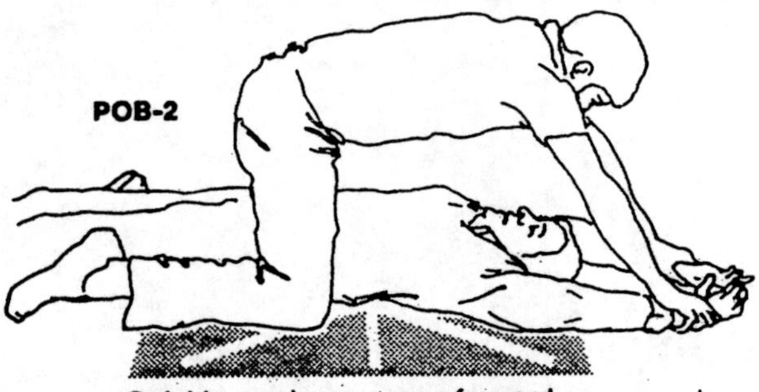

Quickly, push your arms forward, forming a steeple by bringing your open hands together in a point beyond your head. This will cause the attacker's balance point to shift forward. NOTE: Your hands must remain open; a fist tightens your forearm and thus makes movement more difficult. Also, your hands must come together in a point beyond your head, or the attacker's balance may not shift.

POB-3

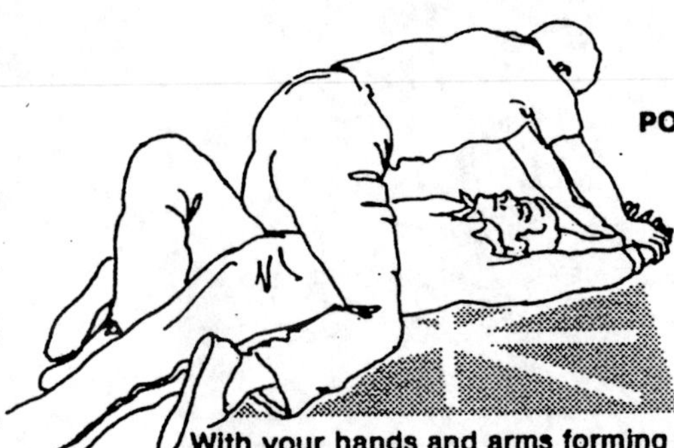

With your hands and arms forming a steeple and the attacker's balance point moved forward, bend your right leg, placing your right foot firmly upon the ground.

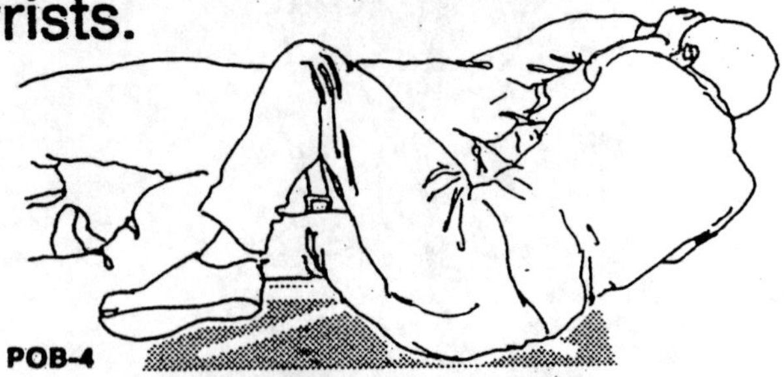

POB-4

Lifting your hips off the ground by pressing down with your right foot, roll the attacker to your left. For extra power, lift your arms, too.

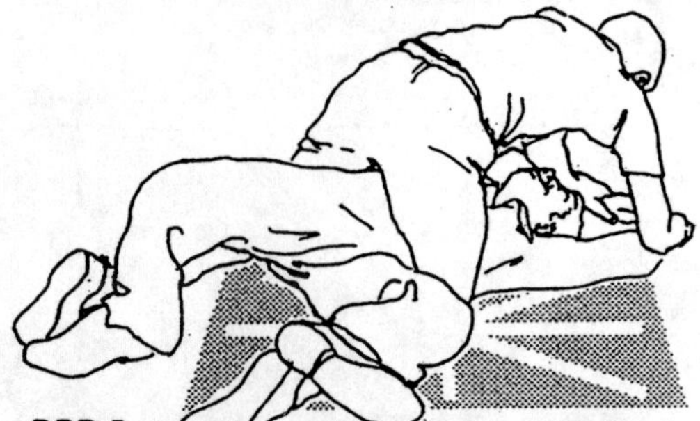

POB-5

As you begin to roll, your left leg should be placed over the attacker's right leg. This action will trap the attacker's leg, thus helping to hold him/her into position.

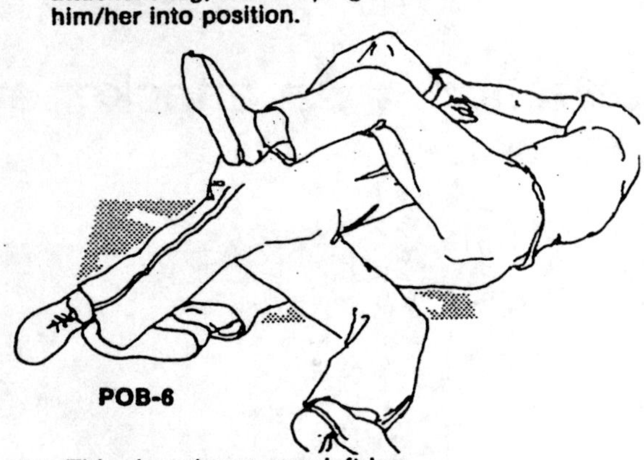

POB-6

This view shows your left leg trapping the attacker's right leg as the roll is being made. Note also that the attacker's legs are spread.

POB-7

After the attacker has been rolled onto his/her side, forcefully bring your knee into the attacker's groin. Use appropriate follow-up procedures.

**Situation:** An attacker holds you on your back by sitting upon your stomach while choking you around the throat with his/her hands.

**Action:**

COB-1

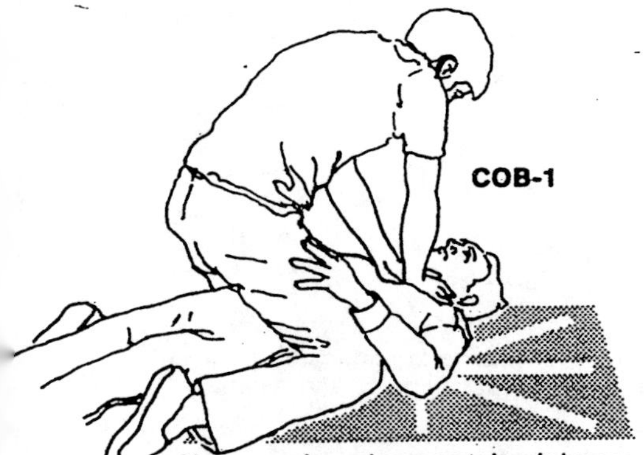

You are pinned on your back by an attacker who is sitting on your stomach and who is also choking you.

COB-2

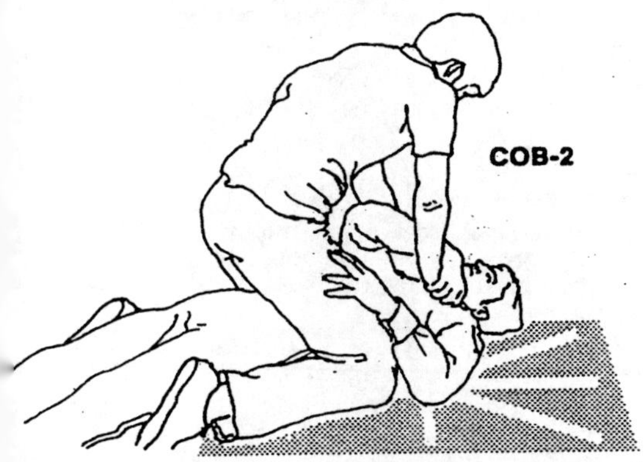

Using your right hand, quickly reach under the attacker's left arm and grasp his/her right hand. Notice that your fingers are being placed under his/her right hand.

COB-3

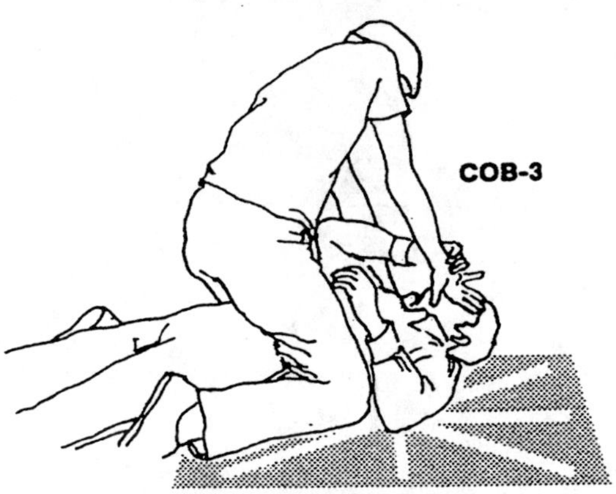

Peel the attacker's right hand from your neck by lifting upward and by turning his/her hand clockwise.

COB-4

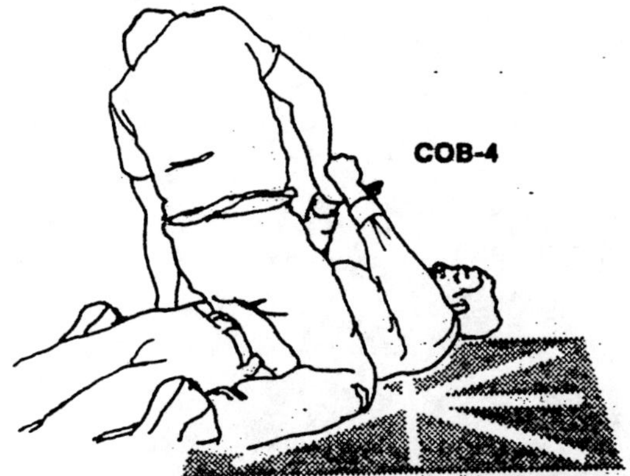

Grasp the attacker's right thumb with your left hand. Bend his/her wrist (counterjoint movement) which will produce pain. Notice that the attacker's right elbow is slightly bent.

COB-5

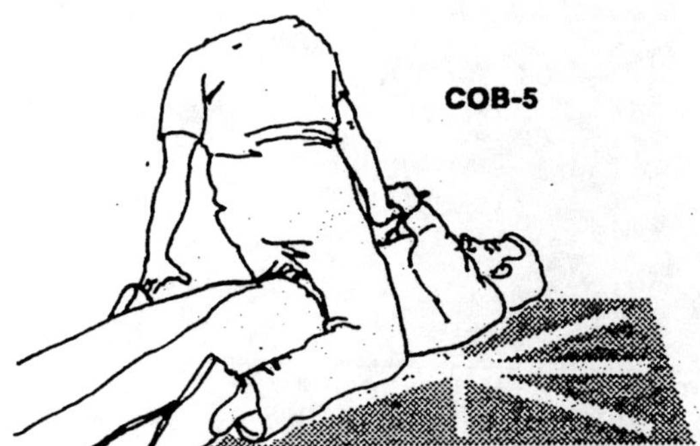

Straighten the attacker's right elbow by turning his/her wrist to the right while applying counterjoint pressure in an effort to break the wrist. In an effort to escape the pain, the attacker should roll to your right, freeing you. Use appropriate follow-up procedures.

**Situation:** An attacker holds you on your back by sitting upon your stomach while choking you around the throat with his/her hands.

**Action:**

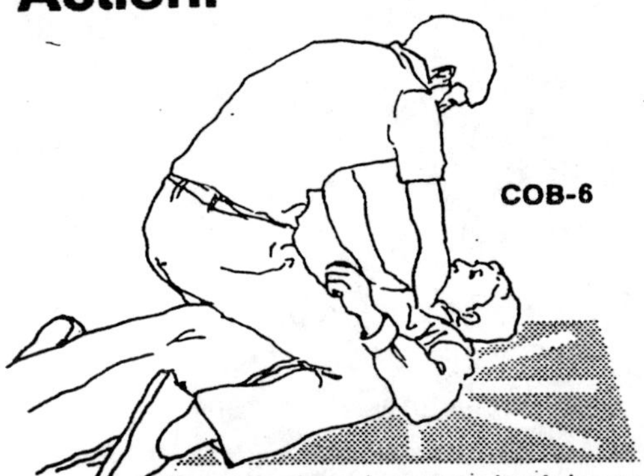

COB-6

You are pinned on your back by an attacker who is sitting on your stomach and who is also choking you.

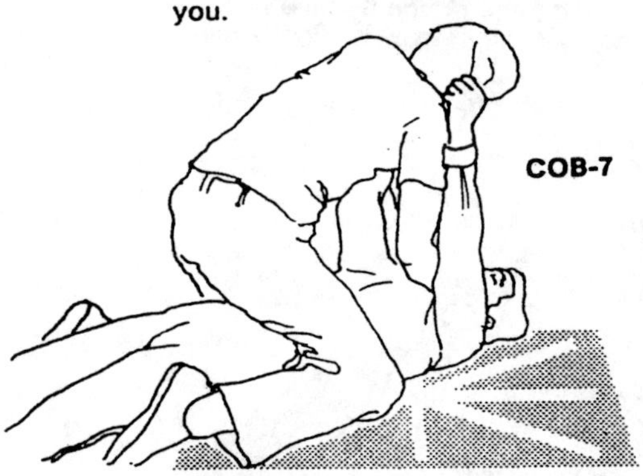

COB-7

Immediately, reach between the attacker's arms with your right hand and grasp his/her chin. Simultaneously, with your left hand, grasp the attacker's hair or ear. Keep your left hand to the outside of the attacker's right arm so that you can reach the head area.

COB-8

Forcefully, twist the attacker's head counterclockwise. This is done by pushing the chin up and to the right with your right hand, while simultaneously pulling the head (really the hair) downward and to the inside with your left hand.

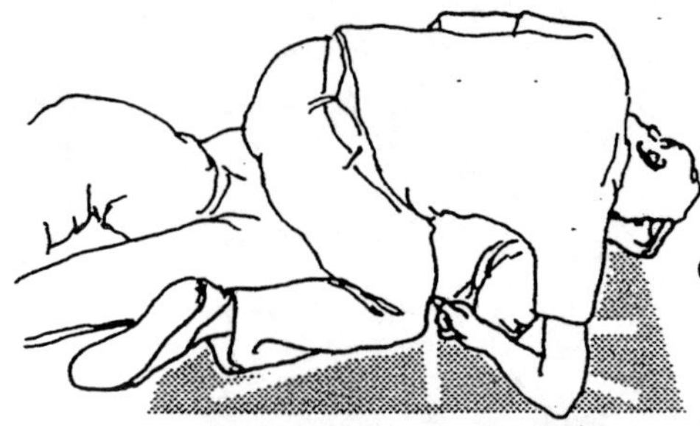

COB-9

Continue twisting the attacker's head until (s)he loses balance and begins to fall to your left.

COB-10

After you have "twisted" the attacker onto the ground alongside you, use the appropriate follow-up procedures.

**Situation:** During a fight you tripped and fell onto your back. Now a person is approaching you to "do you in."

**Action:**

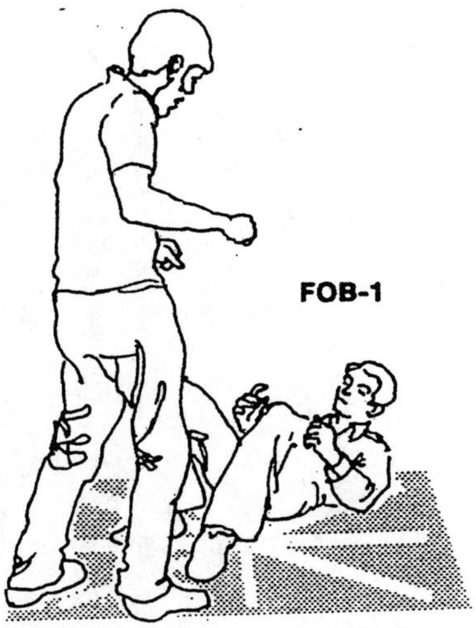

FOB-1

While on your back, a person is approaching to "finish" the fight.

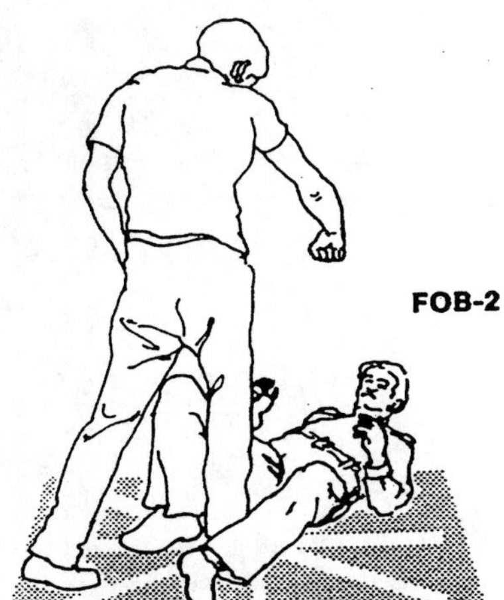

FOB-2

As the person approaches, extend your left leg, hooking your left ankle behind the person's right ankle.

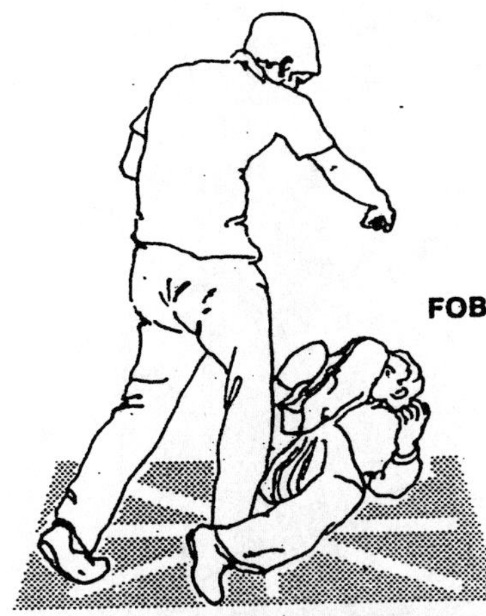

FOB-3

With your left ankle into place, raise your right leg and bend your knee.

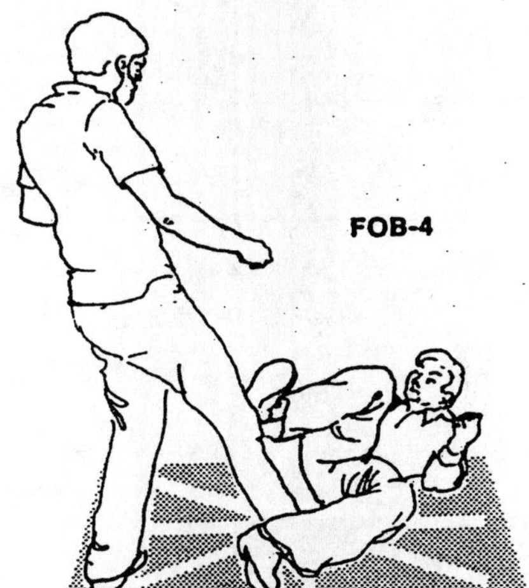

FOB-4

Forcefully push your right foot against the person's leg (just above the knee) while keeping your left ankle in place. This counterjoint movement against the knee will knock the person backward causing him/her to fall. The knee may also be broken. Note: to increase your striking area, you may wish to turn your right foot sideways (toes pointing toward your left side).

**Situation:** Standing in an interrogation position talking with a suspect, (s)he attempts to kick you in the groin.

**Action:**

FGK-1

Standing in an interrogation position, you begin talking to a suspect.

FGK-2

Suddenly, the suspect lifts his/her right foot, attempting to kick you in the groin.

FGK-3

Keeping your back straight, prepare to stop the suspect's kick using an "X" block.

FGK-4

Thrusting your right leg back which serves to move your groin back and away from the kick, stop the suspect's kick using an "X" block technique. The "X" block is created by placing one wrist on top of the other, hands open with fingers together. Remember to keep your eyes on the suspect, not on the kick, The reason: the kick could be a fake, hence you could be set up for a punch to the face. Watching the suspect also lets you see if (s)he has pulled a knife or gun.

FGK-5

Having blocked the suspect's kick, quickly grab the leg by wrapping your hands around his/her ankle. Next stand erect, lifting the suspect's leg to your waist level.

FGK-6

Maintaining your balance by holding onto the suspect's ankle, lift your right foot by bending your knee.

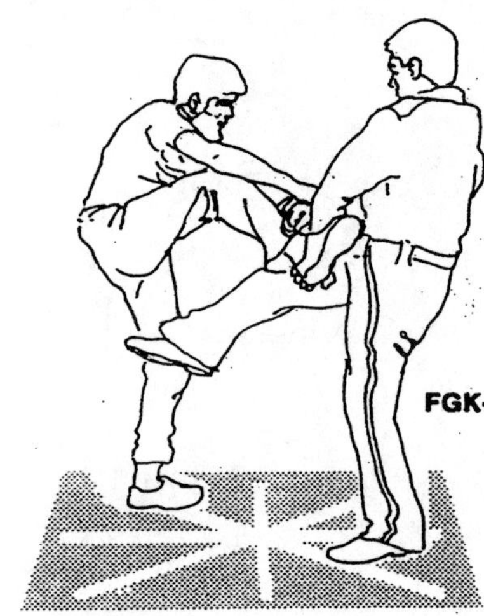

FGK-7

Forcefully, kick the suspect in the groin area. Use appropriate follow-up procedures.

## CHAPTER SIX: CONTROL AND RESTRAINT TECHNIQUES

Controlling an individual through the use of effective yet safe techniques is this section's focus. While there are hundreds of controlling and restraining techniques, we have selected the ones which you can learn and also retain after a few short practice sessions.

When you are practicing the techniques shown in this section, concentrate on combining the various control and restraint holds. Since combat is always changing, versatility and ease in changing from one hold to another is important.

**Situation:** You are walking a suspect in the "position of advantage" when (s)he refuses to go any farther, or begins to offer resistance.

**Action:**

PAK-1

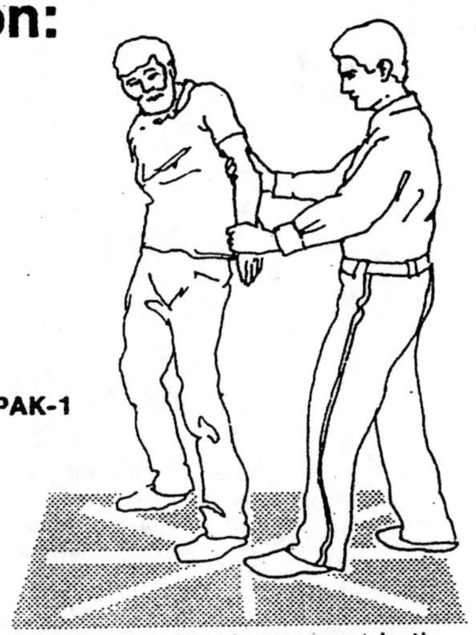

You are walking the suspect in the "position of advantage" when (s)he refuses to cooperate. That is, you are holding the suspect by his/her left wrist with your left wrist, while firmly grasping his/her left bicep with your right hand.

PAK-2

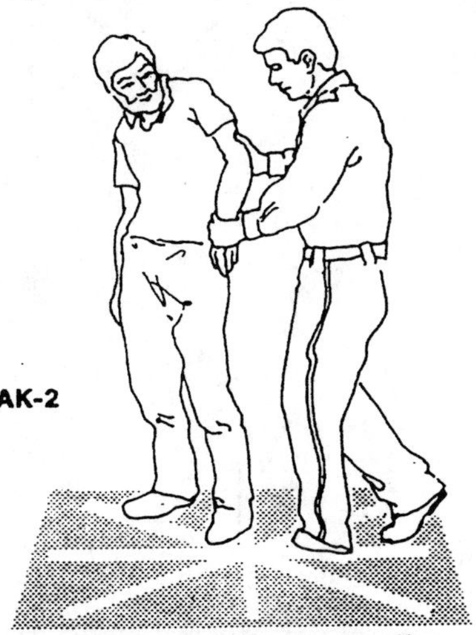

When the suspect begins to offer resistance, bend your right leg at the knee.

PAK-3

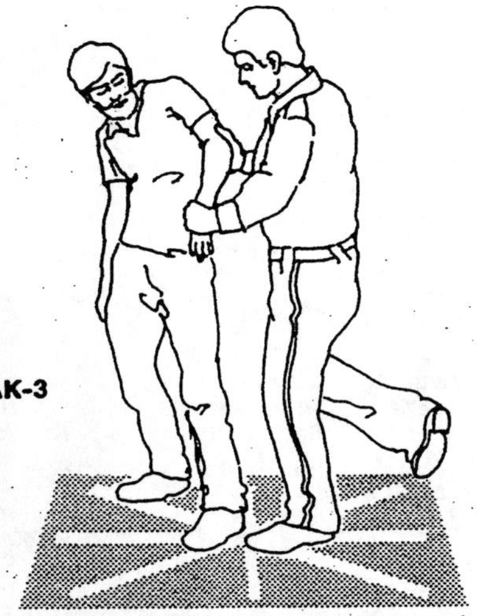

Lift your right foot from the ground so that your leg will be mobile.

PAK-4

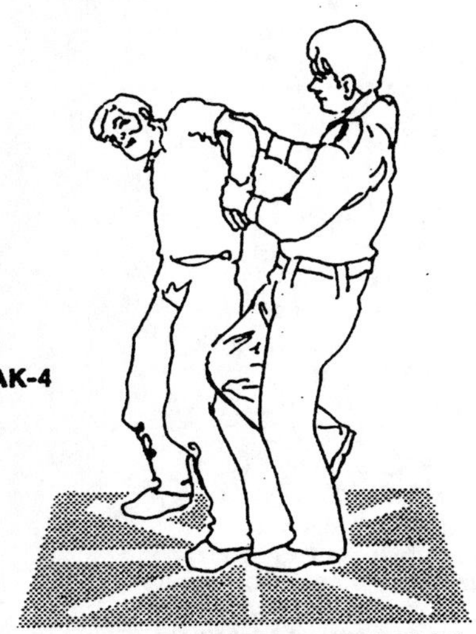

Forcefully strike the suspect's thigh area with your right knee. Your impact point should be on the suspect's trouser seam, about three inches above the knee joint. This action will result in the suspect's leg cramping, rendering him/her unable to walk. Use appropriate follow-up procedures.

**Situation:** You are walking a suspect from the "position of advantage" when (s)he suddenly refuses to go any farther, or begins to offer resistance.

**Action:**

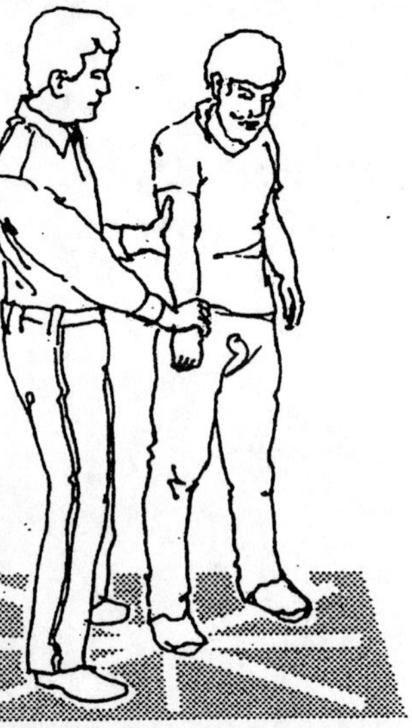

RAL-1

You are walking the suspect from a "position of advantage" when (s)he refuses to cooperate. That is, you are holding the suspect by his/her right wrist with your right hand, while grasping his/her right bicep with your left hand.

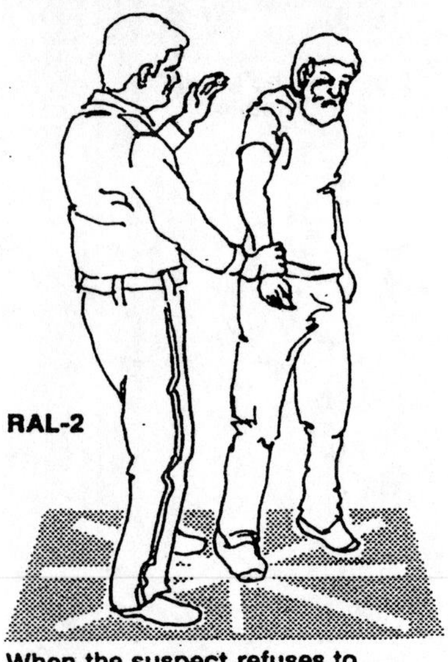

RAL-2

When the suspect refuses to cooperate, remove your left hand from the suspect's bicep. Continuing to hold the suspect's right wrist, bend and raise your left arm at the elbow keeping your left hand open, fingers together. Straighten the person's right arm by pulling it outward with your right hand.

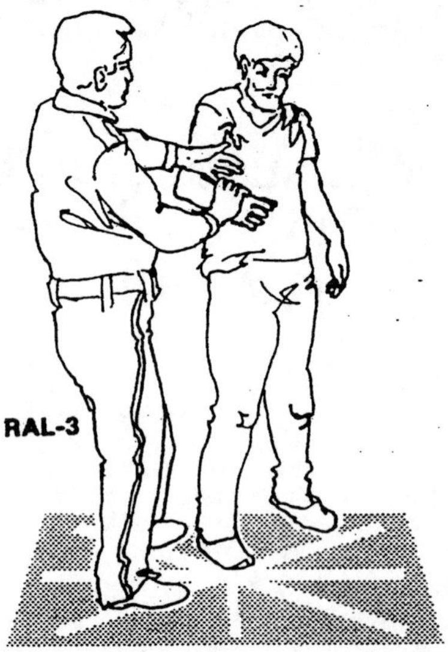

RAL-3

Forcefully "chop" the crook of the suspect's right arm with your left hand, while lifting his/her right wrist to shoulder height using your right hand.

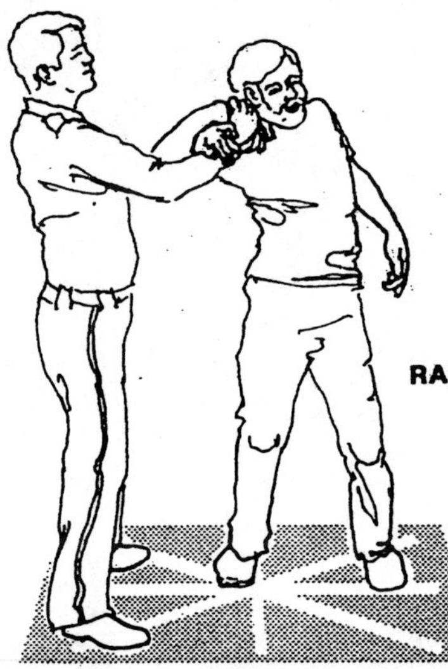

RAL-4

Keeping your left hand in the crook of the suspect's elbow, grasp your right wrist when you get the person's wrist to shoulder height.

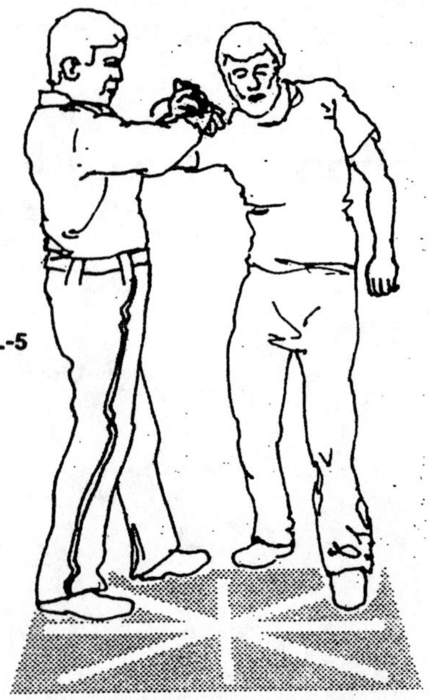

RAL-5

Begin to apply pressure against the person's wrist and shoulder by pushing backward (past the head) and downward on his/her wrist and upward and forward on his/her forearm.

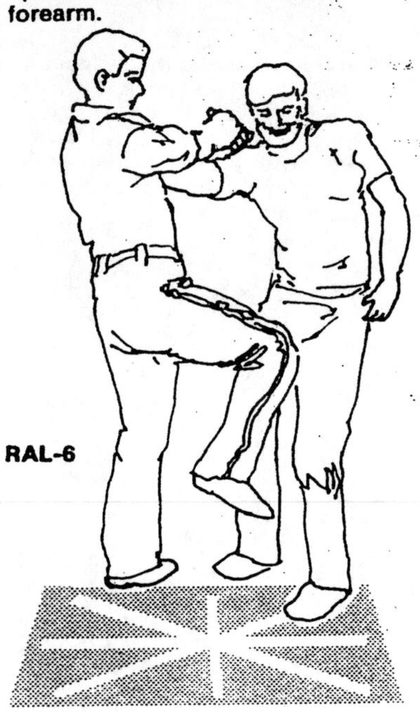

RAL-6

If necessary, i.e., the suspect is resisting you, strike the person in the lower abdominal area with your knee.

RAL-7

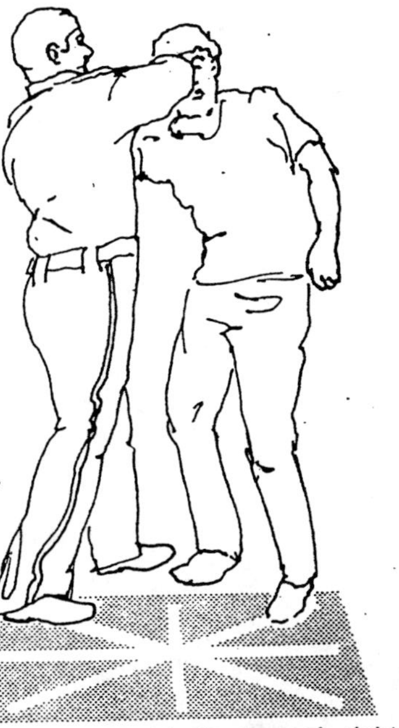

Stepping alongside the person's right foot with your left foot (about one foot apart), face the person. Push the person's wrist downward and backward (past the head) with your right hand, while applying pressure upward and forward on his/her forearm. If necessary, you may strike the person in the face with your right forearm as you complete the reverse arm lock.

RAL-8

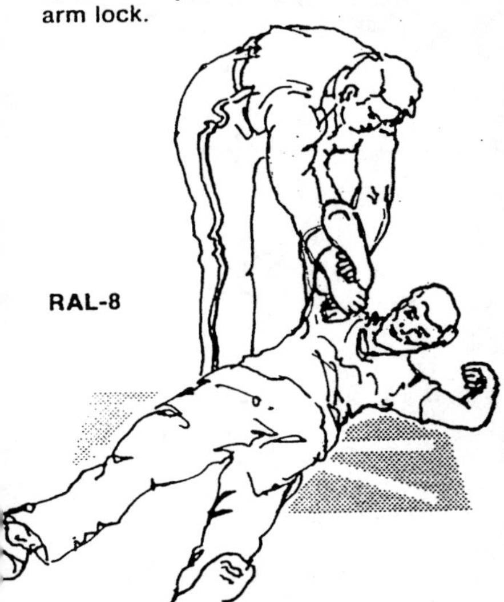

Continue the pressure on the supect's wrist, arm and shoulder until (s)he falls backward upon the ground. Don't remove your hands.

RAL-9

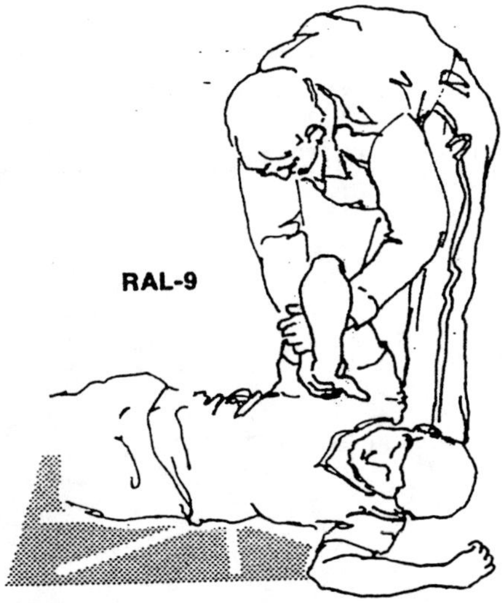

Lift up on the suspect's arm so that (s)he will rest on his/her left side.

RAL-10

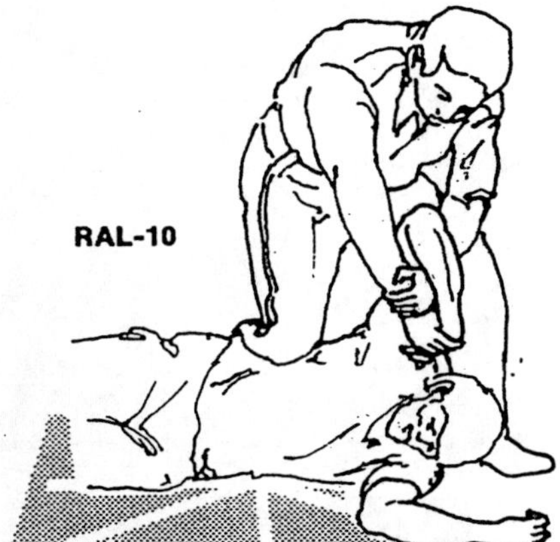

After, (s)he is on the left side, place your right knee upon his/her right rib cage. This action will help to control the person, plus help you to keep good balance. NOTE: Do not drop your knee upon his/her rib cage. The reason: you do not want to crack or break the ribs.

RAL-11

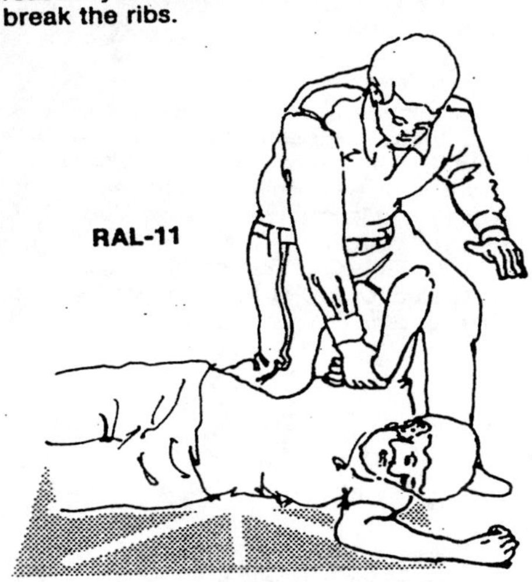

Holding the person's right wrist with your right hand, remove your left hand from your right wrist.

RAL-12

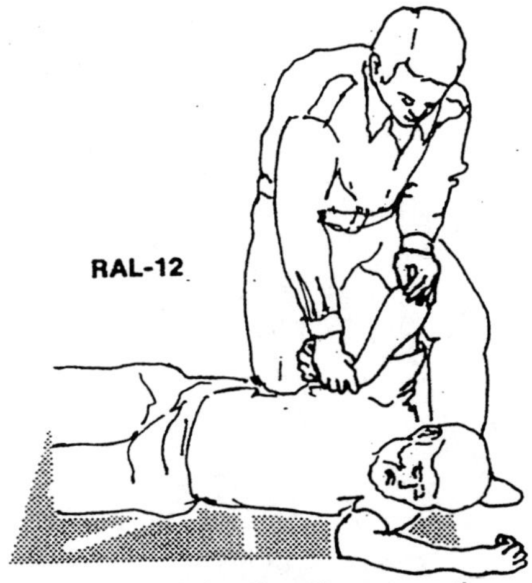

Place your left hand on the suspect's elbow.

RAL-13

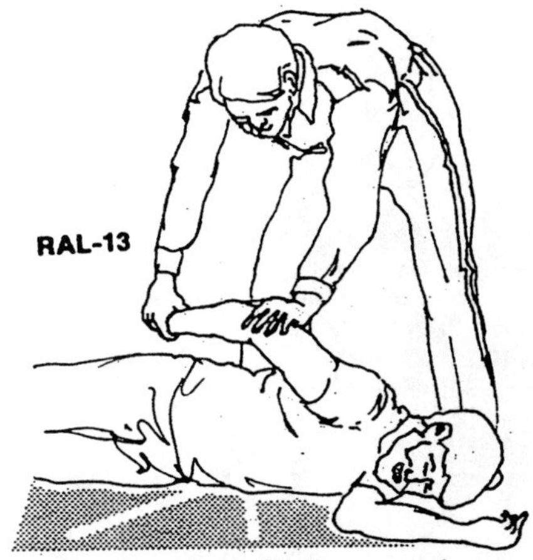

Simultaneously, push the person's elbow toward the ground with your left hand, while pulling his/her right wrist toward your knee using your right hand. This action should cause the suspect to roll onto his/her stomach.

RAL-14

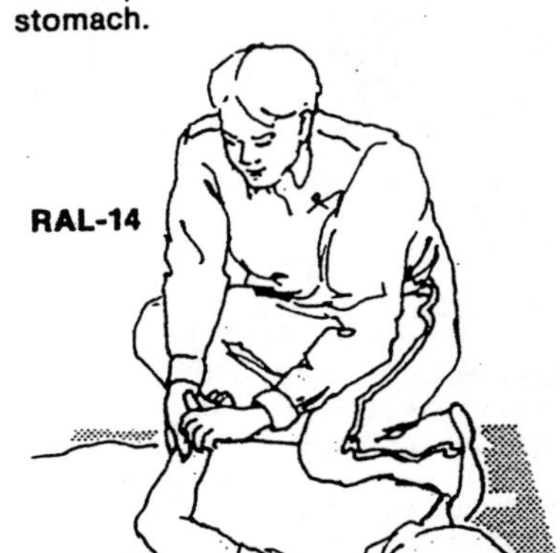

After the suspect is lying flat, kneel upon the suspect so that your left knee is on his/her shoulder blade area. Your right knee may be placed on his/her waist, or upon the ground next to the suspect. Handcuff the suspect's left wrist. Use appropriate follow-up procedures. CAUTION: Do not place your knee on the suspect's neck. The reason: you may cause serious injury to the suspect.

**Situation:** You are walking a suspect in the "position of advantage" when (s)he suddenly refuses to go any farther, or begins to offer resistance.

**Action:**

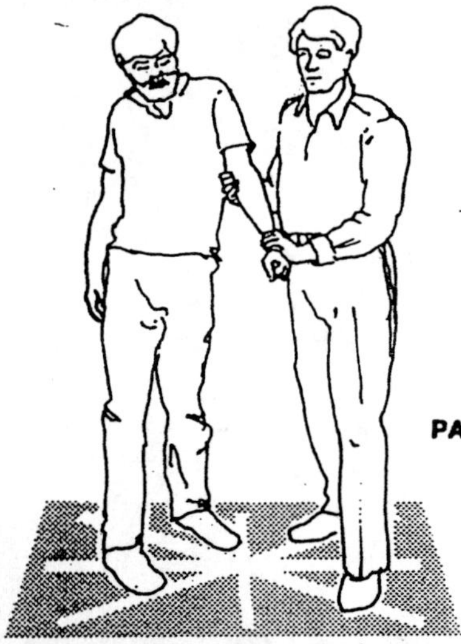

PAD-1

You are walking a suspect from a "position of advantage" when (s)he refuses to cooperate. That is, you are holding the suspect by his/her left wrist with your left hand, while firmly grasping his/her left bicep with your right hand.

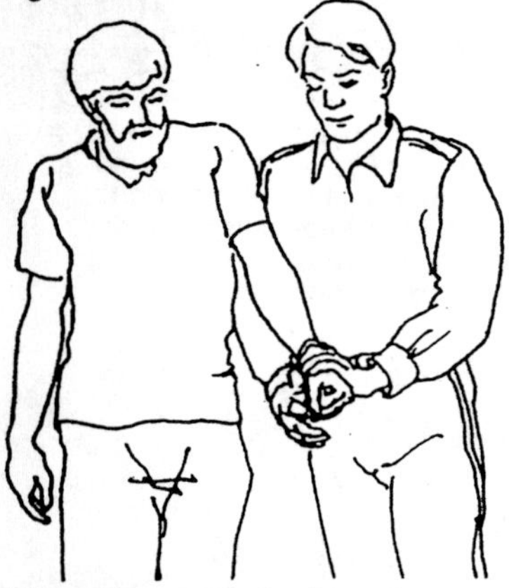

PAD-2

When the suspect refuses to cooperate, remove your right hand from the suspect's bicep. Continuing to hold the suspect's left wrist, insert your right arm between the suspect's body and left arm. Next place the tip of your right index finger over the suspect's left thumbnail.

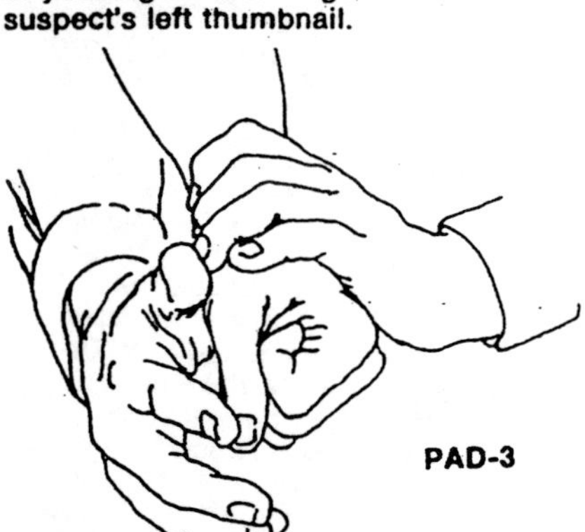

PAD-3

A close-up showing your right index finger being placed on the suspect's left thumbnail.

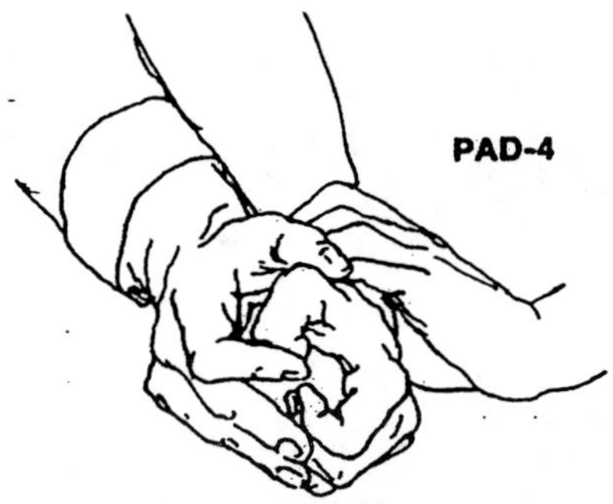

PAD-4

Index finger in place, squeeze the suspect's thumbnail as though squeezing the trigger of a firearm. Your right thumb should be placed behind the suspect's thumb so that it bends at the thumb knuckle. The goal is to produce intense pain in the suspect's left thumb.

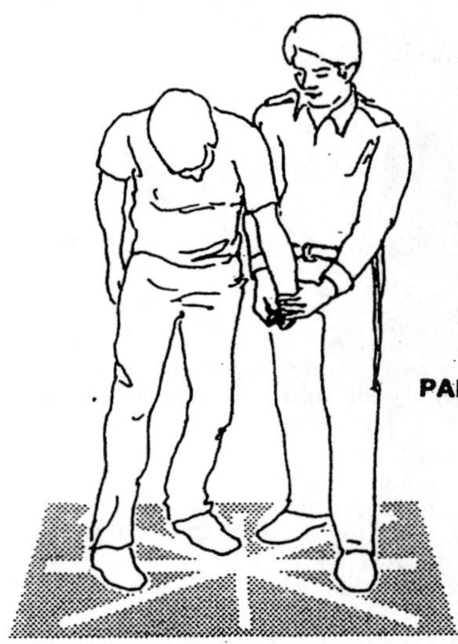

PAD-5

While squeezing the suspect's thumbnail and bending his/her thumb, pull the suspect's left forearm downward and backward causing the suspect to lean forward. Note: You are still standing to the left of the suspect, maintaining good balance, prepared for any sudden actions by the suspect.

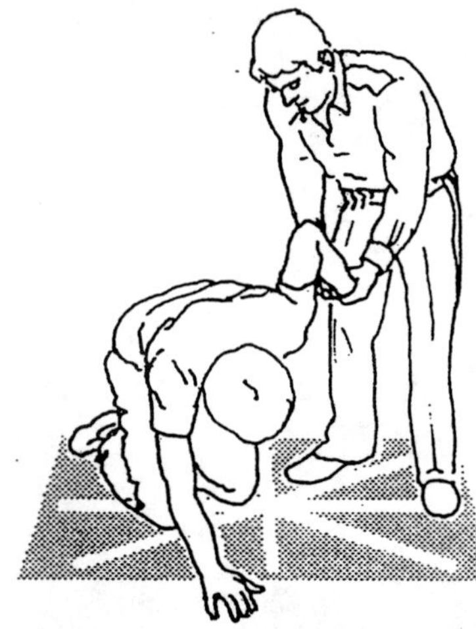

PAD-6

Continue to squeeze and bend the suspect's thumb by pulling him/her forward until his/her knees are on the ground. Keep the suspect's left arm bent at the elbow and away from his/her left side, so that you can effect a handcuffing position. Next, pull the suspect's left arm behind the back, forcing him/her face-down upon the ground.

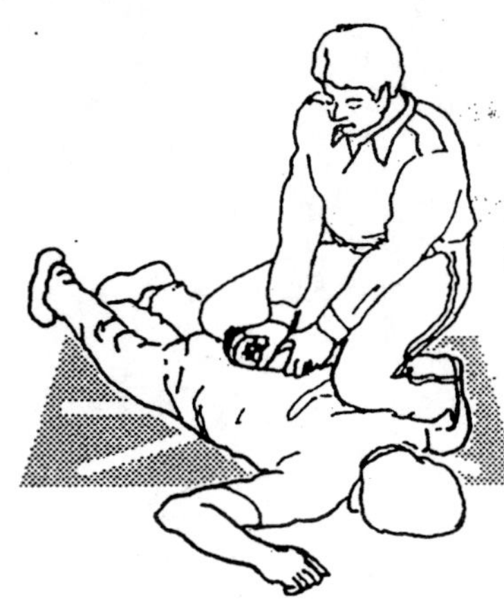

PAD-7

After the suspect is upon the ground, kneel on the suspect. Place your left knee diagonally across the suspect's left shoulder blade area. This will help to keep the suspect flat on the ground. DO NOT PUT YOUR KNEE ON THE SUSPECT'S NECK! The reason: you may slip during the knee's placement and unintentionally seriously damage or break the neck. The suspect's arm should be "trapped" between your two legs. Handcuff the trapped wrist first, then handcuff the other wrist.

**Situation:** You are walking a suspect from the "position of advantage" when (s)he suddenly refuses to go any farther, or begins to offer resistance.

**Action:**

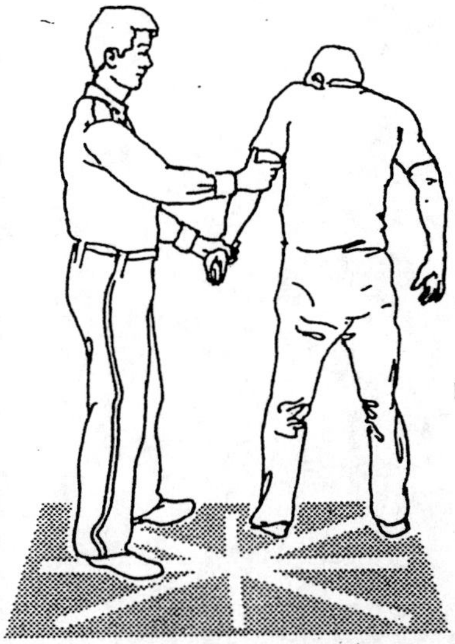

BHL-1

You are walking the suspect from a "position of advantage" when (s)he refuses to cooperate. That is, you are holding the suspect by his/her left bicep with your right hand.

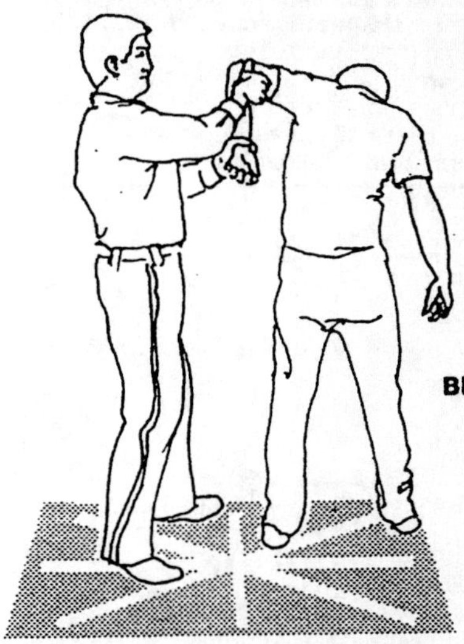

BHL-2

To apply the technique, pinch the underside of the suspect's bicep with your right thumb and index finger. Simultaneously, lift the suspect's arm using your left hand, causing the arm to bend at the elbow. NOTE: Should the suspect try to punch you with his/her right hand, the only thing struck will be his/her own left elbow. Hence, a built-in safety feature.

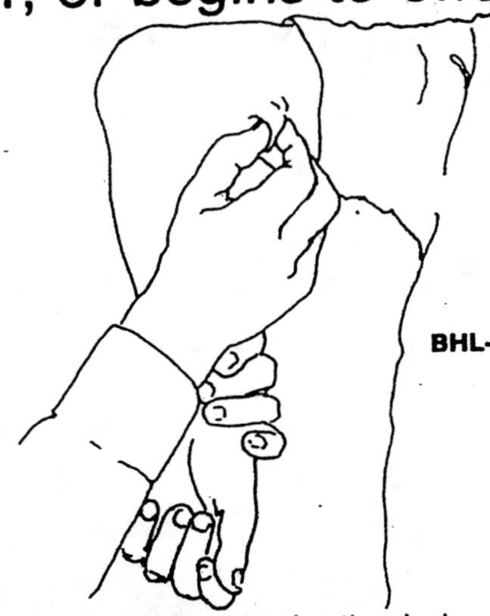

BHL-3

A close-up view showing the pinch. The lesser amount of skin pinched, the better. The reason: pinching a lot of skin causes less pain than pinching just a little.

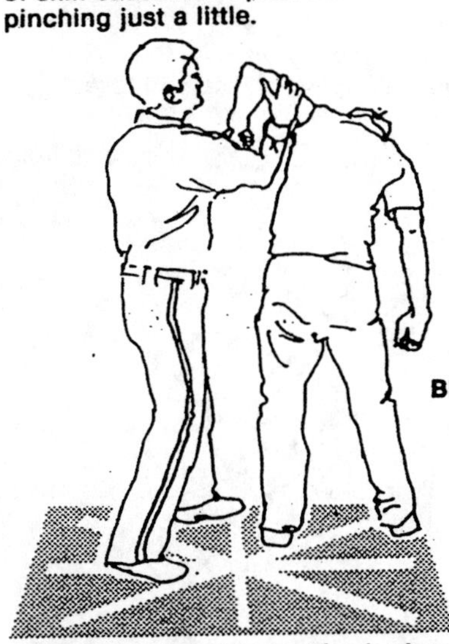

BHL-4

The suspect's left arm raised, place your right hand on the suspect's bicep. NOTE: Slapping your right hand into place will cause the suspect to lurch forward, easing the technique application.

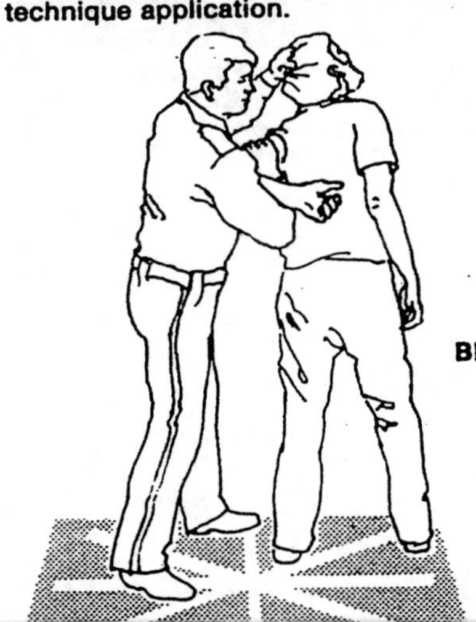

BHL-5

Using your left hand, grab the suspect's hair, left ear, or shirt (coat) collar. The reason: to firmly control the suspect. If you fail to grasp the suspect's hair, ear or collar, there is a chance that (s)he can escape the armlock.

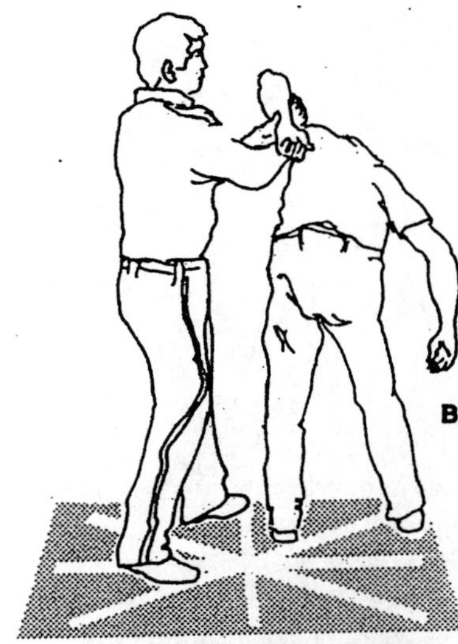

BHL-6

With your right hand in place, use your left hand to lift the suspect's forearm over your right arm.

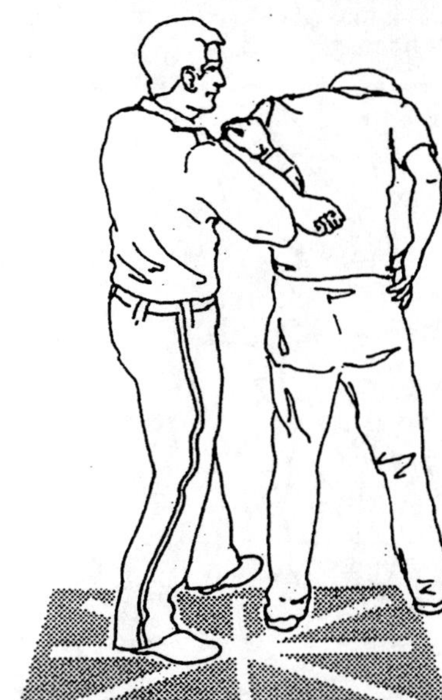

BHL-7

After lifting the suspect's forearm over your right arm, release your left hand. Attempt to cradle the suspect's wrist area in the crook of your right arm. Continue to fold the suspect's left arm behind and up his/her back.

**Situation:** You are walking a suspect from the "position of advantage" when (s)he suddenly refuses to go any farther, or begins to offer resistance.

**Action:**

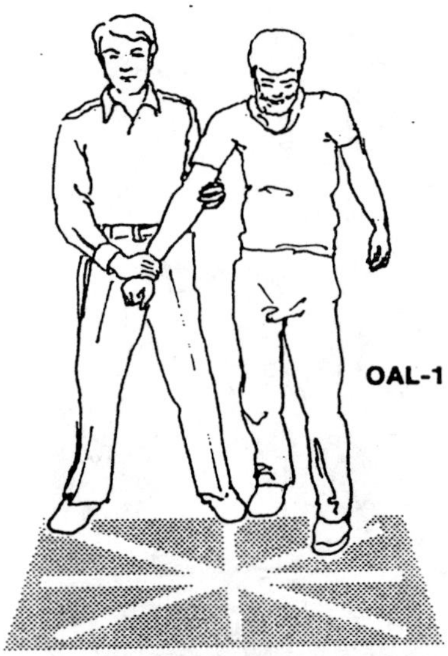

OAL-1

You are walking the suspect from a "position of advantage when (s)he refuses to cooperate. That is, you are holding the suspect by his/her right wrist with your right hand, while grasping his/her right bicep with your left hand.

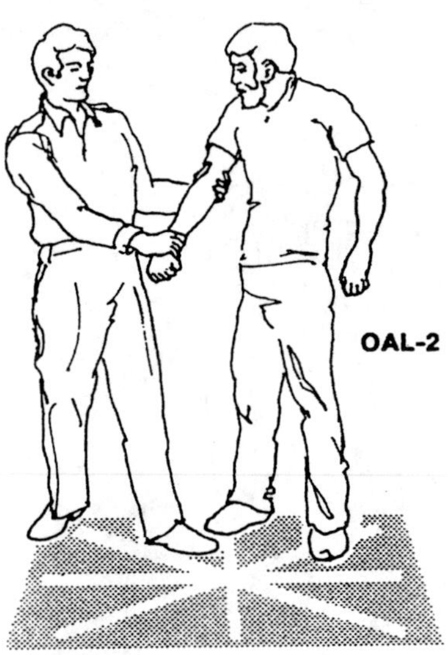

OAL-2

When the suspect refuses to cooperate, pull the person's arm toward you.

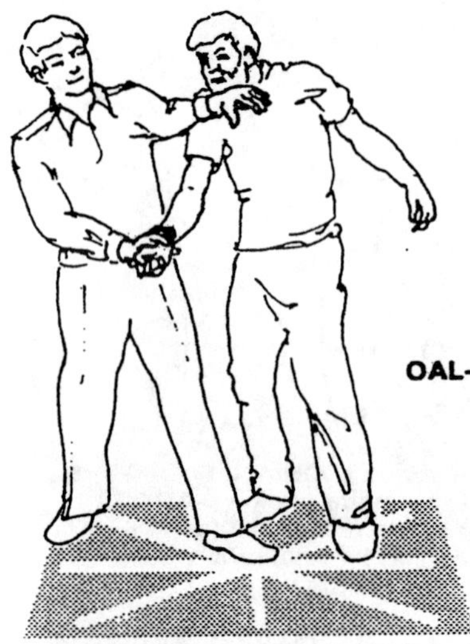

OAL-3

Remove your left arm, placing it over the suspect's arm. Simultaneously, straighten the person's arm by pulling it forward with your right hand.

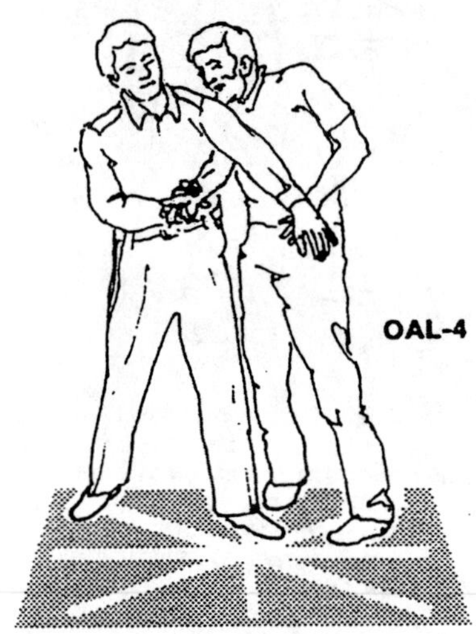

OAL-4

Wrap your left arm around the suspect's right arm. Your forearm should be placed above the person's elbow for good leverage.

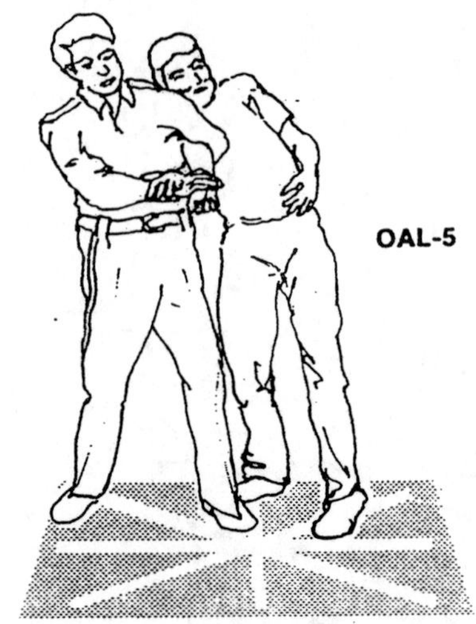

OAL-5

Grasp your right wrist with your left hand. Keeping the suspect's elbow straight and with your left forearm above it, flex your left foream while pulling the suspect's wrist downward with your right hand. This action should create intense pain in the suspect's elbow area. If necessary, you can break the person's elbow. Use appropriate follow-up procedures.

**Situation:** You are walking a suspect in the "position of advantage" when (s)he forcefully tries to escape.

**Action:**

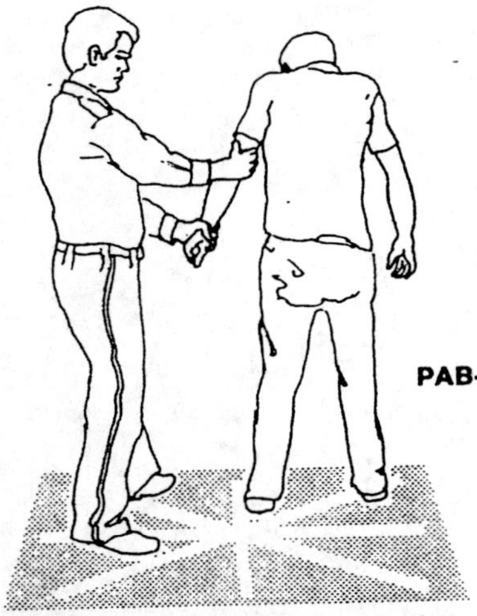

PAB-1

You are walking the suspect in the "position of advantage". That is, you are holding the suspect by his/her left wrist with your left hand, while firmly grasping his/her left bicep with your right hand.

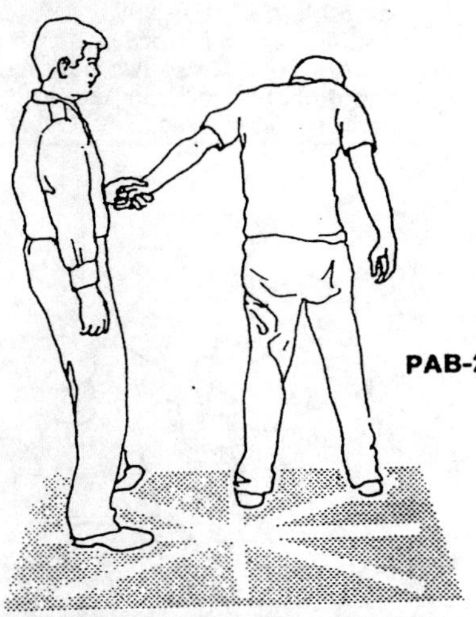

PAB-2

Suddenly, the suspect makes an escape attempt. (S)he begins to escape your firm grasp. Notice that the suspect's left elbow is pointing upward.

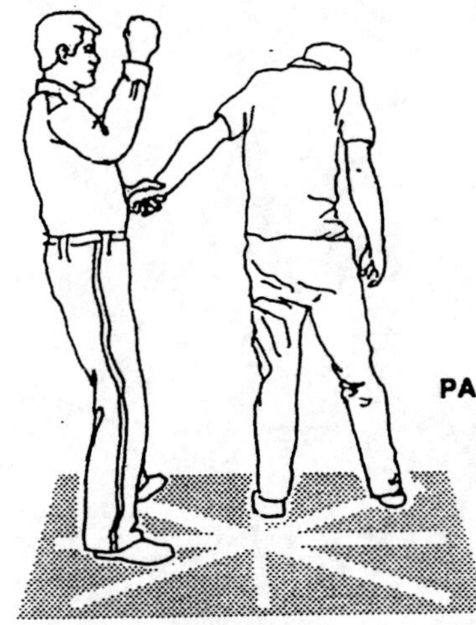

PAB-3

Quickly, raise your right arm, bending it at the elbow.

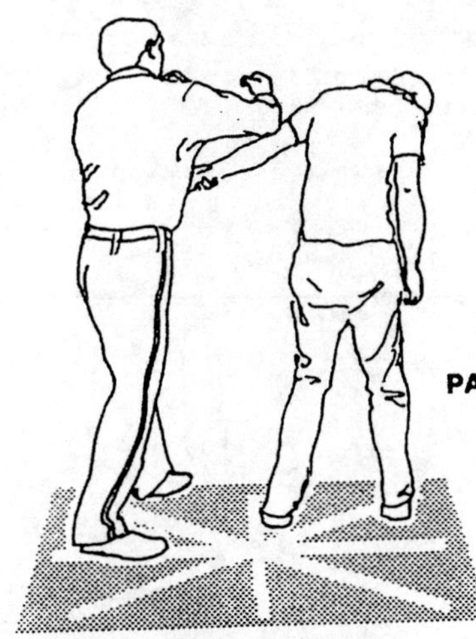

PAB-4

Forcefully drop your right arm so that your forearm strikes the suspect's arm just above the elbow. This action will probably break the suspect's elbow, and/or force him/her to the ground. Use appropriate follow-up procedures.

**Situation:** You must control and restrain a person whom you have just placed under arrest, but who refuses to comply with your order.

**Action:**

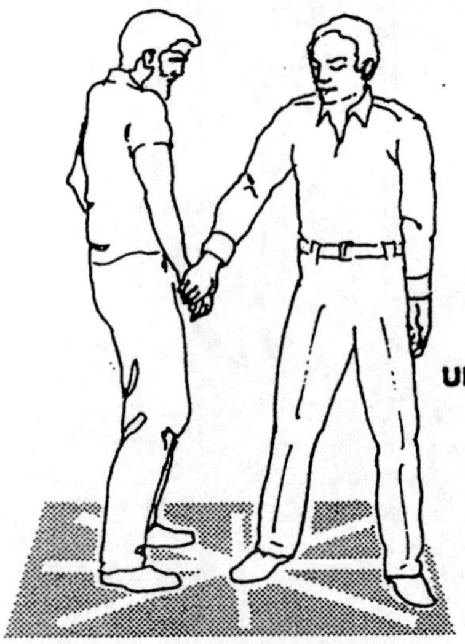

UDW-1

Grasp the suspect's right hand with your right hand - palm down.

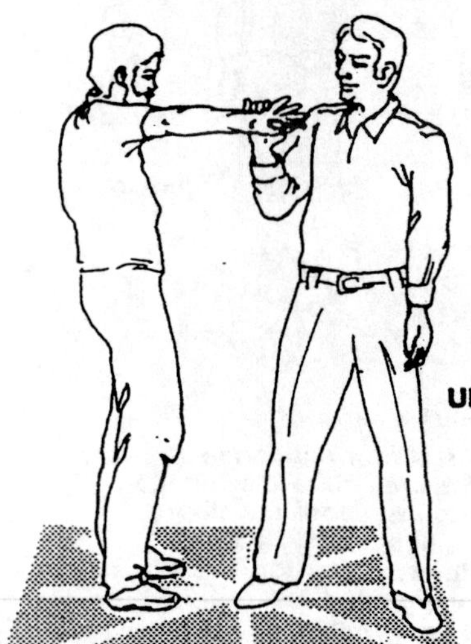

UDW-2

Quickly raise the suspect's arm to your shoulder height, turning his/her arm until you can see the suspect's palm. NOTE: Keep the suspect's arm straight so (s)he cannot bend it.

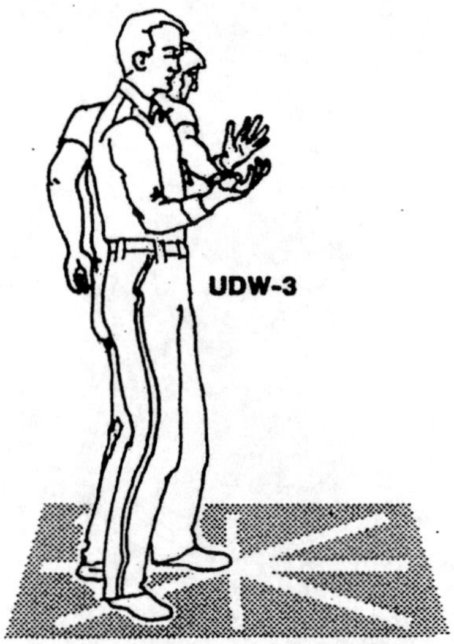

UDW-3

Make a quarter turn by pivoting on your left foot so that you are standing on the right side of the suspect. The suspect's right palm should be pointed upward, hand flat. Your left wrist should be placed in front of and against the person's right wrist.

UDW-4

A front view showing the proper placement of your left wrist.

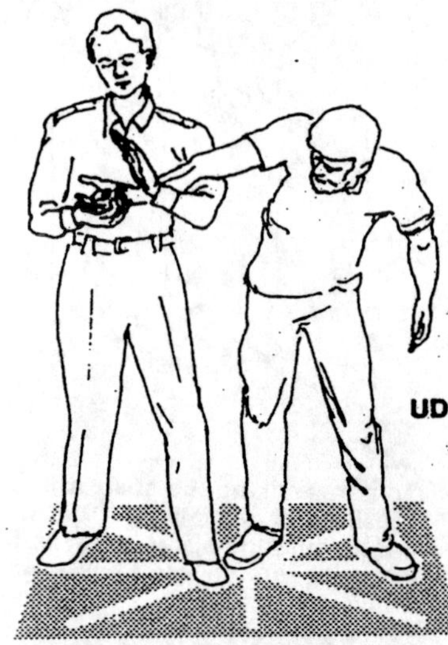

UDW-5

Using your right hand, push the suspect's right hand to the left, bending it at the wrist. Remember to keep his/her palm upward, hand flat. Simultaneously, draw your left wrist toward you. These two actions should cause intense pain in the person's wrist area.

UDW-6

To control the person with one hand, grasp his/her right hand with your left hand. Keep pressure applied to the person's wrist by pulling his/her right hand to the left.

UDW-7

To walk the individual, raise his/her upward. Pain compliance is kept through the pressure on the person's wrist. Use appropriate follow-up measures.

**Situation:** Standing alongside a suspect, you grasp his/her fingers in an attempt to effect a control hold.

**Action:**

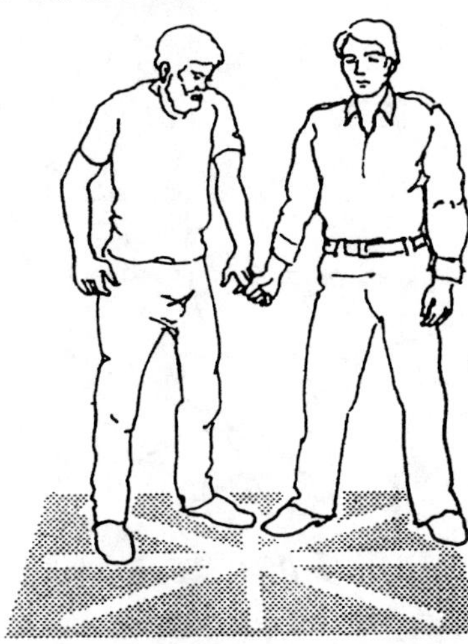

CFG-1

While standing next to the suspect, you grasp the fingers on his/her left hand with your right hand.

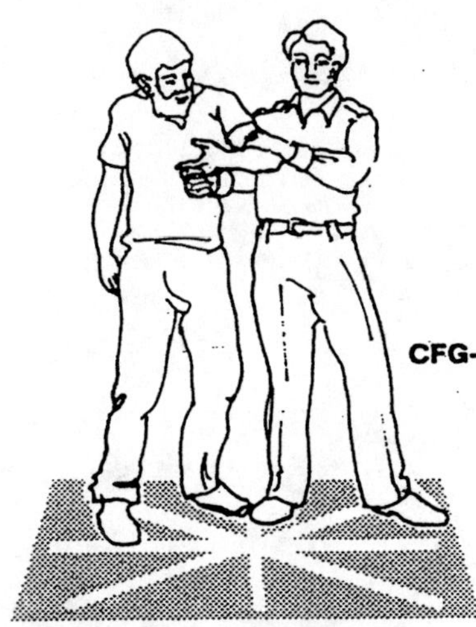

CFG-2

Bending the fingers backward causing his/her left hand to become arc-shaped, raise the suspect's arm while grasping his/her elbow area with your right arm. Your goal is to place the suspect's elbow and bicep area between your right arm and your rib cage.

CFG-3

After the suspect's arm is in place, continue counterjoint pressure using the fingers. Use appropriate follow-up procedures.

**Situation:** A driver refuses to exit his/her vehicle.

**Action:**

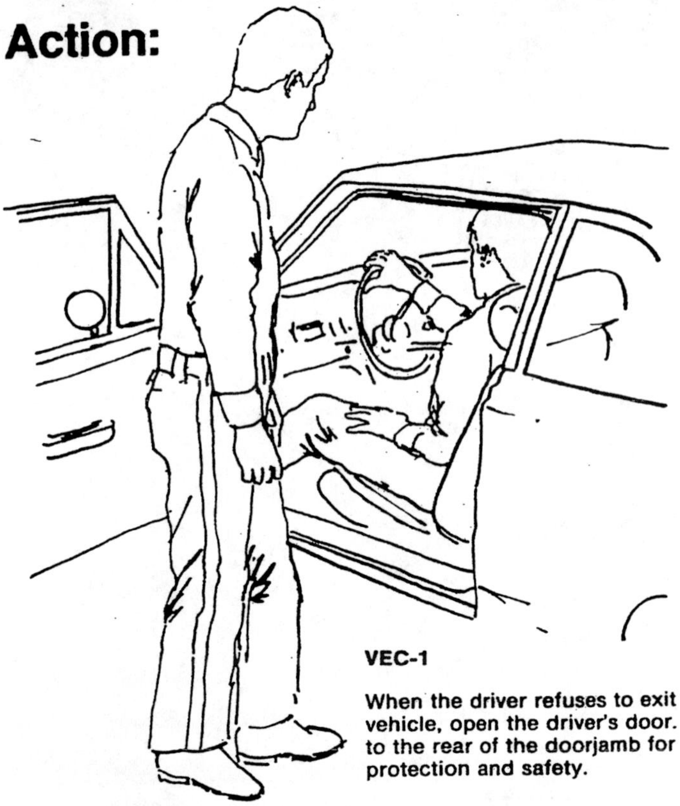

**VEC-1**

When the driver refuses to exit the vehicle, open the driver's door. Stand to the rear of the doorjamb for protection and safety.

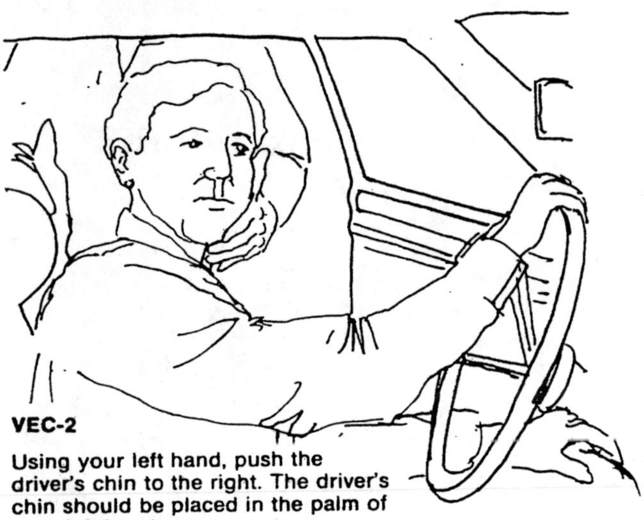

**VEC-2**

Using your left hand, push the driver's chin to the right. The driver's chin should be placed in the palm of your left hand.

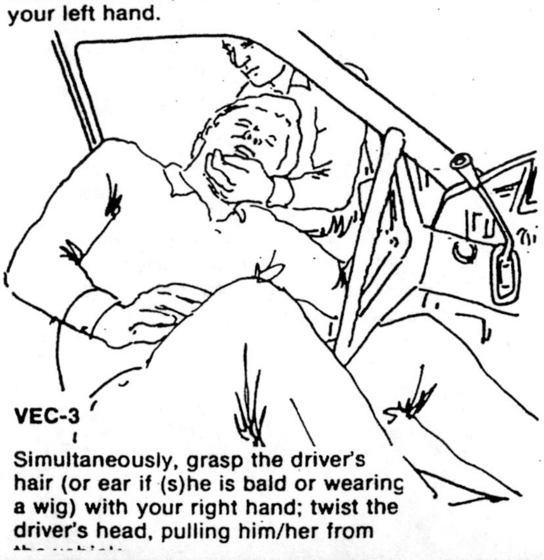

**VEC-3**

Simultaneously, grasp the driver's hair (or ear if (s)he is bald or wearing a wig) with your right hand; twist the driver's head, pulling him/her from

**VEC-4**

A side-view showing the removal of the driver. NOTE: If the driver is wearing a seatbelt or harness, you must give him/her time to unbuckle it.

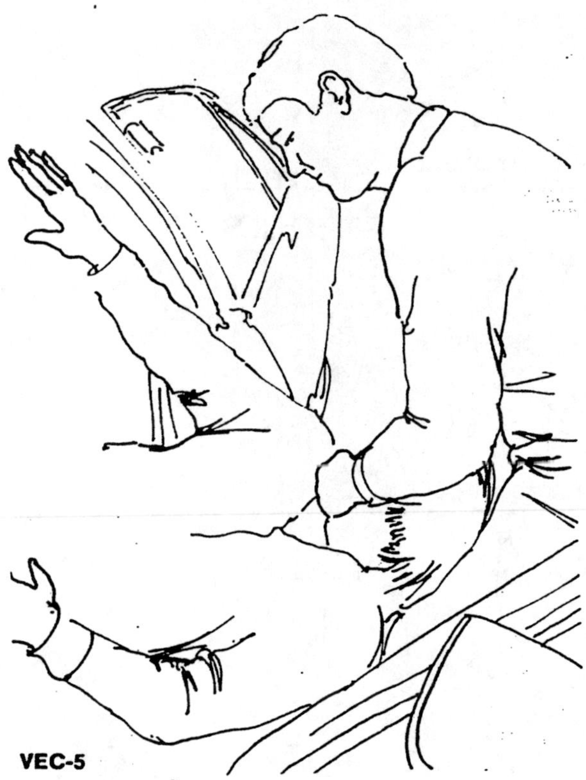

**VEC-5**

As you twist the driver's head, pull him/her from the vehicle. (S)He will come out stomach up so that you can check for any weapons which may be in the waistband. Use appropriate follow-up procedures.

**Situation:** You must remove a seated person who is offering passive resistance.

**Action:**

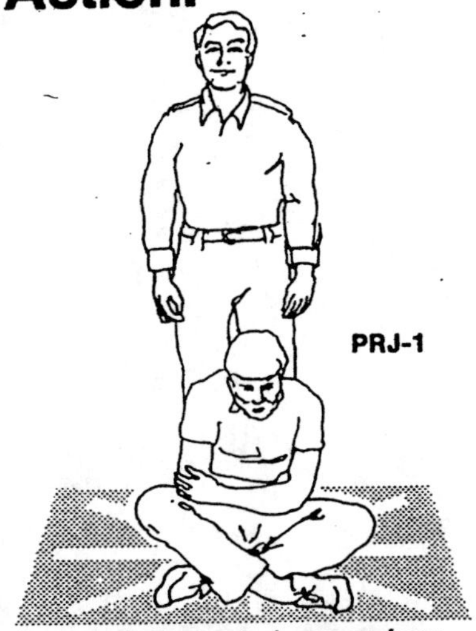

PRJ-1

Approach the seated person from behind so that (s)he cannot see you and cannot see what you're doing.

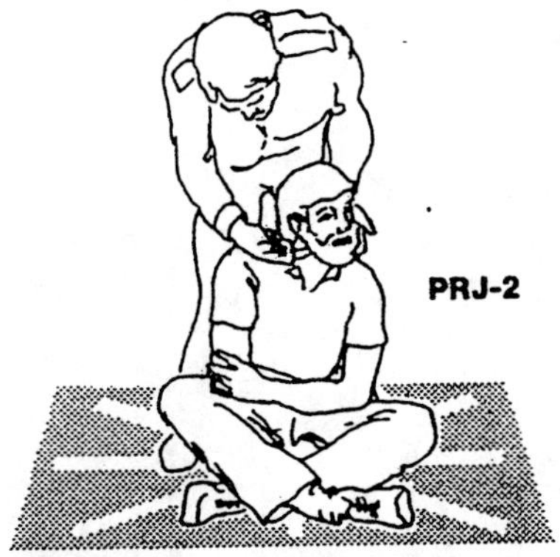

PRJ-2

Bending forward at your waist, insert one of your fingers under each side of the person's jaw hinge.

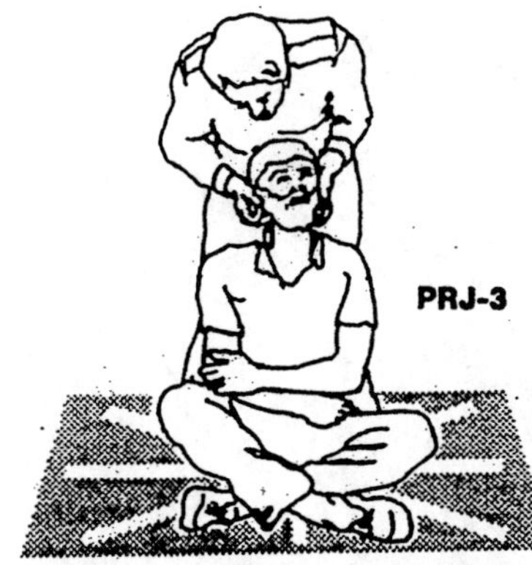

PRJ-3

Pushing your fingers both inward and upward, lift the person to his/her feet. Use appropriate follow-up procedures.

**Situation:** You must remove a seated person who is offering passive resistance.

**Action:**

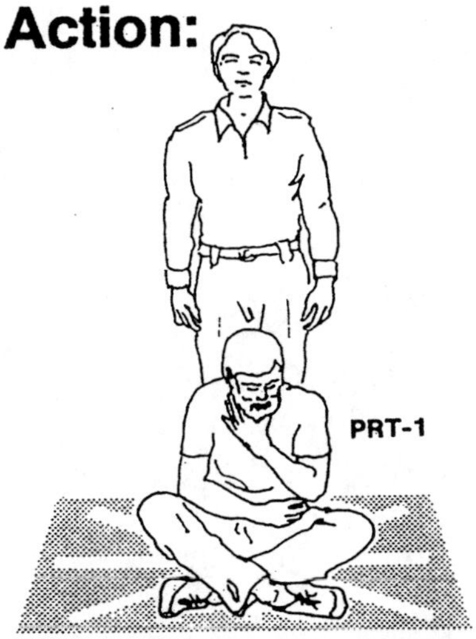

PRT-1

Approach the seated person from behind so that (s)he cannot see you and cannot see what you're doing.

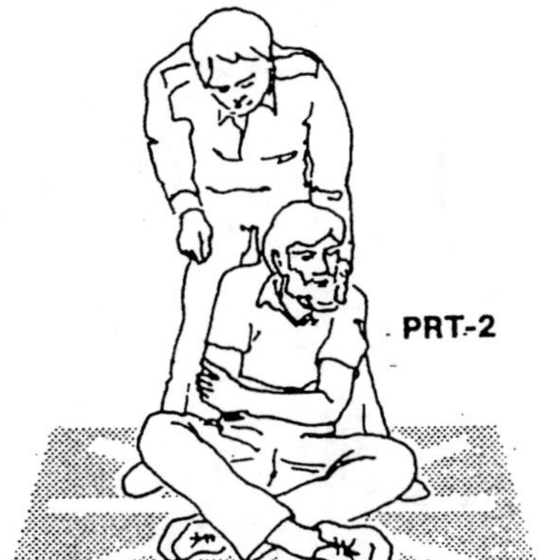

PRT-2

Bending forward at your waist, "cup" the person's chin in your left hand, tilting the person's head backward until it is resting against your chest.

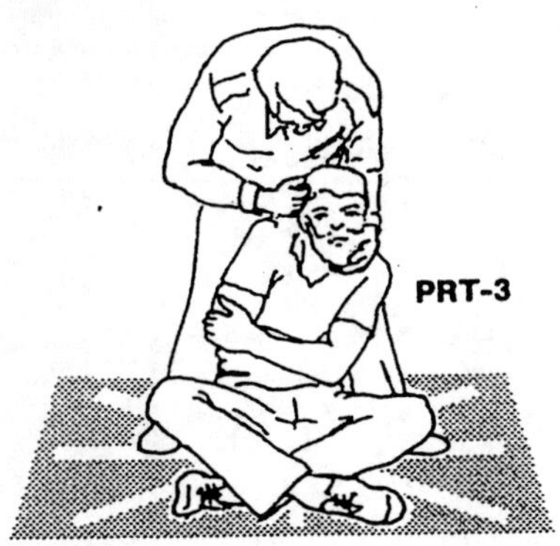

PRT-3

Cupping the person's chin, make a fist with your right hand.

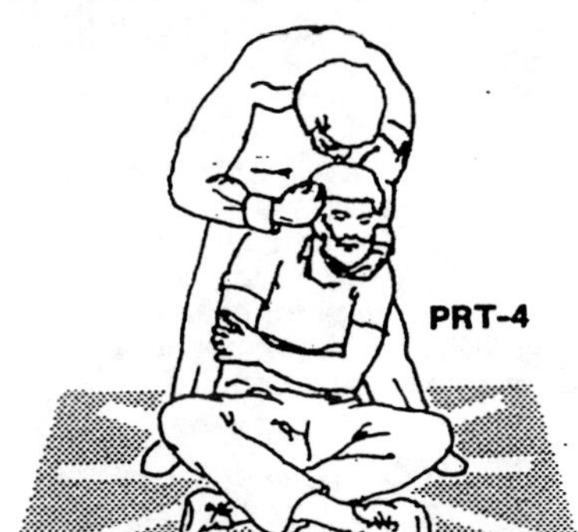

PRT-4

Press your right fist tightly against the person's head, so that your middle knuckle is placed against the right temple area.

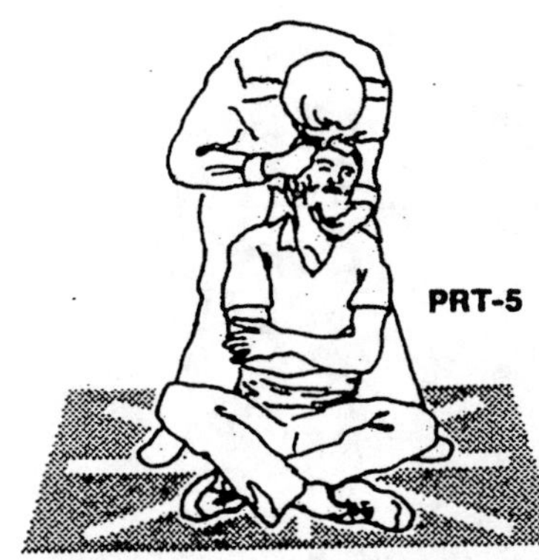

PRT-5

Forcefully apply pressure to the person's temple area using the large knuckle of your right hand. DO NOT PUNCH OR STRIKE THE TEMPLE AREA AS THIS MAY CAUSE SEVERE INJURY or cause death to the person. While applying pressure to the temple area (this causes severe pain), lift the person to his/her feet by pulling against the chin. Remember, his/her head is being supported by your chest area. Use appropriate follow-up procedures.

**Situation:** You are responding to the aid of an officer who is fighting a suspect or to the aid of a third party.

**Action:**

RHS-1

Approach the suspect from behind so that (s)he can't see you. Stand so that you are in an interrogation position.

RHS-2

Bending your right arm at the elbow, point your right fingers to the left. For ease in technique application, keep your arm at shoulder height.

RHS-3

Extend your arm forward so that the top of your hand will slap the person's head. IMPORTANT: Keep your right hand open; do not make a fist. The reason: to prevent serious injury to the suspect.

RHS-4

Slap the person's head (at the base of the skull) using the top side of your right hand. The forcefulness of your slap will depend upon the situation. A hard slap, for example, will, most likely, render the person momentarily unconscious.

RHS-

Use appropriate follow-up procedures.

**Situation:** A person attempts to punch you in the face with a left handed punch.

**Action:**

BLP-1

A person attempts to punch you in the face with a left handed punch.

BLP-2

Quickly raise your right arm, blocking the person's punch. Use appropriate follow-up procedures.

**Situation:** A person attempts to punch you in the face with a left handed punch.

**Action:**

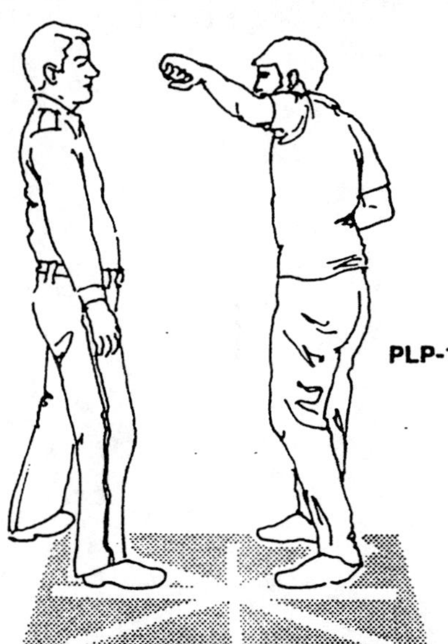

PLP-1

A person attempts to punch you in the face with a left handed punch.

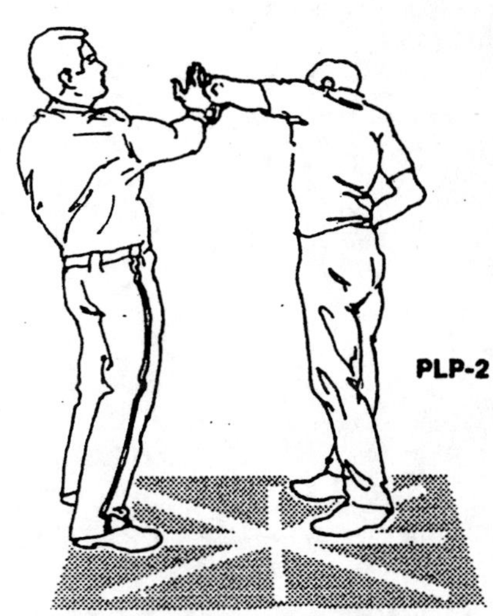

PLP-2

Quickly, step backward with your right foot. Parry the punch by "tapping" the person's left wrist with your open (fingers together) right hand. Use appropriate follow-up procedures.

## CHAPTER SEVEN: DISARMING—CLUBS

If someone attacks you with a club and you have time to draw your weapon, do it. Meet deadly force with deadly force; however, if there isn't enough time to draw your weapon, use one of the techniques contained in this section.

Regardless of the technique chosen by you, make sure that you disarm the suspect so that (s)he can't attack you for a second time using the same weapon. Oh, and don't forget, should you injure the suspect during his/her attack, you still have an obligation to give him/her medical attention.

**Situation:** A person attempts to strike you in an over-the-head manner with a pipe, stick, or other bludgeon.

**Action:**

WRO-1

A person who is holding a club raises his/her right arm in preparation to strike you on the head.

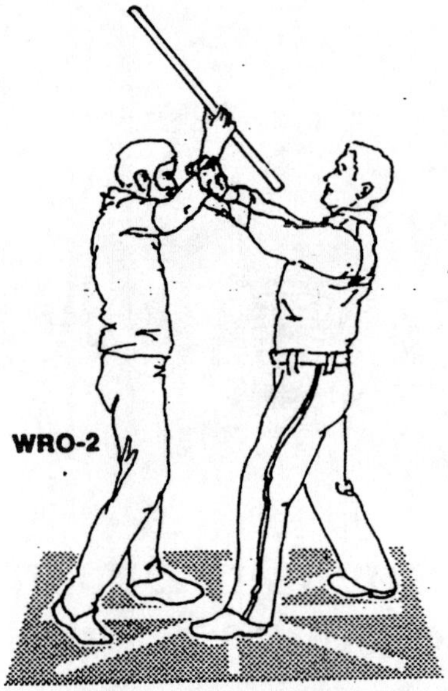

WRO-2

As the person strikes, step into the attack, thrusting your arms upward, blocking the wrist using an "X" block. For safety reasons, you must block the person's wrist, not the person's forearm as shown.

WRO-3

Failure to thrust your arms upward and to block the forearm will result in your being hit on the head by the club.

**Situation:** A person attempts to strike you in an over-the-head manner with a pipe, stick or other bludgeon.

**Action:**

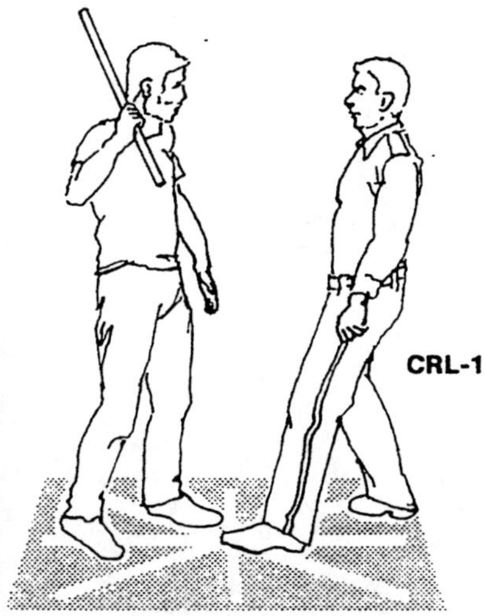

CRL-1

A person who is holding a club raises his/her right arm in preparation to strike you on the head.

CRL-2

As the person strikes, prepare to step into the attack in an effort to "stuff" it. That is, you want to block the attack before the person's arm gains momentum.

CRL-3

Step into the attack with your left foot, while thrusting your arm upward blocking the wrist. Use an "X" block.

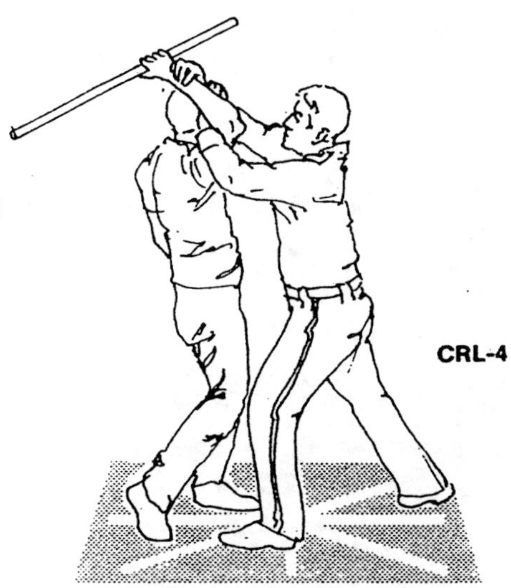

CRL-4

Grasp the person's right wrist with your right hand. Then, grab your right wrist with your left hand by inserting your left hand under the person's right forearm. Apply pressure against the person's wrist and shoulder by pushing backward (past the head) and downward on his/her wrist and upward and forward on his/her forearm.

CRL-5

Step alongside the person's right foot with your left foot (about one foot apart). This will give you better balance and better leverage. Continue the pressure on the person's wrist, arm and shoulder until (s)he falls backward upon the ground.

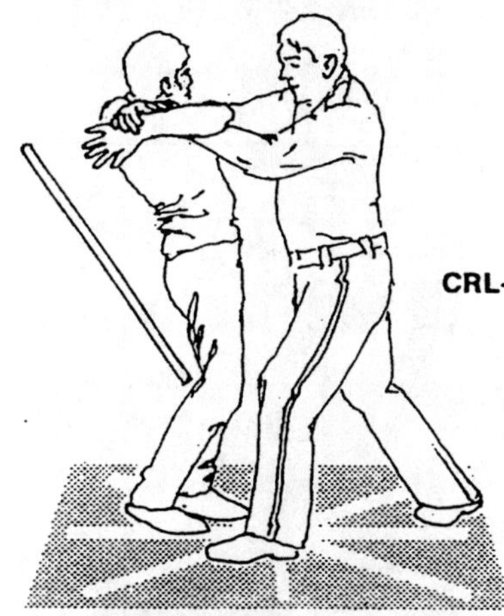

CRL-6

A forceful application of the reverse armlock should dislocate or break the shoulder. This action should make the person drop the club. If you do not dislocate or break the person's shoulder, use appropriate follow-up procedures, such as those shown in RAL-8 through RAL-14.

**Situation:** A person attempts to strike you in an over-the-head manner with a pipe, stick or other bludgeon.

**Action:**

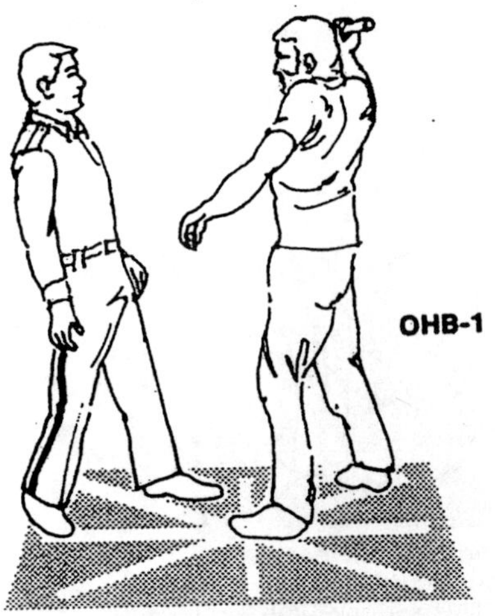

OHB-1

A person who is holding a club raises his/her right arm in preparation to strike you on the head.

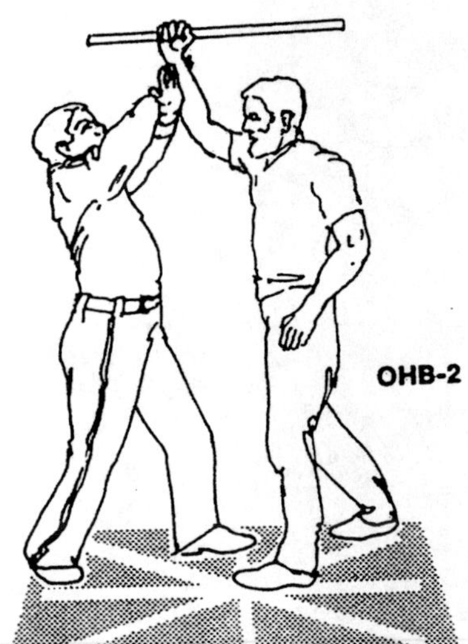

OHB-2

As the person strikes, step into the attack, thrusting your arms upward, blocking the person's wrist using an "X" block.

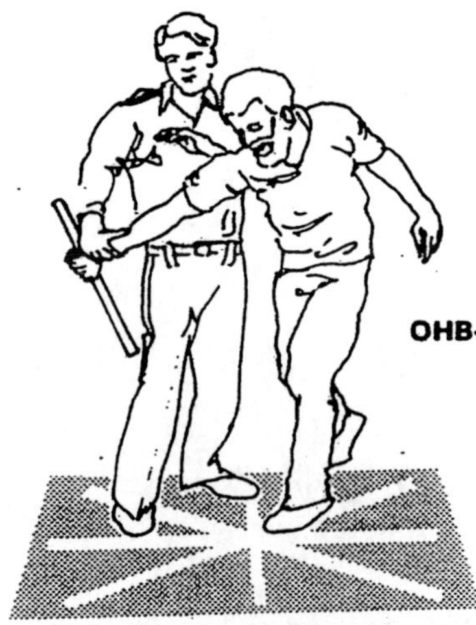

OHB-3

Having blocked the attack, quickly make a quarter turn to the rear with your right foot as you hold onto the person's wrist with your right hand.

OHB-4

Draw the person's wrist into and against your right pelvic bone area with your right hand. The reason: so that you aren't accidentally struck in the groin with the club. Having made a fist with your left hand, raise your left arm in preparation for the delivery of a strike to the person's bicep.

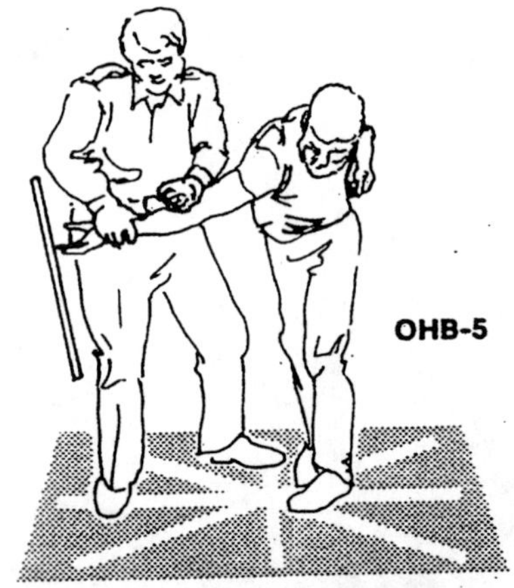

OHB-5

Using your right hand, rotate the person's wrist so that his/her elbow is facing you. Then, deliver a forceful forearm strike to the person's arm, just above the elbow. This action should break the person's elbow causing him/her to drop the club. Use appropriate follow-up procedures.

**Situation:** A person attempts to strike you with a club using a baseball-type swing.

**Action:**

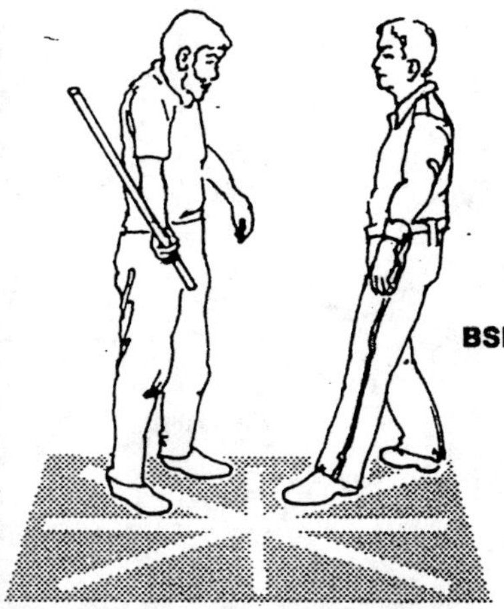

BSB-1

A person who is holding a club attempts to strike you on your left side, using a baseball-type swing.

BSB-2

As the person swings, raise your left arm, stepping into the attack so that the person's forearm strikes your rib area.

BSB-3

Place your right hand—palm down—upon the person's right shoulder, while wrapping your left arm over the person's arm. Your left arm should be placed above the person's elbow for superior leverage.

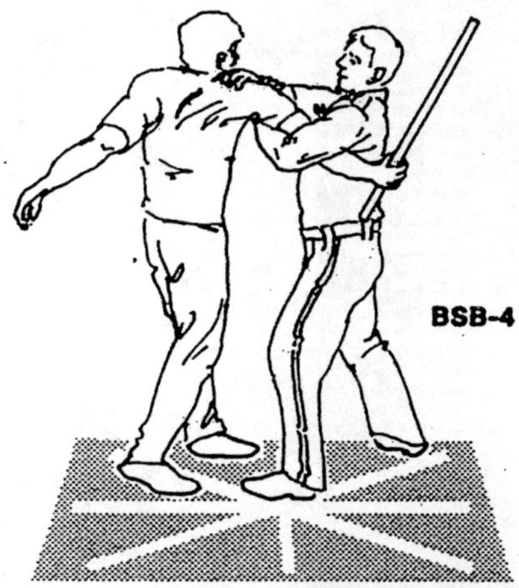

BSB-4

Next, grasp your right wrist with your left hand. Begin to apply upward pressure against the person's elbow by tensing and flexing your left forearm.

BSB-5

Pushing on your right wrist with your left hand, while flexing your left forearm should break the person's elbow. Remember to keep your left forearm above the person's elbow for maximum counterjoint pressure. This action should make the person drop the club. Use appropriate follow-up procedures.

**Situation:** A person holding a club in the right hand swings it, backhand-style, in an attempt to strike you on the right side.

**Action:**

BHB-1

A person holding a club in his/her right hand attempts to hit you on your right side as (s)he swings it—backhand-style.

BHB-2

As the person swings, step into the attack and grab the person's right wrist with your right hand. If you miss the person's wrist, don't worry. Stepping into the attack places the club behind you.

BHB-3

After grabbing the person's right wrist, quickly make a quarter turn to the rear with your right foot. Draw the person's wrist into and against your right pelvic bone area. The reason: so that you aren't accidentally struck in the groin with the club. Raise your left arm in preparation for the delivery of a strike to the person's elbow.

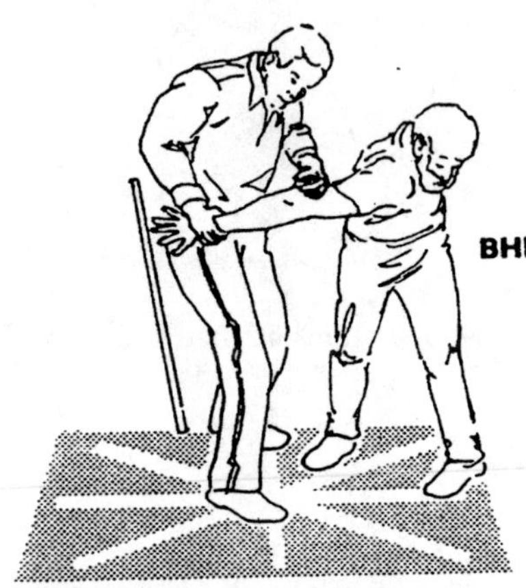

BHB-4

Using your right hand, rotate the person's wrist so that his/her elbow is facing you. Next, deliver a forceful forearm strike to the person's arm, just above the elbow. This action should break the person's elbow causing him/her to drop the club. Use appropriate follow-up procedures.

## CHAPTER EIGHT: DISARMING—KNIFE

When you see the suspect pull a knife, draw your weapon. Fast! A knife is nothing to play with, even if you're a highly trained martial artist. You might as well face it, you are probably going to get cut in a knife fight, unless you first render the suspect so incapacitated that (s)he can't attack you.

Should you be unable to draw your weapon or baton, the techniques shown in this section should prove valuable. Since speed is important in disarming your attacker, practice these techniques with a little more zest.

**Situation:** You are confronted from the front by a person who is holding a knife in his/her right hand. The knife is inverted.

**Action:**

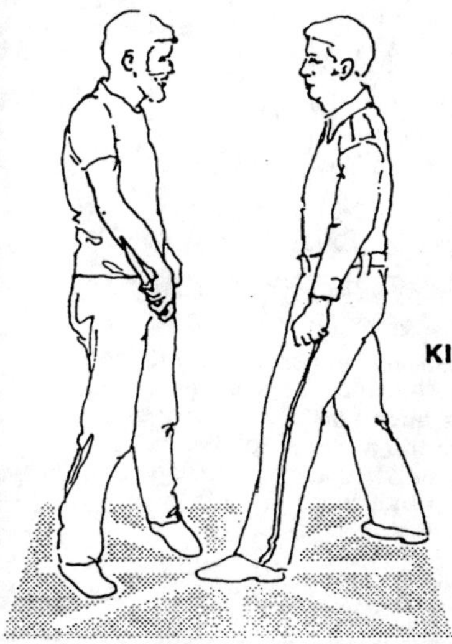

KIL-1

A person confronts you from the front while holding a knife in his/her right hand. The knife is being held in an inverted manner. DO NOT ATTEMPT TO DISARM THE PERSON. IF YOU DO, YOU WILL MOST LIKELY BE KILLED OR AT THE VERY LEAST SEVERELY INJURED. IF YOU HAVE A FIREARM, DRAW IT, IF NOT, MOVE AWAY. FAST!!!

KIL-2

Holding a knife in an inverted manner gives the attacker many ways to cut you. As shown, (s)he can quickly slash at you, cutting you with the blade.

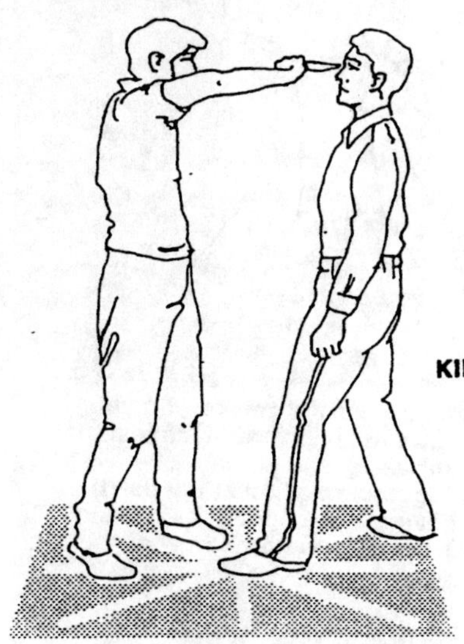

KIL-3

In a flash, (s)he can reverse direction stabbing you in the eye or cutting you with the other edge, before you can defensively react.

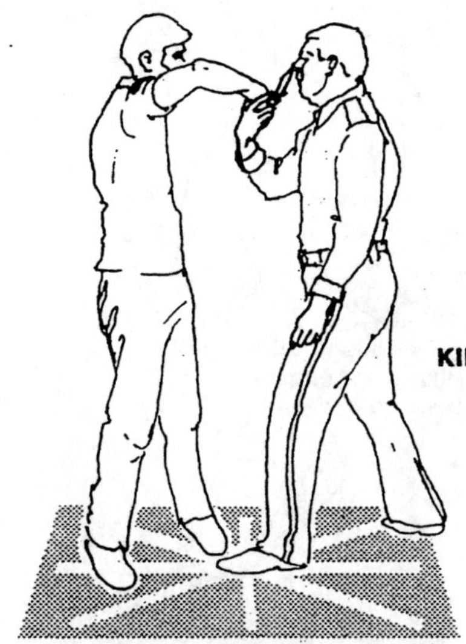

KIL-4

Attemping to grab the person's wrist or arm will only get you hurt. An inverted knife is too hard to control through standard defensive tactics.

KIL-5

Even a backhand attack can be deadly, should you attempt to block it.

**Situation:** A person attempts to stab you in an over-the-head manner with a knife.

**Action:**

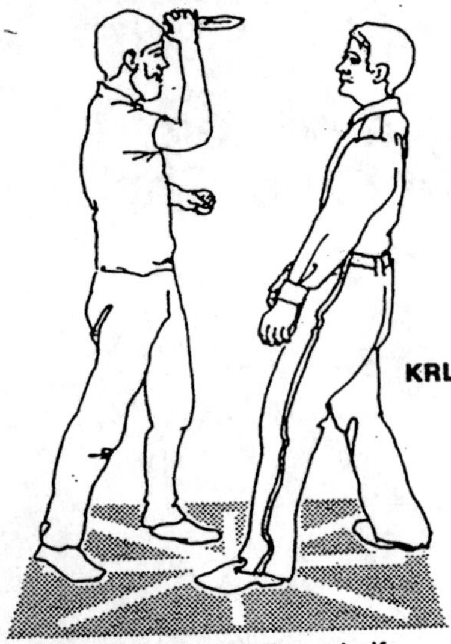

KRL-1

A person who is holding a knife raises his/her right arm in preparation to stab you.

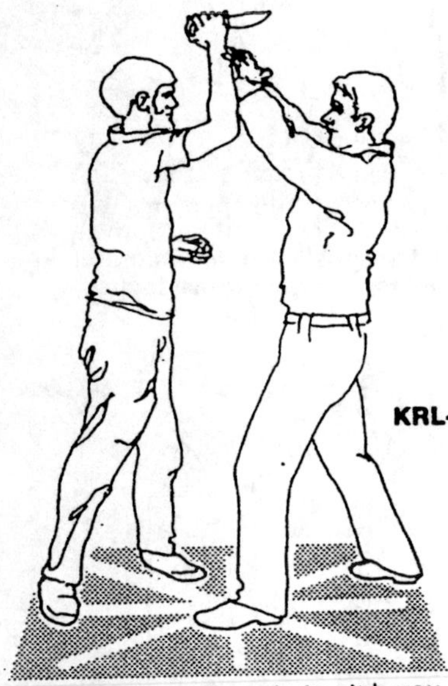

KRL-2

As the person attempts to stab you, prepare to step into the attack in an effort to "stuff" it. That is, you want to block the attack before the person's arm gains momentum. Stepping into the attack with your left foot, thrust both of your arms upward, blocking the wrist. Use an "X" block.

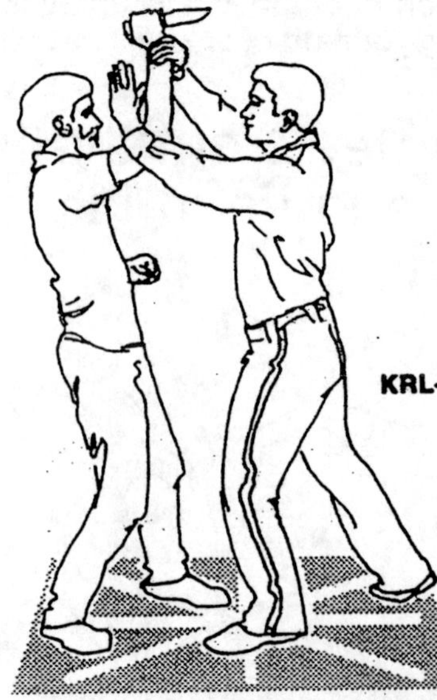

KRL-3

Having temporarily stopped the person's right arm, grasp the person's right wrist with your right hand. Then, grab your right wrist with your left hand by inserting your left hand under the person's right forearm.

KRL-4

Grasping your right wrist with your left hand, apply pressure against the person's wrist and shoulder by pushing backward (past the head) and downward on his/her wrist and upward and forward on his/her forearm.

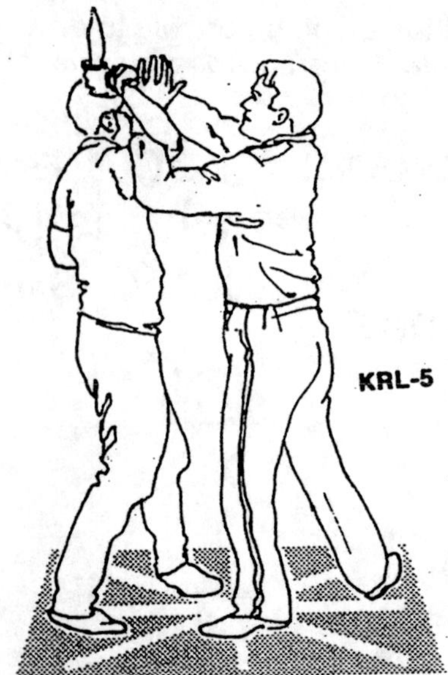

KRL-5

Step closer to the person's right foot with your left foot. This will give you better balance and better leverage. Continue the pressure on the person's wrist, arm and shoulder until (s)he falls backward upon the ground.

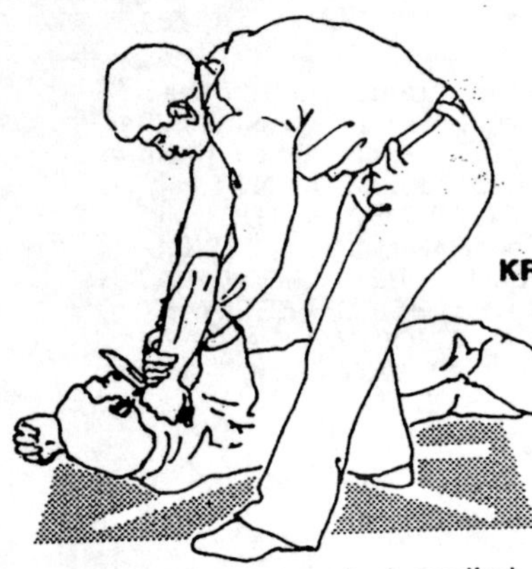

KRL-6

Keep the reverse arm lock applied while the person is lying on the ground.

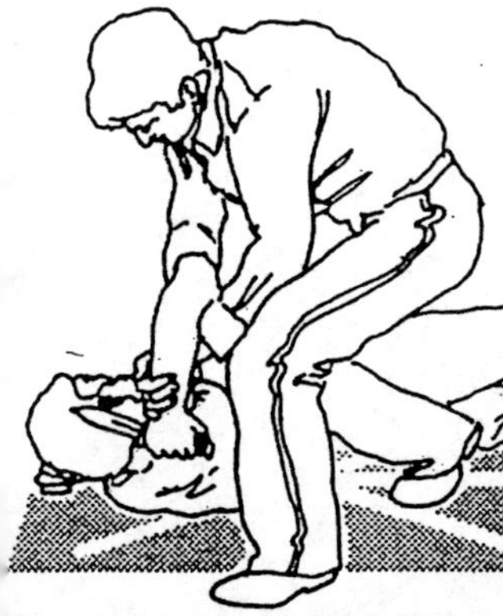

KRL-7

Forcefully drop your right knee upon the person's rib cage. This action may either crack or break the ribs. The results are generally severe pain and shortness of breath.

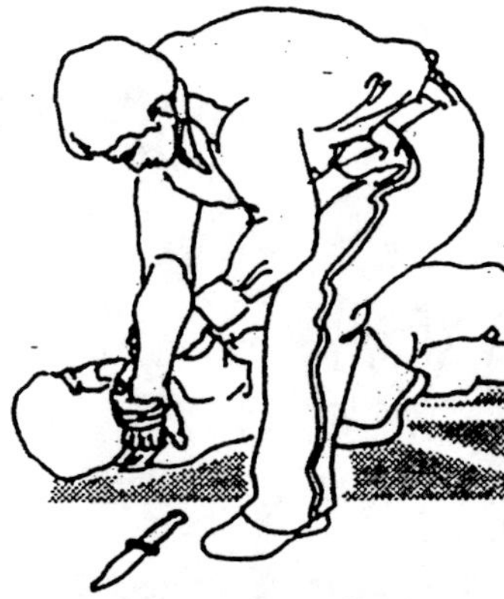

KRL-8

Continue the application of the reverse arm lock until the person has dropped the knife. A forceful application of the reverse arm lock should dislocate or break the shoulder. This action should make the person drop the knife. If you do not dislocate or break the person's shoulder, after the knife has been dropped, use appropriate follow-up measures, such as those shown in RAL-8 through RAL-14.

## Situation: A person holding a knife in the right hand, attempts to stab you in the stomach.

## Action:

KWL-1

A person holding a knife in the right hand, attempts to stab you in the stomach.

KWL-2

As the person pushes the knife forward, make a quarter turn by stepping back with your right leg. Simultaneously, parry the person's lunge by grasping his/her right wrist and hand (thumb pointed down, but on the top and in the center of his/her right hand). The quarter turn motion will move your body away from the knife's intended path; the grasping of the person's wrist and hand puts you in better control of the

KWL-3

Having grasped the person's right wrist with your left hand, next grasp the person's right hand with your right hand. Your right fingers will grasp the "drumstick" of the thumb, with your right thumb being placed on the center of the person's right hand.

KWL-4

Next, make a quarter turn by stepping backward with your left leg. Simultaneously, bend the person's right wrist backward and twist it to your left. DO NOT PUSH the person's wrist and hand toward the elbow, as this will only brace the right hand against his/her right shoulder area.

KWL-5

Forcefully, apply pressure downward and to your outside on the person's right wrist. This action, most likely, will cause the wrist to break and the person's right hand to open, dropping the knife. Use appropriate follow-up procedures.

**Situation:** A person holding a knife in the right hand, attempts to stab you in the stomach.

**Action:**

KIS-1

A person holding a knife in the right hand, attempts to stab you in the stomach.

KIS-2

As the person pushes the knife forward, make a quarter turn by stepping back with your left leg. Simultaneously, grasp the person's right wrist with your right hand (thumb is on top of the wrist). The quarter turn motion will move your body away from the knife's intended path; the grasping of the person's wrist puts you in better control of the situation.

KIS-3

Having grasped the person's right wrist, push it to your left, raising his/her arm, while stepping under the arm with your right leg.

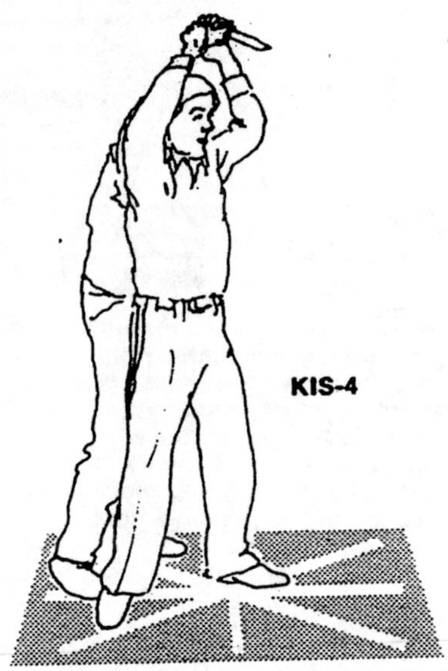

KIS-4

Grasp the person's right wrist with your right hand. Make a 360° turn while holding onto the wrist with both of your hands.

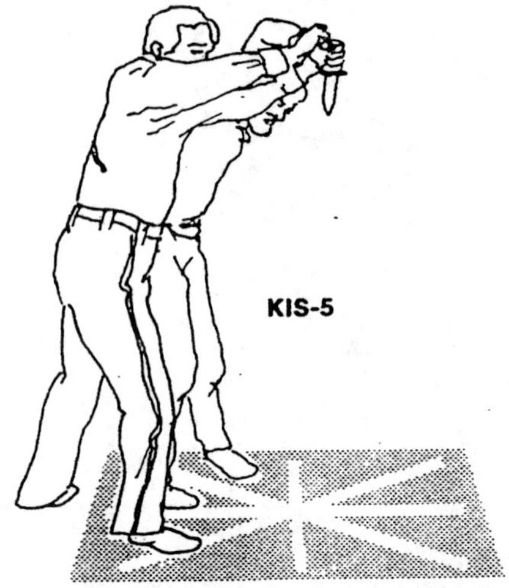

KIS-5

As you complete the 360° turn, step behind the person with your left leg. Position the person's arm by slightly bending and twisting it so that the knife blade is pointing downward.

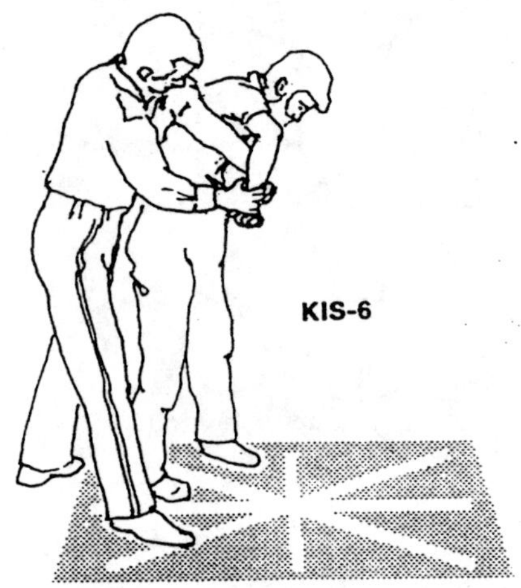

KIS-6

Forcefully, turn the person's arm and wrist into his/her body, so that (s)he is impaled by the knife.

**Situation:** A person holding a knife in the right hand, attempts to stab you in the stomach.

**Action:**

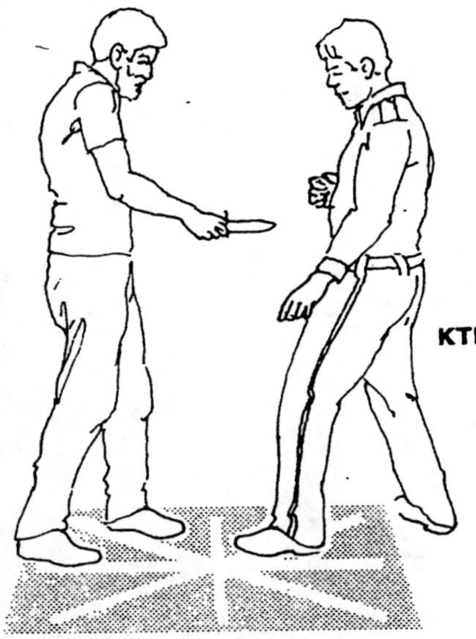

KTL-1

A person holding a knife in the right hand, attempts to stab you in the stomach.

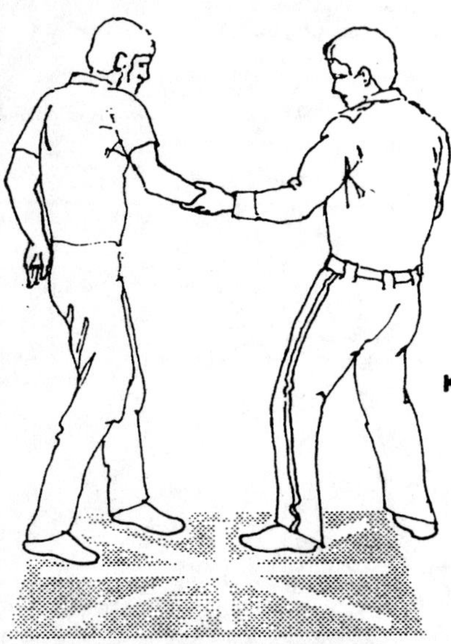

KTL-2

As the person pushes the knife forward, make a quarter turn by stepping back with your right leg. Simultaneously, grasp the person's right wrist with your left hand (thumb on top of the wrist). The quarter turn motion will move your body away from the knife's intended path; the grasping of the person's wrist puts you in better control of the situation.

KTL-3

Having grasped the person's right hand, push it to your right, raising his/her arm, stepping under the arm with your left leg. Grasp the person's right wrist with your right hand. Make a 360° turn while holding onto the wrist with both of your hands.

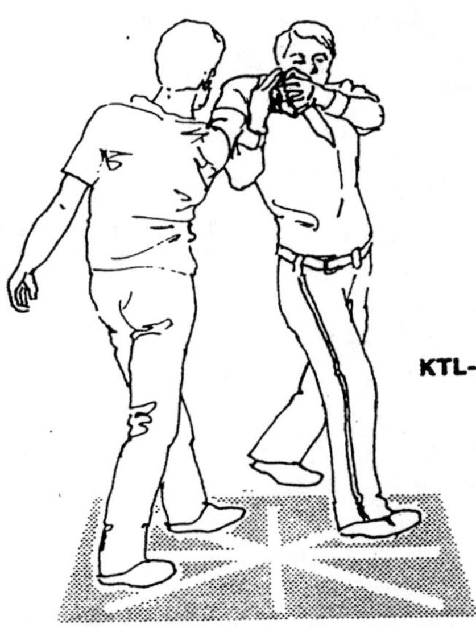

KTL-4

As you complete the 360° turn, bend the person's arm so that the knife is pushed behind the person's shoulder area.

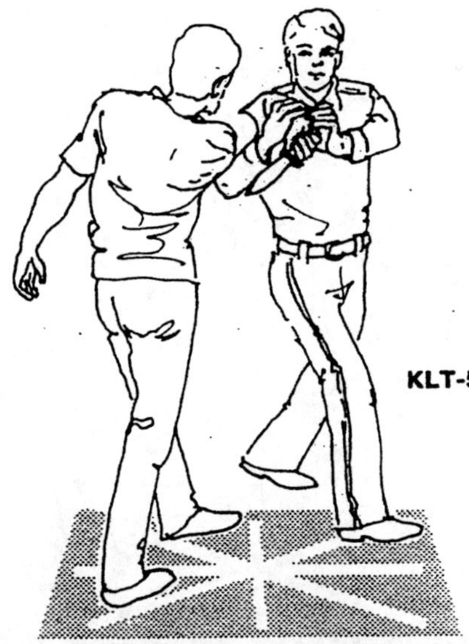

KLT-5

Forcefully, apply pressure downward and backward to the person's wrists. Doing so will lift his/her elbow and should dislocate or break the shoulder. The person should also fall backward onto the ground. This action should make the person drop the knife. Use appropriate follow-up procedures.

**Situation:** A person holding a knife in the left hand attempts to stab you in the stomach.

**Action:**

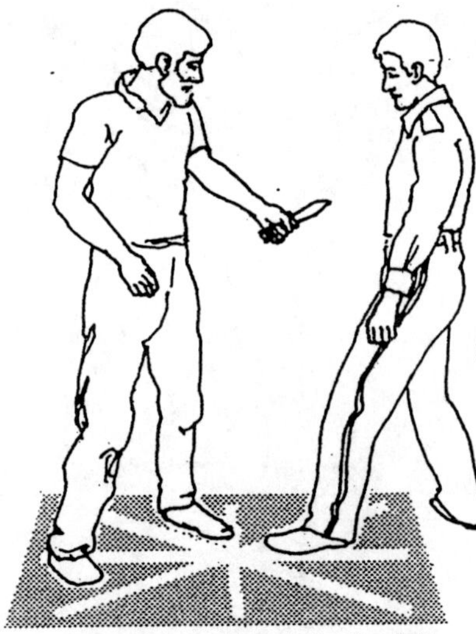

SKB-1

A person holding a knife in the left hand attempts to stab you in the stomach.

SKB-2

As the person pushes the knife forward, make a quarter turn by stepping back with your left leg. Simultaneously, grasp the person's left wrist with your right hand (thumb is on top of the wrist). The quarter turn motion will move your body away from the knife's intended path; the grasping of the person's wrist puts you in better control of the situation.

SKB-3

Stepping into the person with your right leg, grasp the person's wrist with your left hand, too. Pulling the person's wrist forward, force his/her arm to straighten, while placing the person's arm on top of your right shoulder.

SKB-4

After the attacker's arm is straight, pull him/her into you, so that his/her bicep is atop your shoulder, his/her elbow is pointed toward the ground, and his/her left hand is palm upward. If the attacker is shorter than you, bend your knees to compensate for the height difference. Forcefully pull down on the person's wrist, while simultaneously straightening your legs. This should result in the breaking of the attacker's elbow. CAUTION: If the attacker is a lot taller than you, this technique may not work as well.

**Situation:** A person, holding a knife in the right hand, attempts to cut you with a horizontal slashing motion.

**Action:**

KAL-1

A person, holding a knife in the right hand, raises it in an attempt to cut you using a horizontal slashing motion.

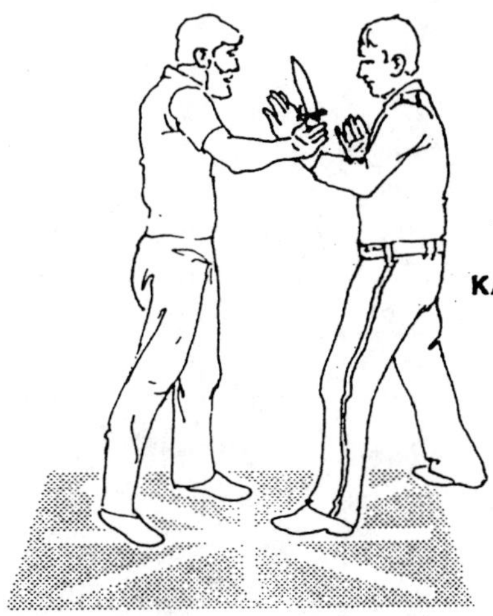

KAL-2

As the person begins to slash, raise your left arm and step into the person.

KAL-3

Raise your left arm so that the person's right forearm impacts against your left rib cage. Begin to wrap your left arm over the person's arm above his/her elbow.

KAL-4

Place your right hand--palm down--on the person's right shoulder. With your left forearm above the person's elbow for superior leverage, grasp your right wrist with your left hand. Apply upward pressure to the person's elbow by tensing and flexing your left arm.

KAL-5

Forcefully push on your right wrist with your left hand, while flexing your left forearm causing the person's elbow to break. Remember to keep your left forearm above the person's elbow for maximum counterjoint pressure.

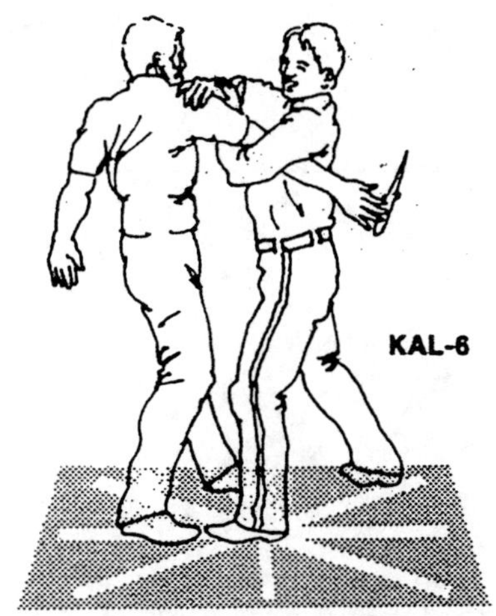

KAL-6

This action should break the elbow, and should make the person drop the knife. Use appropriate follow-up procedures.

**Situation:** A person holding a knife in the right hand, attempts to cut you with a backhand slashing motion.

**Action:**

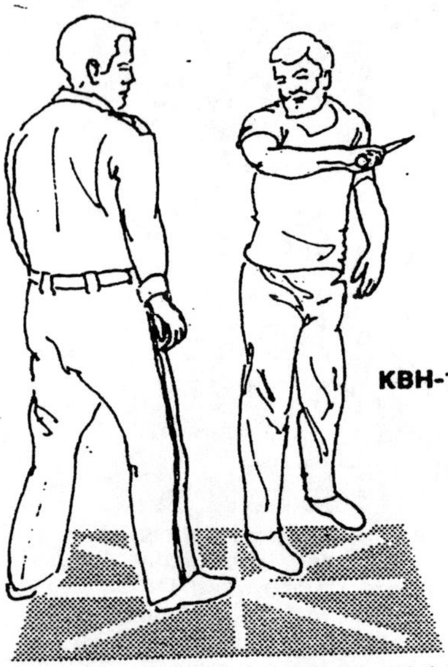

KBH-1

A person holding a knife in the right hand, raises it in an attempt to cut you using a backhand slashing motion.

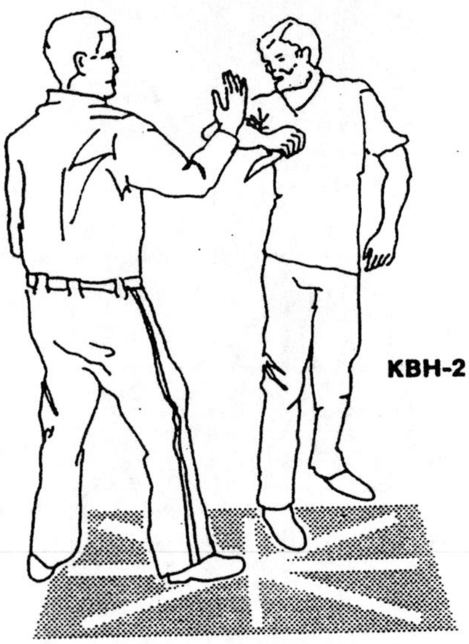

KBH-2

As the person slashes, step into the attack with your left foot, and grab the person's right wrist with your right hand. If you miss the person's wrist, the knife will go to your outside. You should still block the knife arm with your right arm.

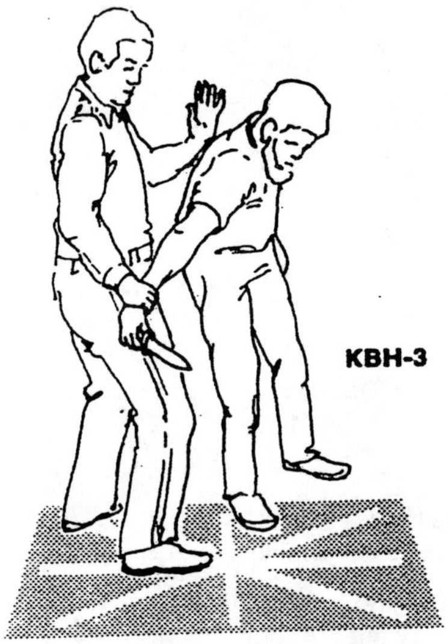

KBH-3

After grabbing the person's right wrist, quickly make a quarter turn to the rear with your right leg. Draw the person's wrist into and against your right pelvic bone area. The reason: so that you aren't accidentally cut by the knife. Raise your left arm to deliver a strike to the person's elbow.

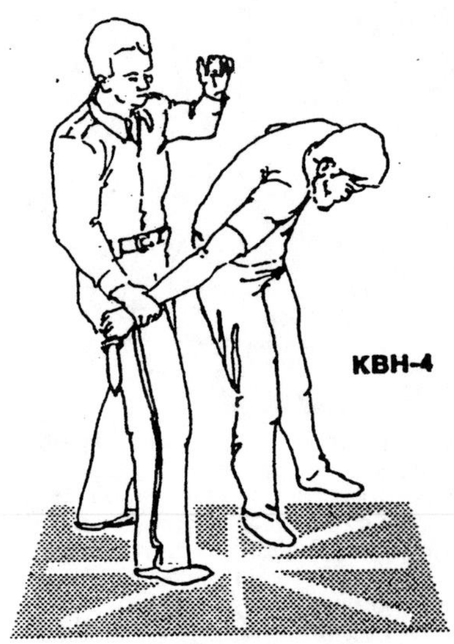

KBH-4

Using your right hand, rotate the person's right wrist so that his/her elbow is facing you.

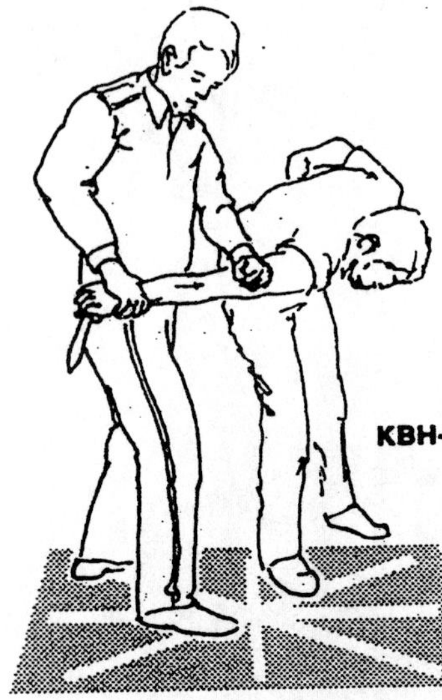

KBH-5

Next, deliver a forceful forearm strike to the person's arm, just above the elbow.

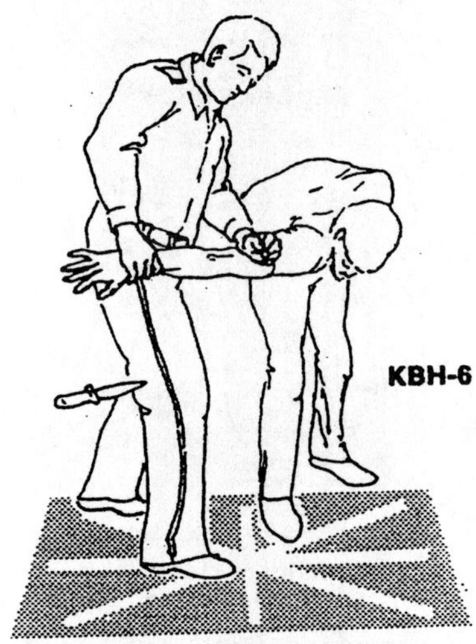

KBH-6

This action should break the person's elbow causing him/her to drop the knife. Use appropriate follow-up procedures.

## CHAPTER NINE: DISARMING—FIREARM

DO NOT ATTEMPT to disarm a suspect unless your life or the life of a third party is in imminent danger. The reason: there is no reason to be shot, especially if the suspect had no original plans to shoot you.

The techniques in this section are based upon a concept called ZONE THEORY®. Basically, your disarming technique must match the "zone" in which the firearm is located. For example, a firearm which is touching your right shoulder blade area is located in ZONE FOUR. Hence, the technique you use should be designed for ZONE FOUR. ZONE THEORY® is discussed in more detail during our instructor courses. At this time, there is no reason to bog you down with confusing detail.

In summary, just remember that disarming is an art, not a science. The more you practice these techniques, the better they will work for you. So get to it.

**Situation:** While wearing a cross-draw holster, you attempt to arrest a person.

**Action:**

CDK-1

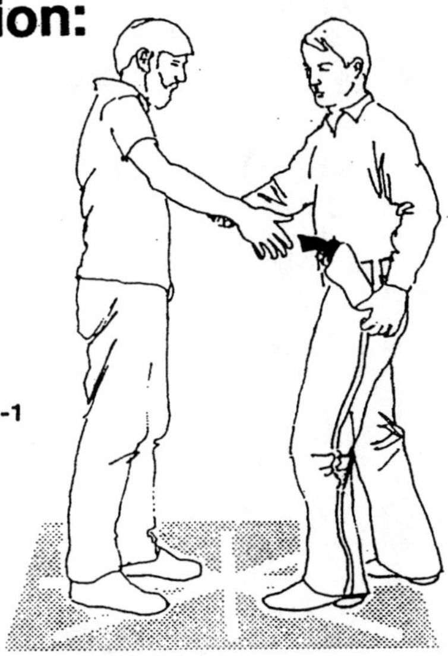

While wearing a cross-draw holster, you attempt to arrest a person by motioning for him/her to come with you.

CDK-2

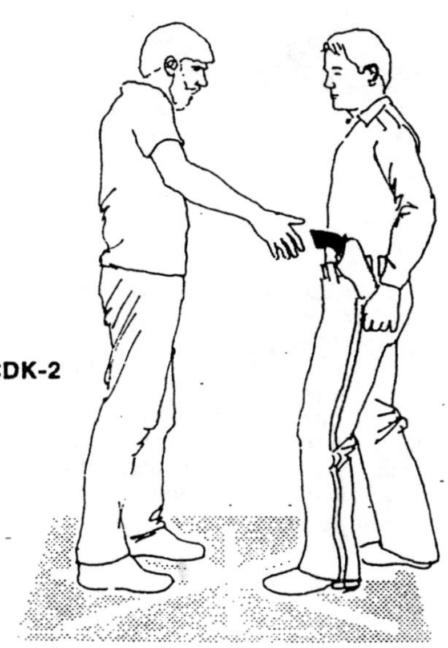

Quickly, the person reaches toward your revolver using his/her right hand.

CDK-3

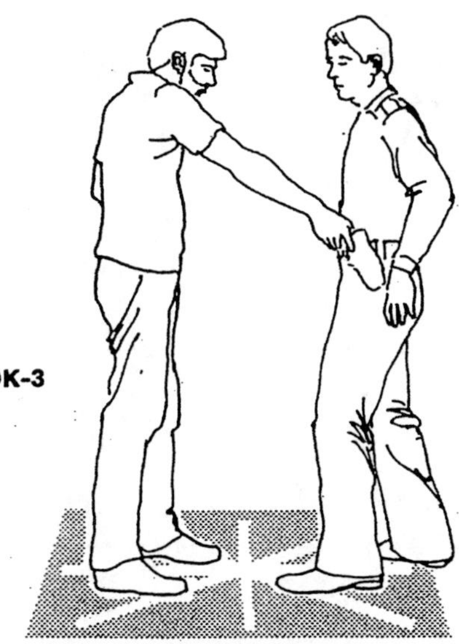

The person grasps your service weapon with his/her right hand.

CDK-4

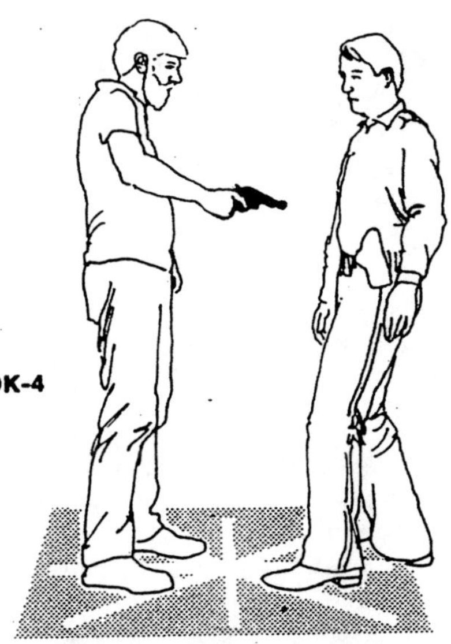

Smootnly and easily the person removes your weapon. For this reason, the wearing of a cross draw holster is not recommended.

**Situation:** While talking to a suspect, (s)he reaches for your weapon, drawing it upside down.

**Action:**

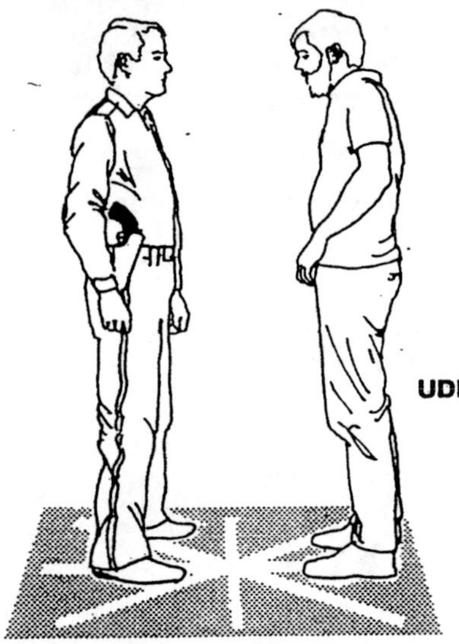

UDD-1

While talking to a suspect, you notice him/her looking at your holstered weapon.

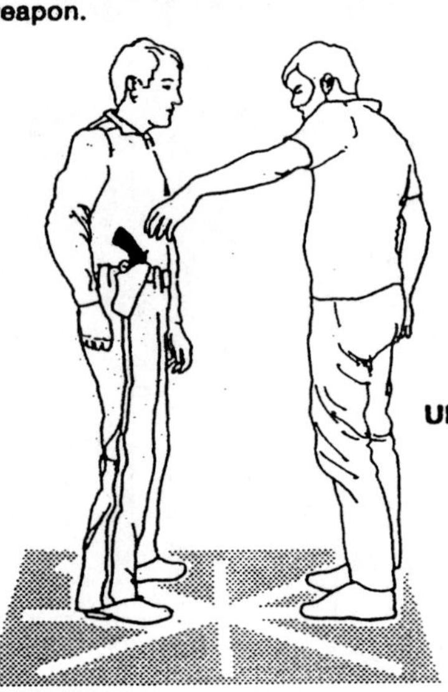

UDD-2

Quickly, the suspect reaches for your weapon with his/her left hand.

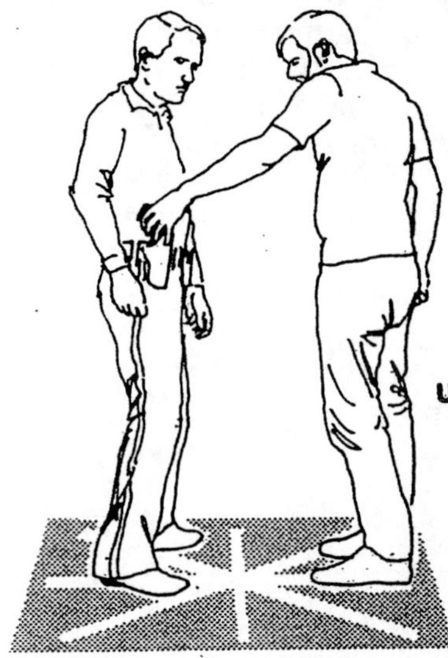

UDD-3

Before you can step backward, (s)he grasps the weapon placing his/her fourth finger on the trigger.

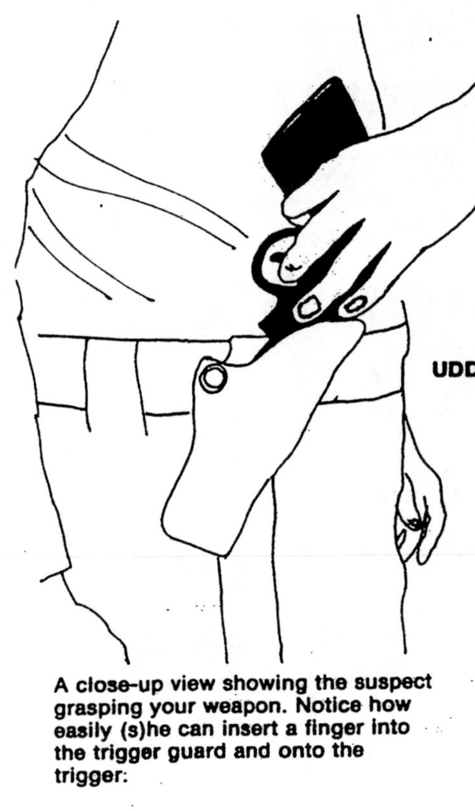

UDD-4

A close-up view showing the suspect grasping your weapon. Notice how easily (s)he can insert a finger into the trigger guard and onto the trigger:

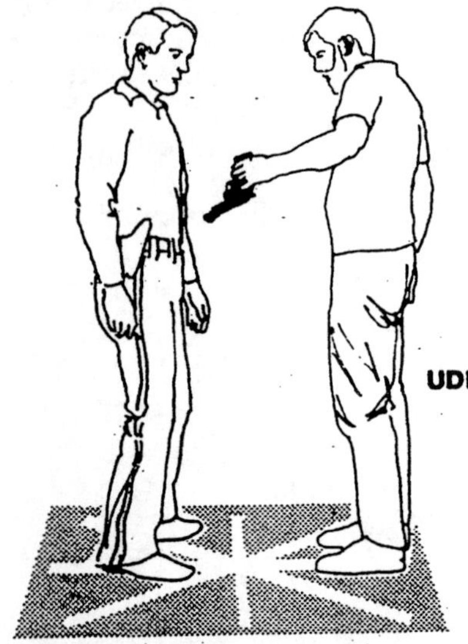

UDD-5

In a flash, (s)he removes your weapon from its holster, shooting you while the weapon is held upside down.

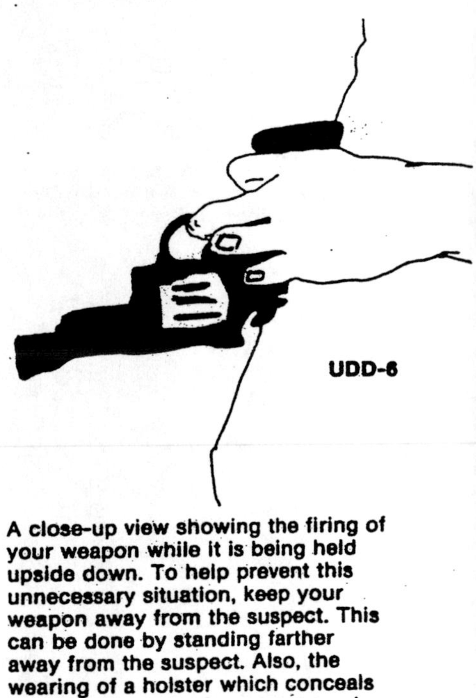

UDD-6

A close-up view showing the firing of your weapon while it is being held upside down. To help prevent this unnecessary situation, keep your weapon away from the suspect. This can be done by standing farther away from the suspect. Also, the wearing of a holster which conceals the trigger guard of your weapon is recommended.

**Situation:** A person who is holding a handgun in his/her right hand points it at your stomach, and tells you to raise your hands.

**Action:**

HGA-1

A person who is holding a handgun in his/her right hand points it at your stomach, and tells you to raise your hands.

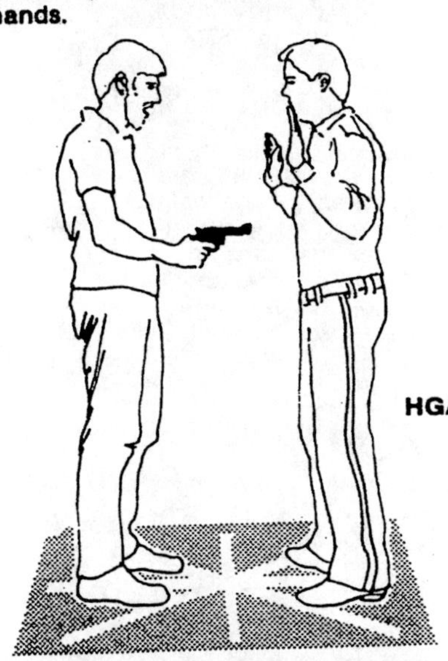

HGA-2

Only raise your hands to head level. Keeping your elbows bent, place your hands just slightly in front of your face. These actions will let you use your hands to grasp the weapon quickly, and without "telegraphing" your intentions.

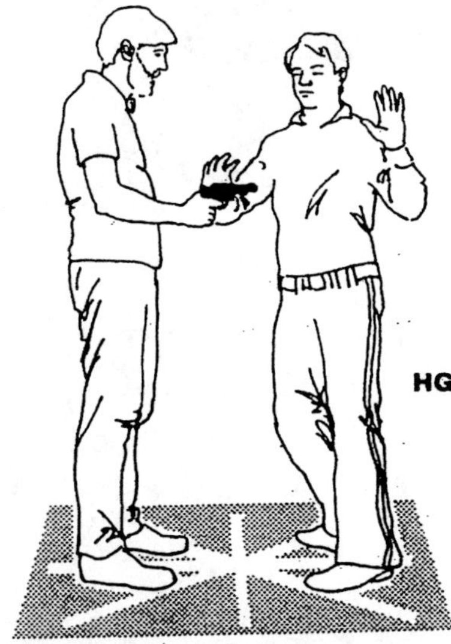

HGA-3

Quickly, thrust your right hand toward the cylinder of the weapon, while simultaneously twisting your body to the right. Twisting your body to the right should remove you from the line of fire.

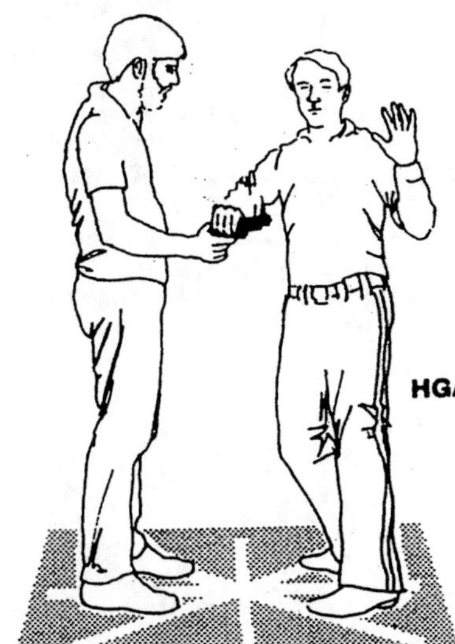

HGA-4

Firmly grasp the cylinder of the weapon with your right hand. Grasping it firmly will prevent it from turning. Also, as you grasp the cylinder, push the weapon to your left moving it yet farther away from you.

HGA-5

Another view showing the grasping of the cylinder with your right hand.

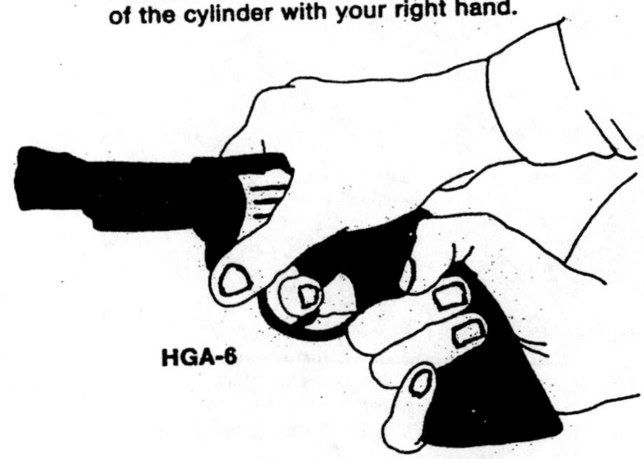

HGA-6

A close-up view showing the proper grasp of the cylinder with your right hand. Notice that your thumb is pointed downward. The reasons: so that it is a natural grasp from the hands up position, and so that you will be able to continue this technique.

HGA-7

There is a possibility that the weapon had been cocked by the suspect prior to his/her pointing it at you.

HGA-8

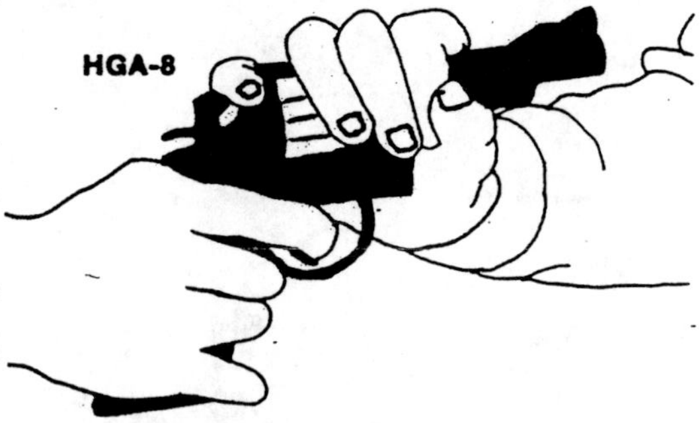

A close-up view showing the proper way to grasp a cocked weapon. When grasping the cylinder, place your little finger between the hammer and the frame. This action will prevent the hammer from dropping on either the primer or the firing pin.

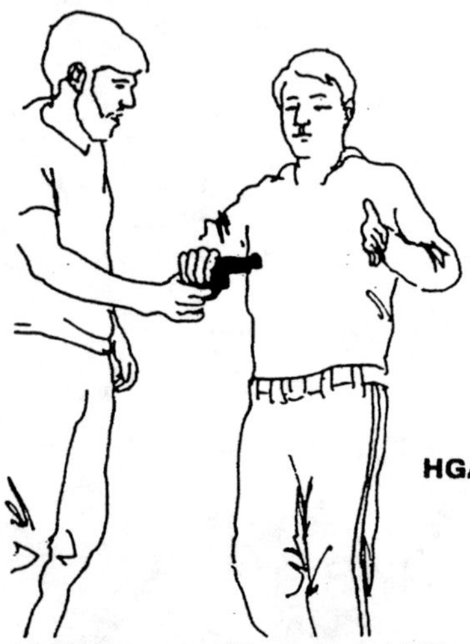

HGA-9

Having grasped the cylinder with your right hand, prepare to grasp the barrel with your left hand. Notice that your left thumb is pointed upward.

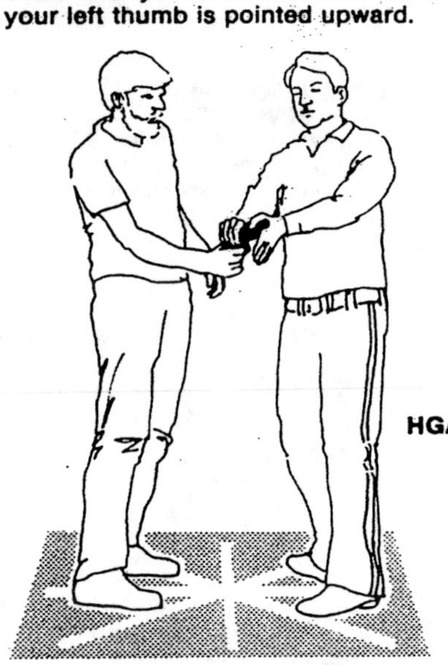

HGA-10

Grasp the barrel of the weapon with your left hand. The barrel should be placed against the web of your left hand.

HGA-11

A close-up view showing the proper positioning of your hands. Keep your hand away from the bore in case the gun should discharge.

HGA-12

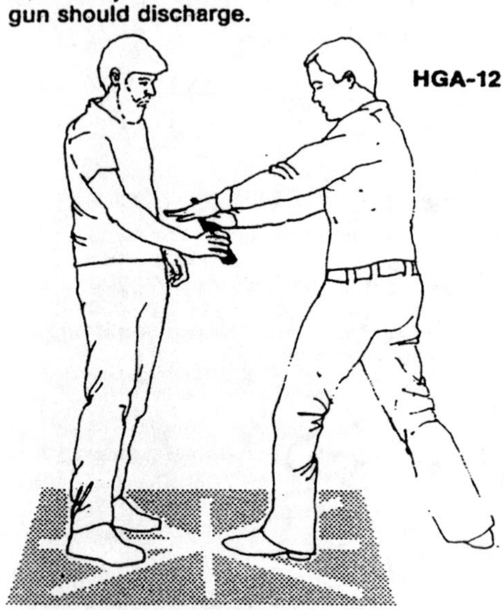

Twist the barrel toward the person by pushing on it with your left hand, while simultaneously twisting it with your right hand.

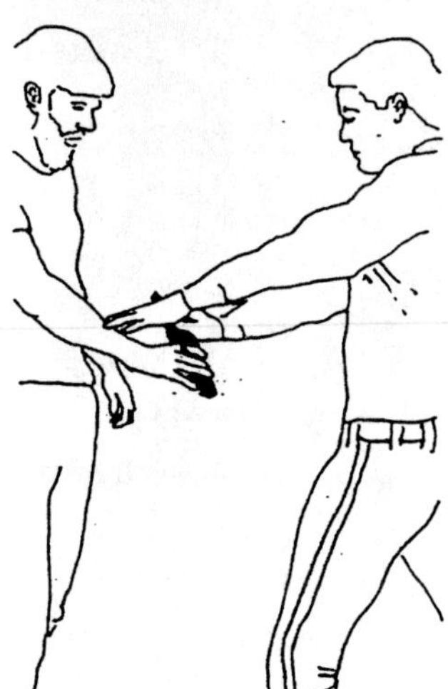

HGA-13

Another view showing the same twisting motion.

HGA-14

A close-up view showing the same twisting motion. Notice that the trigger guard is being turned into the web between the index and middle finger. Twisting the weapon in the manner should break and/or amputate the person's right index finger.

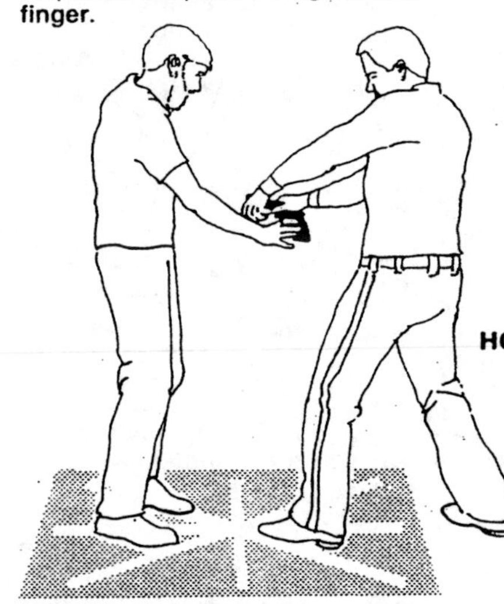

HGA

Having twisted the barrel of the weapon into the person, forcefully pull the weapon toward you. Simultaneously, step backward with your right leg. These actions should break and/or amputate the person's right index finger. Use appropriate follow-up procedures.

**Situation:** A person who is holding a handgun in his/her right hand points it at your stomach, and tells you to raise your hands.

**Action:**

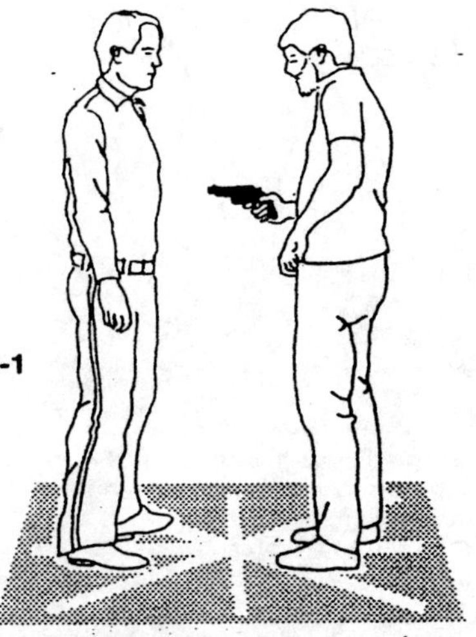

HGR-1

A person who is holding a nandgun in his/her right hand points it at your stomach and tells you to raise your hands.

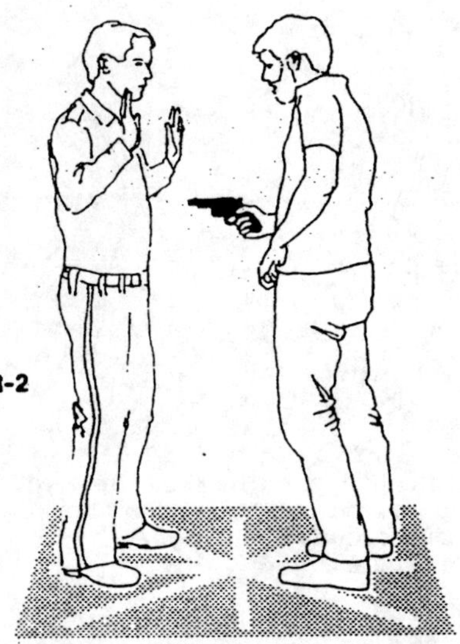

HGR-2

**Only** raise your hands to head level. Keeping your elbows bent, place your hands just slightly in front of your face. These actions will let you use your hands to grasp the weapon quickly, and without "telegraphing" your intentions.

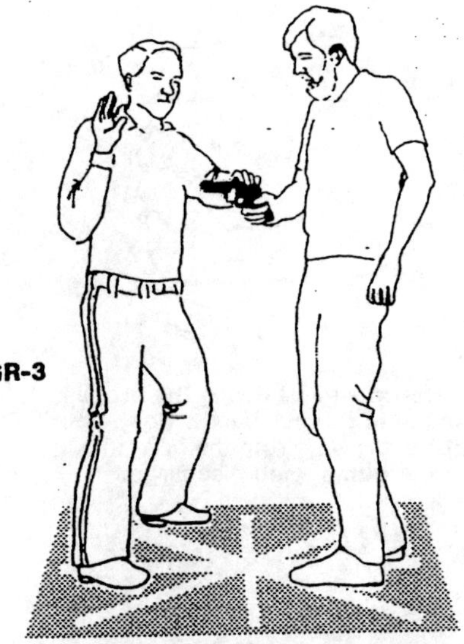

HGR-3

Quickly, thrust your left hand toward the cylinder of the weapon, while simultaneously twisting your body to the left. Twisting your body to the right should remove you from the line of fire.

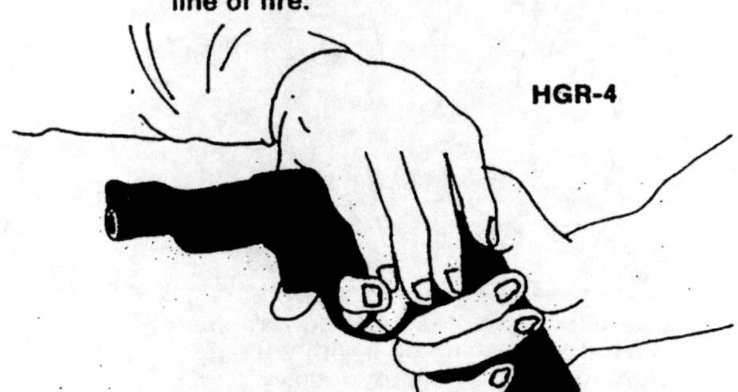

HGR-4

A close-up view showing how to firmly clasp the cylinder of the weapon with your left hand. Grasping it firmly will prevent it from turning. Also, as you grasp the cylinder, push the weapon to your right moving it farther away from you.

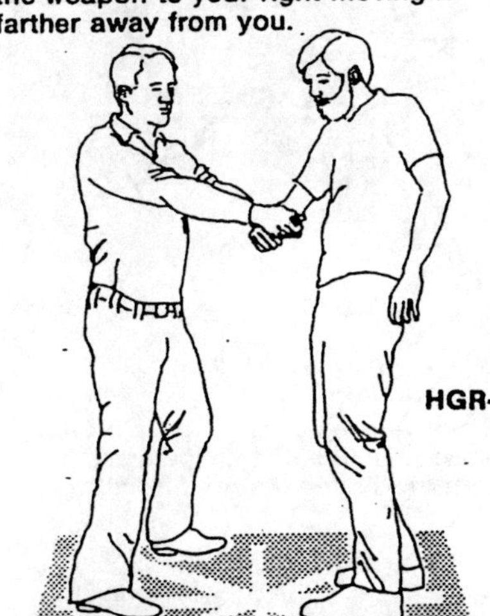

HGR-5

Having grasped the cylinder with your left hand, prepare to grasp the barrel with your right hand. Notice that your right thumb is on top of the barrel.

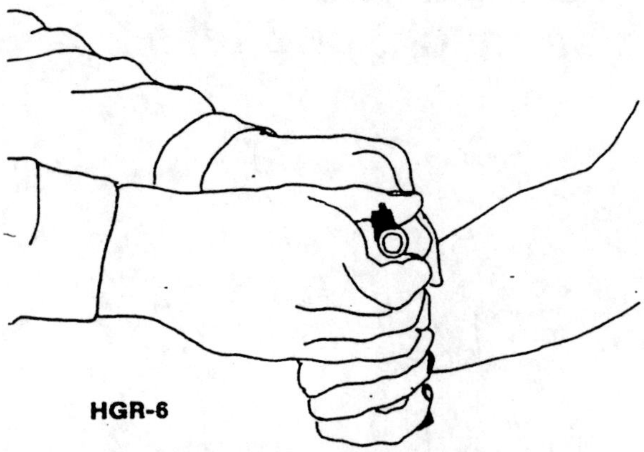

**HGR-6**

A close-up view showing the proper positioning of your hands. Keep your right hand away from the bore in case the gun should discharge.

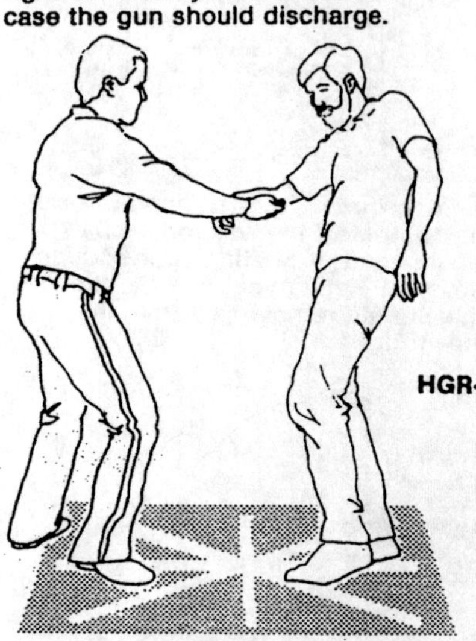

**HGR-7**

Forcefully, twist the barrel toward the person by pushing on it with your right hand, while simultaneously twisting your left hand.

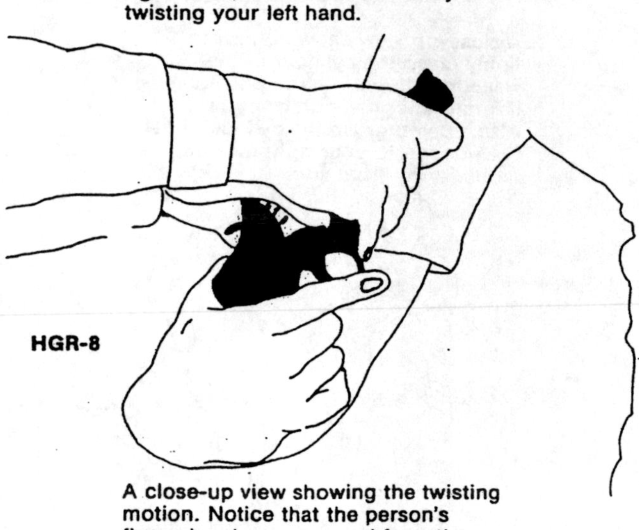

**HGR-8**

A close-up view showing the twisting motion. Notice that the person's finger has been removed from the trigger.

**HGR-9**

Having twisted the barrel of the weapon into the person, forcefully pull the weapon toward you. Simultaneously, step backward with your right leg.

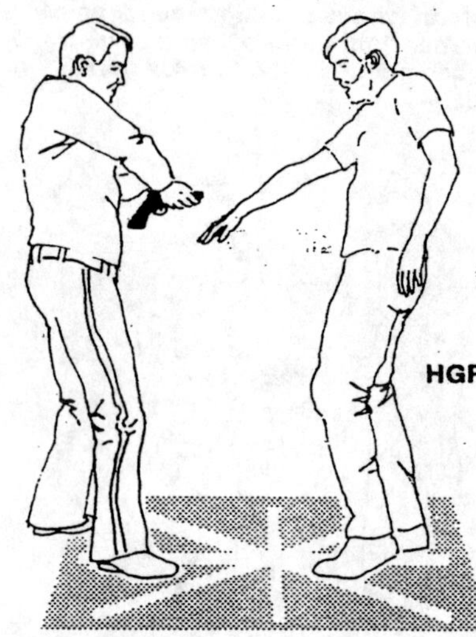

**HGR-10**

The action in HGR-9 should remove the weapon from the person's grasp. Use appropriate follow-up procedures.

Defensive Tactics DTI Institute

**Situation:** A person who is holding a handgun in his/her right hand points it at you at approximately head level, and tells you to raise your hands.

**Action:**

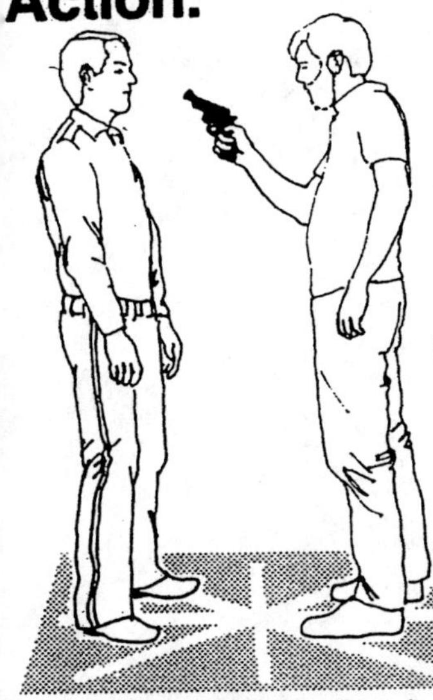

HGF-1

A person holding a handgun in his/her right hand points it at you at approximately head level and tells you to raise your hands.

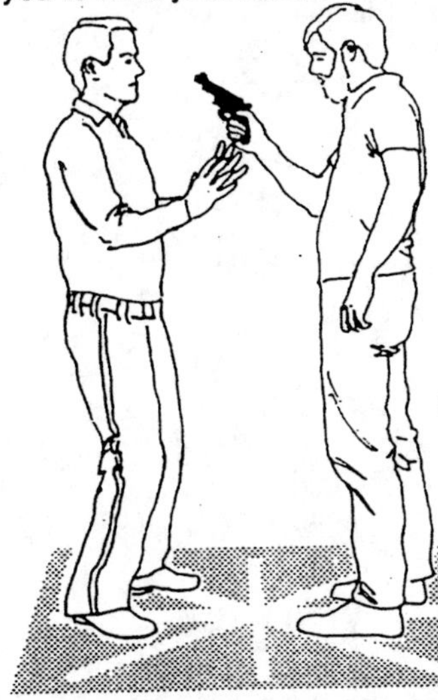

HGF-2

Begin to raise both of your hands. Keep your hands open so that you can grasp the weapon. Since (s)he is looking for movement, take advantage of it.

HGF-3

Forcefully grasp the weapon and push it upward. Your right hand must grasp the cylinder so that it cannot turn. Your left hand will grasp the barrel of the weapon.

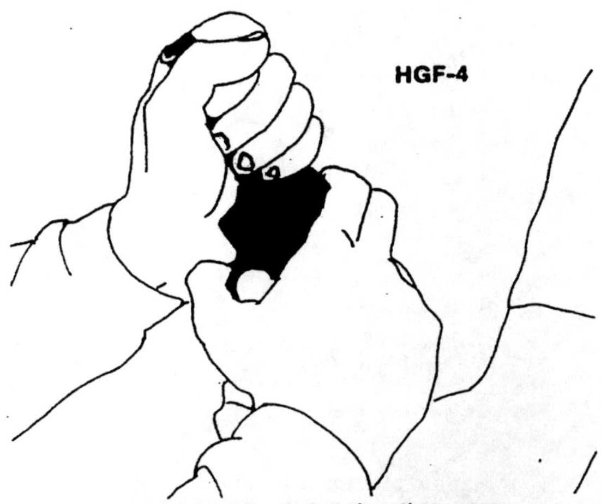

HGF-4

A close-up view showing the proper placement of your hands. Notice that the barrel of the weapon is "cradled" in the webbing of your left hand. Also, your left and right hand positions are extremely important, since you will be pushing the barrel into the person. If your hands are not placed as shown, it may be difficult to push the weapon.

HGF-5

Push the barrel of the weapon toward the person's head. This can easily be done by rotating your hands away from you. After the barrel has been pointed toward the person, forcefully pull the weapon downward, while simultaneously stepping backward with one leg. This action should remove the weapon from the person's hand.

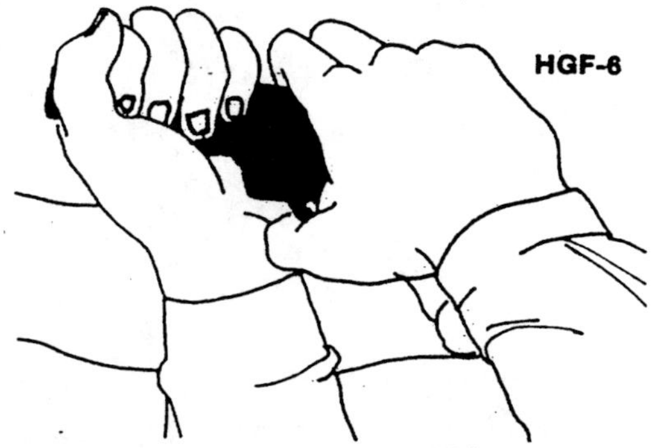

HGF-6

A close up view showing the pushing of the barrel toward the person. Note the position of your hands.

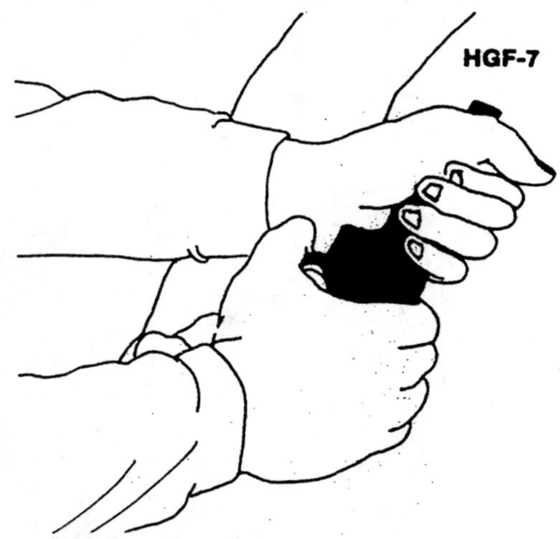

HGF-7

A close up view showing the positition of the barrel prior to your pulling downward on the weapon removing it from the person's hand.

HGF-8

Keeping the barrel pointed toward the person, forcefully pull the weapon downward and into you. This action should remove the weapon from the person's right hand. Use appropriate follow-up procedures.

**Situation:** A person who is holding a handgun in his/her right hand places it against your back.

**Action:**

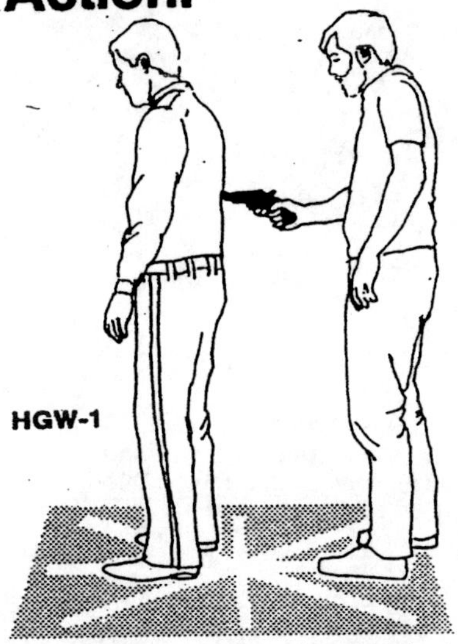

HGW-1

A person places a handgun against your back.

HGW-2

Casually turn your head until you can see which hand is holding the weapon.

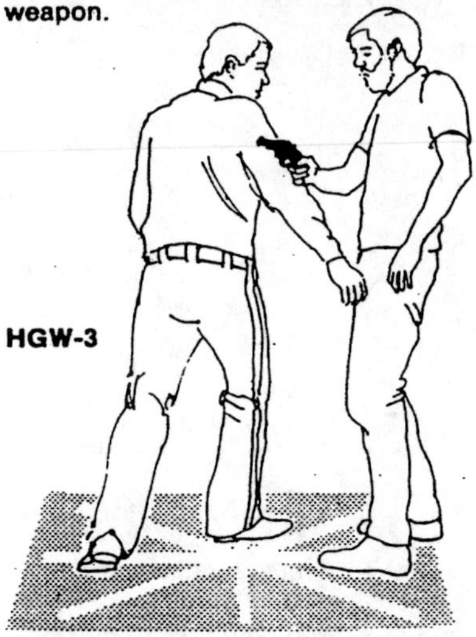

HGW-3

Seeing that it is being held in the right hand, make a quarter turn into the attacker by stepping backward with your right foot. Simultaneously, turn your upper body to the right so that your right elbow bumps the weapon. NOTE: Keep your right arm against the weapon so that the person cannot move the weapon to the right.

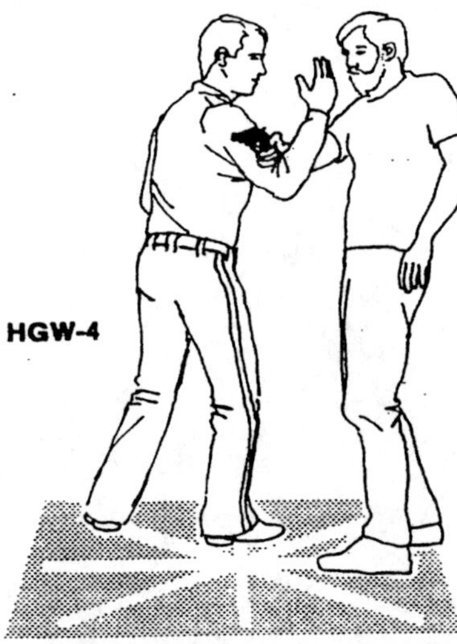

HGW-4

Having made a quarter turn, bend your right arm at the elbow, bringing your right arm under the person's right arm. The person's weapon should be "cradled" in the crook of your right arm.

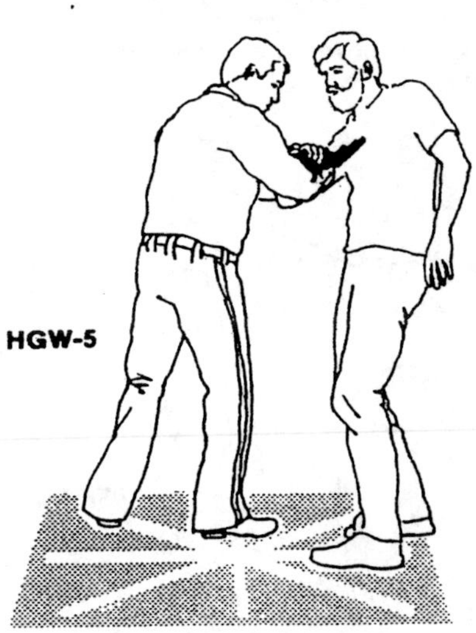

HGW-5

Forcefully, chop the person's elbow joint with your right hand. NOTE: Keep your right hand open so that it will fit into the person's crook of the arm.

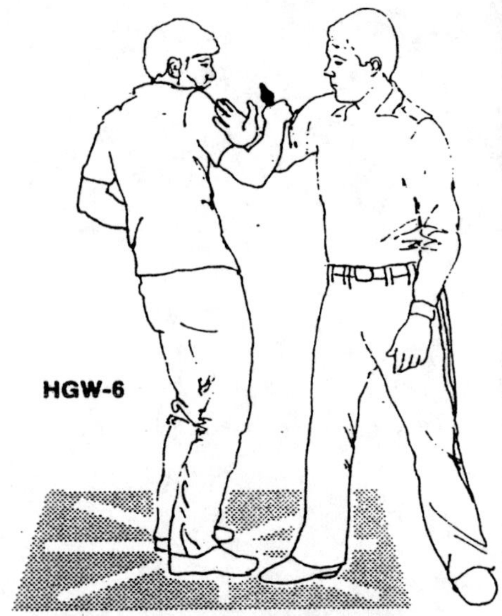

HGW-6

A side view of HGW-5. Note the position of your right hand. Also note that the person's right hand is trapped between your right bicep and forearm, with the handgun pointed away from you.

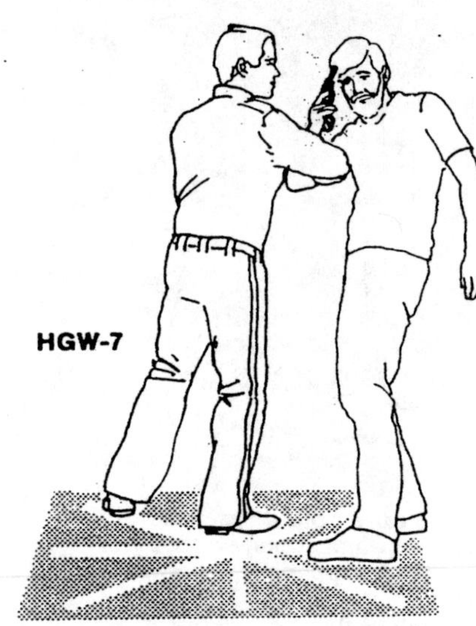

HGW-7

Forcefully, pull your right hand and arm downward. This action will force the person's right arm downward, while simultaneously forcing the weapon upward, smashing the attacker in the face.

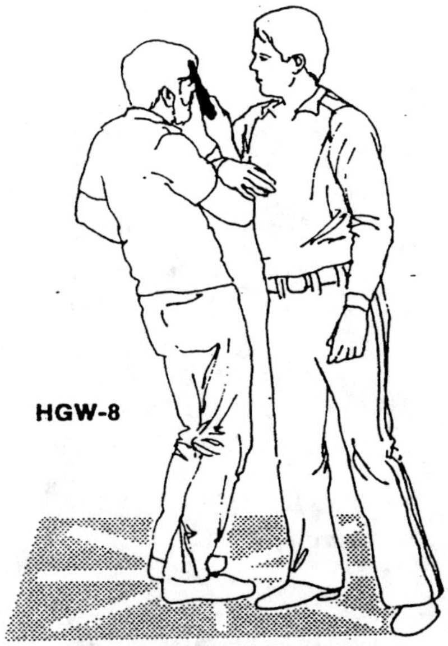

HGW-8

A side view of HGW-7 showing your hand and arm positions. Notice that the barrel and the frame of the weapon strike the person in the face.

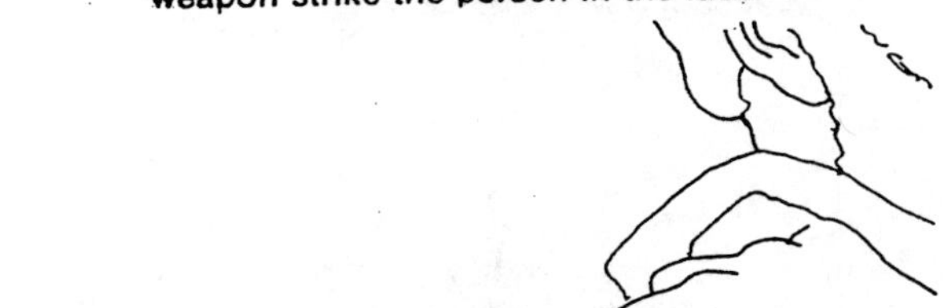

HGW-9

A close-up showing the position of the firearm which has been pushed past the person's head.

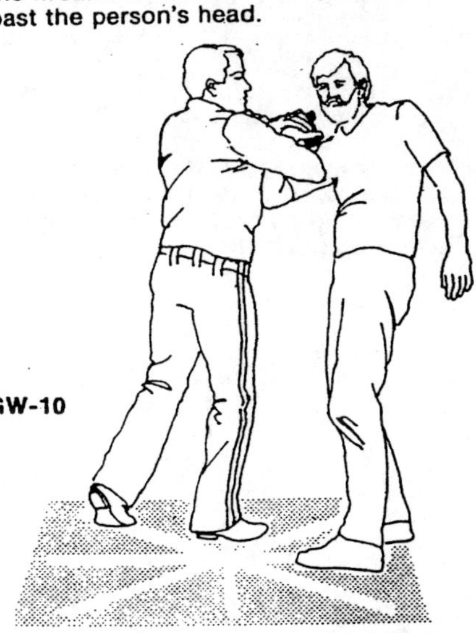

HGW-10

Quickly grasp the person's right wrist with your left hand. Apply a reverse wrist lock to the person's right hand, forcing the weapon past the right side of the person's head.

HGW-11

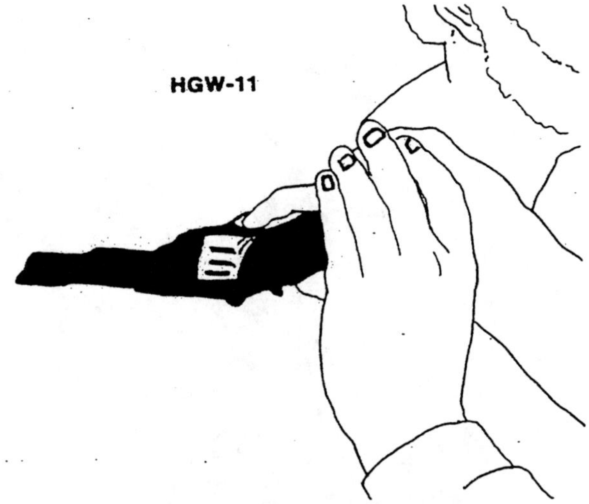

A close-up showing your left hand grasping the person's right hand.

HGW-12

A side view of HGW-9. Notice that when the wrist lock is applied the person becomes unbalanced.

HGW-13

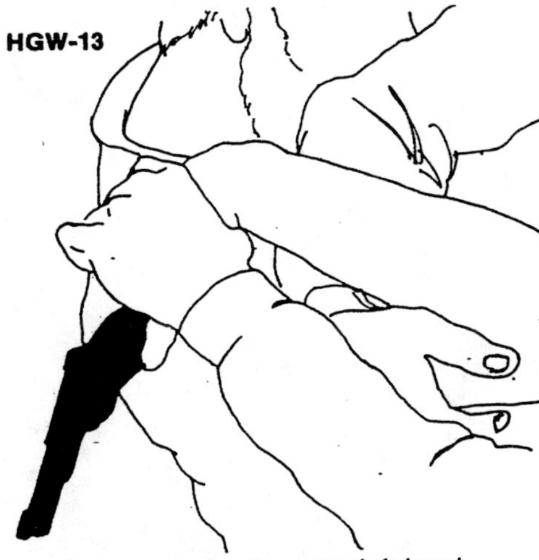

A close-up showing your left hand bending the person's right hand backward.

HGW-14

Holding the person's right hand with your left hand, grasp the barrel of the weapon with your right hand. Pull the barrel toward the ground.

HGW-16

A side view of HGW-11. Grasp the barrel of the weapon so that your right hand isn't placed over the end of the barrel where it could be shot should the weapon discharge.

HGW-15

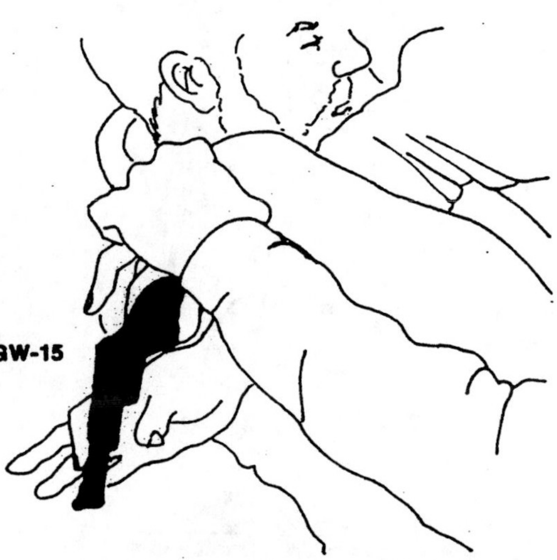

A close-up showing your right hand grasping the barrel of the weapon.

HGW-17

Continuing pressure against the person's right wrist with your left hand, forcefully pull the weapon downward, removing it from the person's right hand. Use appropriate follow-up procedures.

**Situation:** A person who is holding a handgun in his/her right hand places it against your back.

**Action:**

HGL-1

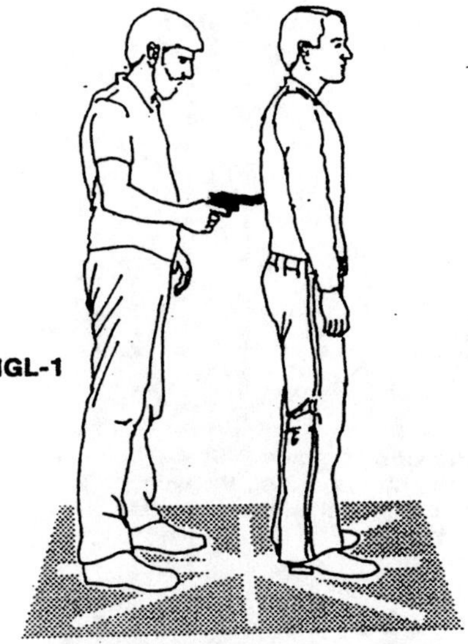

A person places a handgun against your back.

HGL-2

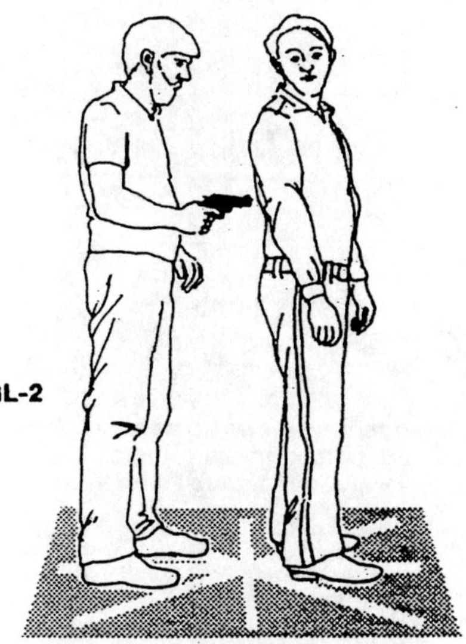

Casually turn your head until you can see which hand is holding the weapon.

HGL-3

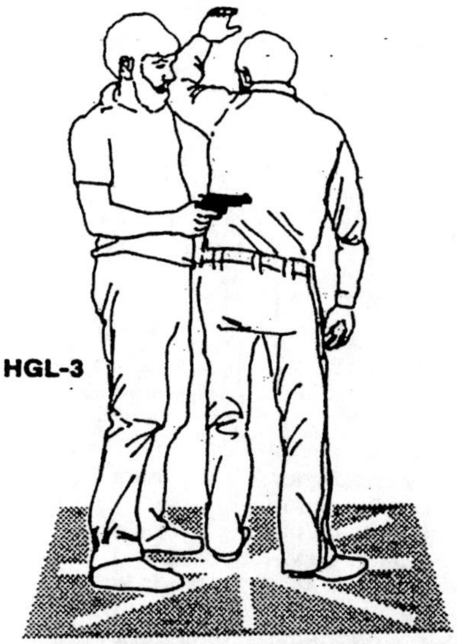

Seeing that it is being held in the right hand, make a quarter turn into the attacker by stepping backward with your left foot. Simultaneously, turn your upper body to the left while raising your left arm to shoulder height. These actions will remove you from the line of fire.

HGL-4

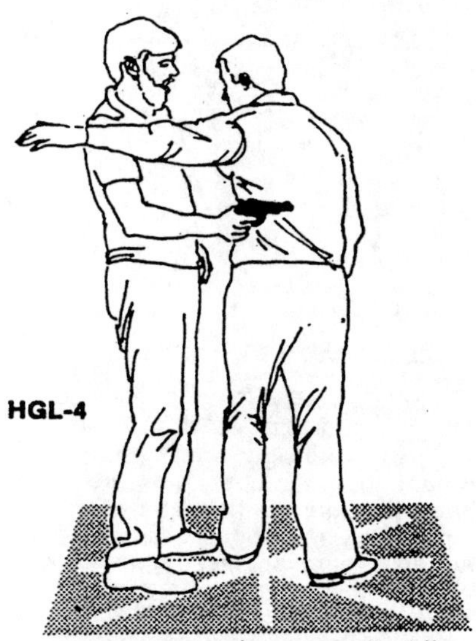

Continue turning to your left while placing your left arm over the person's right arm. Notice that the weapon's barrel is on your left side protruding past your back.

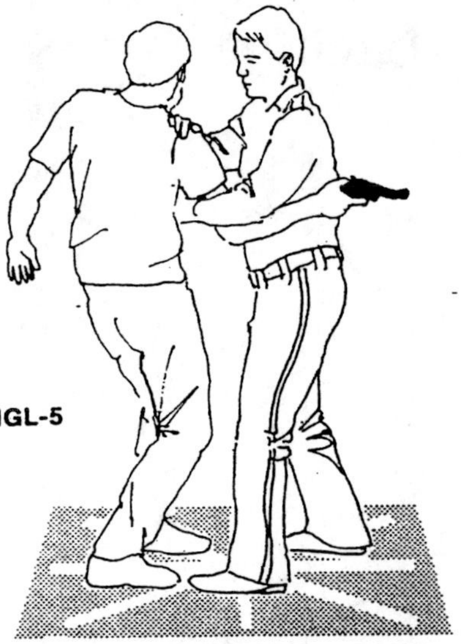

HGL-5

Quickly wrap your left arm over the person's right arm, while simultaneously placing your right hand—palm down—upon the person's right shoulder. Your left forearm must be placed above the person's right elbow for superior leverage.

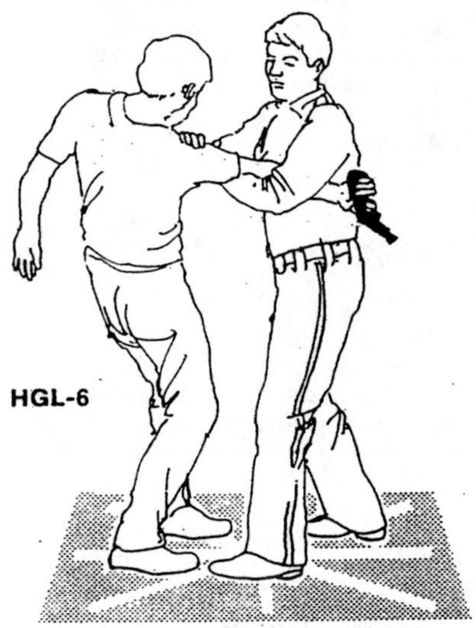

HGL-6

Next grasp your right wrist with your left hand. Begin to apply pressure against the person's right elbow with your left forearm. Remember to keep your left forearm against the person's elbow for maximum counterjoint pressure. This action should break the person's right elbow, causing him/her to drop the weapon.

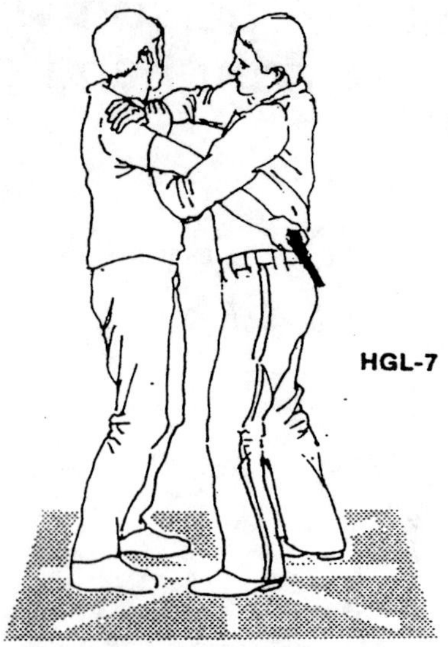

HGL-7

A side view showing HGL-6. Notice that the hand holding the weapon is held firmly against your left side.

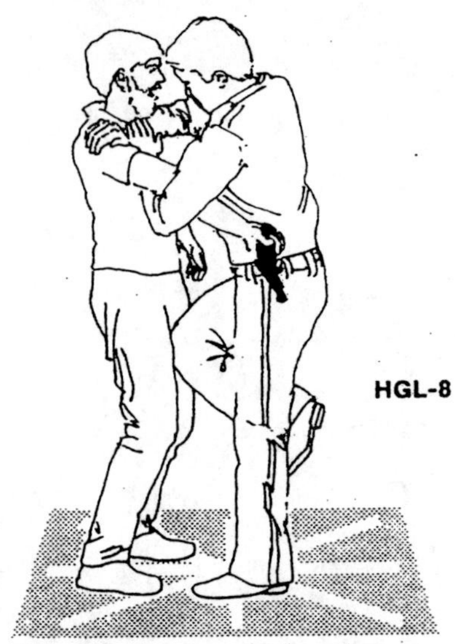

HGL-8

If necessary, you may forcefully strike the person in the groin or in the lower abdominal area with your right knee.

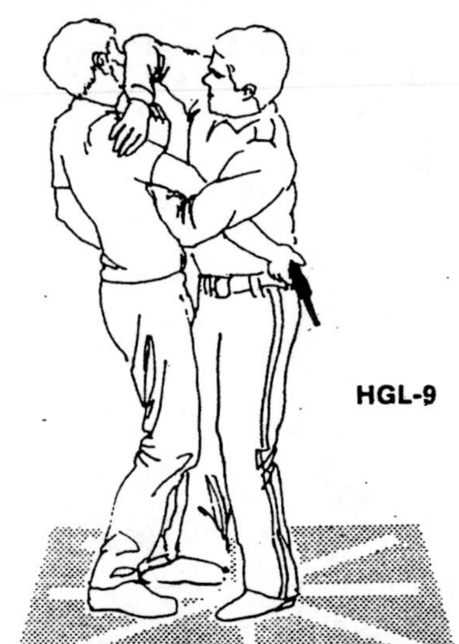

HGL-9

You may also strike the person in the face with your right forearm.

**Situation:** A person who is holding a handgun in his/her right hand places it against your back.

**Action:**

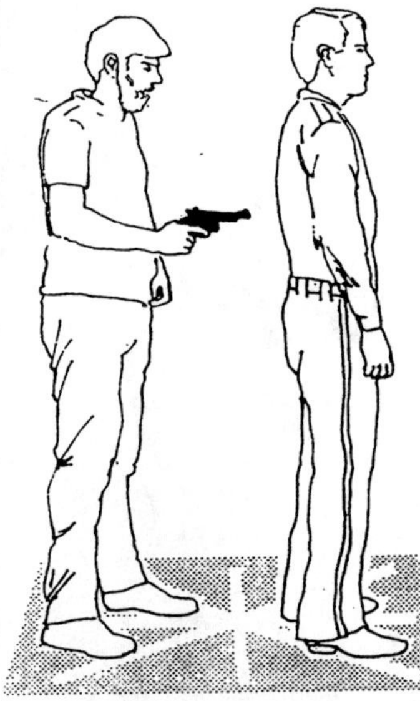

HGE-1

A person places a handgun against your back.

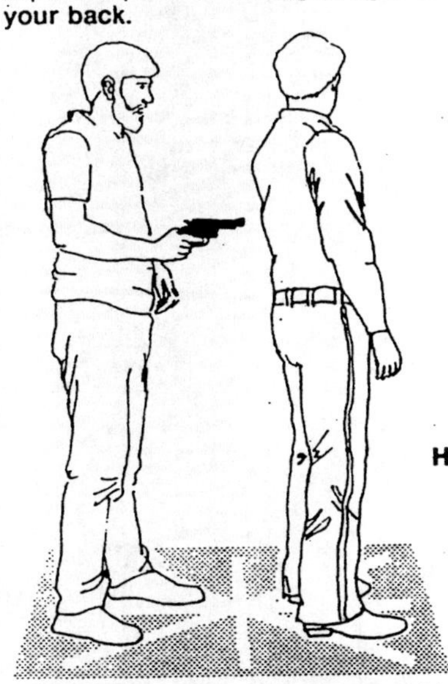

HGE-2

Casually turn your head to see which hand is holding the weapon.

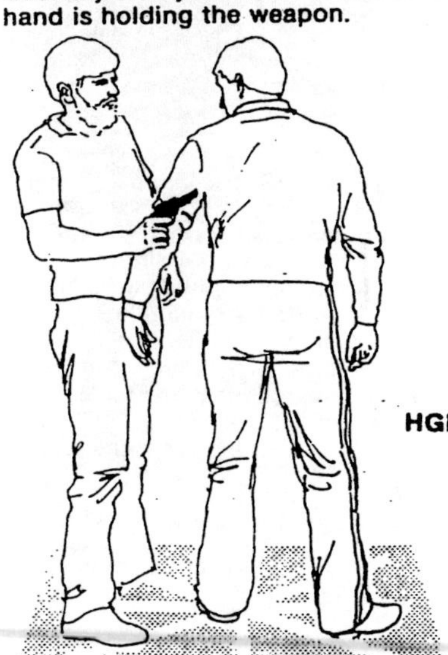

HGE-3

Seeing that the weapon is being held in the right hand, quickly make a quarter turn by stepping backward with your left foot. Simultaneously, turn your upper body to the left bumping the person's right arm with your left elbow. These actions should remove you from the line of fire.

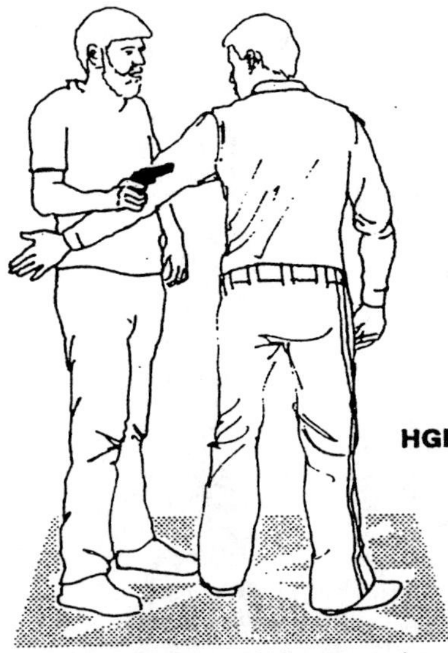

HGE-4

Quickly, place your left arm under the person's right arm. Notice that the weapon is pointing away from you, and cannot be swung to your right, because your left arm is blocking this movement.

HGE-5

Next, wrap your left arm around the person's right arm. Notice that the person's right arm is rotated toward you causing the weapon to also rotate.

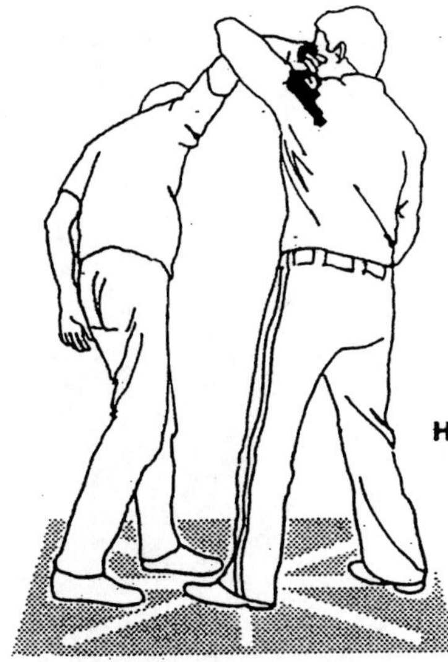

HGE-6

Lift the person's arm upward with your left arm. Notice that the weapon is placed on your left shoulder.

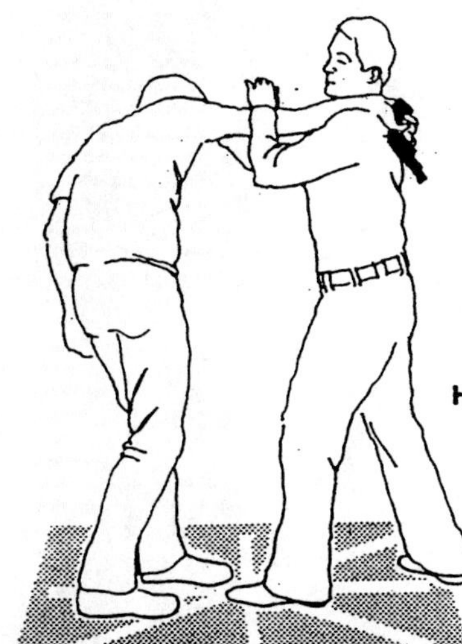

HGE-7

Having lifted the person's arm upward, rotate his/her arm until you can see the elbow. Forcefully, pull the suspect's elbow downward, causing it to break. Breaking the elbow should cause the person to drop the weapon. Use appropriate follow-up procedures.

DTI

**Situation:** A person who is holding a handgun in his/her right hand places it against the back of your head and tells you to raise your hands.

**Action:**

HGB-1

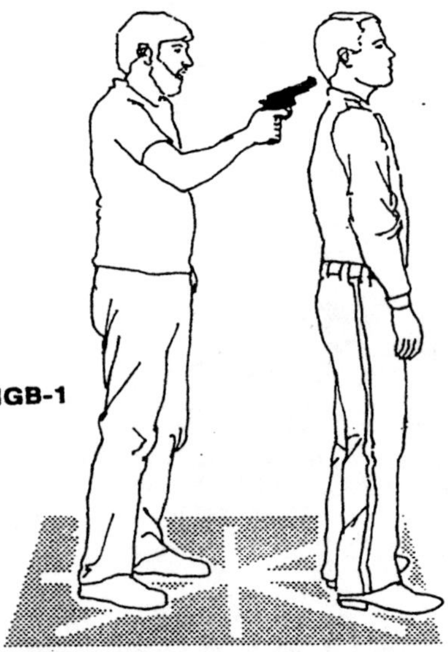

A person places a handgun against the back of your head and tells you to raise your hands.

HGB-2

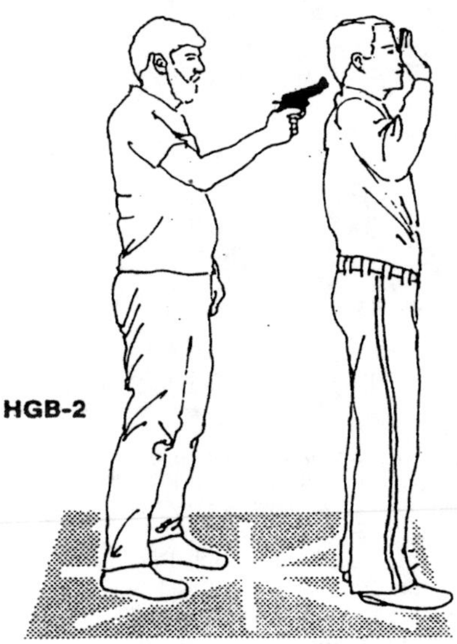

**Only** raise your hands to head level. Keeping your elbows bent, place your hands just slightly in front of your face. These actions will let you use your forearm to move the weapon away from the back of your head.

HGB-3

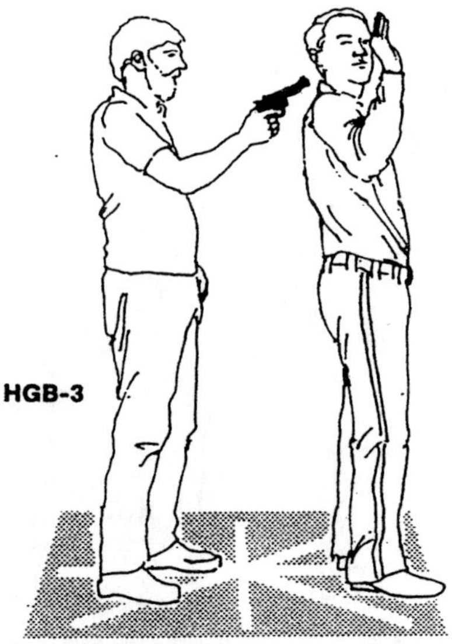

Casually, turn your head to see which hand is holding the weapon.

HGB-4

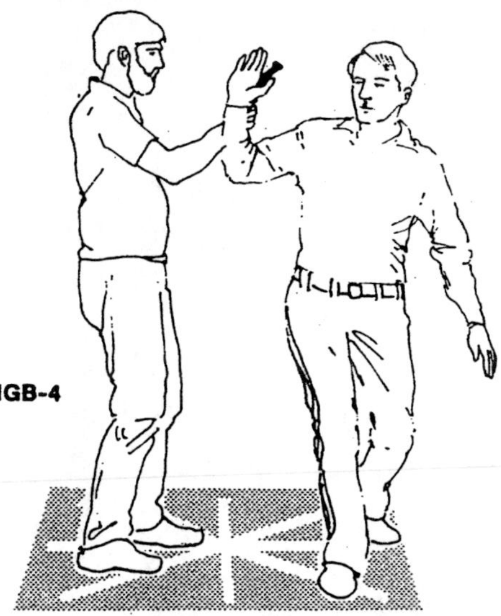

Seeing that the weapon is being held in the right hand, quickly make a 180° turn by stepping backward with your right foot. Turning the upper part of your body to the right, bump the person's right arm with your right forearm. This can be easily done by keeping your right arm bent as you turn into the person. These actions should remove you from the line of fire.

HGB-5

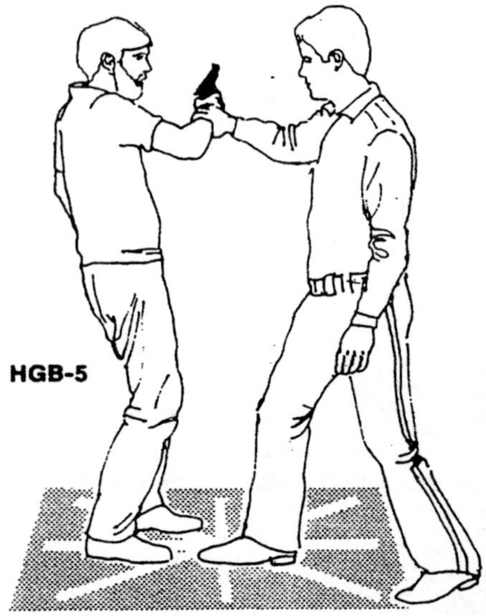

As you complete your 180° turn grasp the person's right wrist with your right hand.

HGB-6

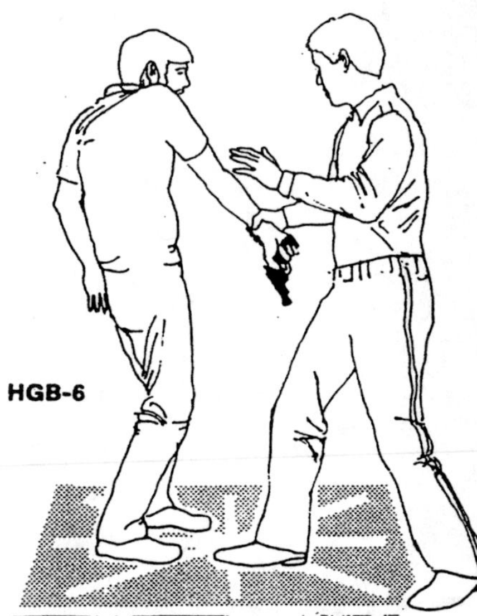

Quickly rotate the person's wrist away from you so that his/her elbow is facing you, while pulling his/her arm toward the ground. Notice that his/her arm is pulled until it is straight so that (s)he is slightly unbalanced. These actions should point the barrel of the weapon toward the ground for safety reasons.

HGB-7

After grabbing the person's right wrist, quickly make a quarter turn to the rear using your right foot. Draw the person's wrist into and against your right pelvic bone area. The reason: so that the barrel of the firearm is pointing away from and to the outside of you.

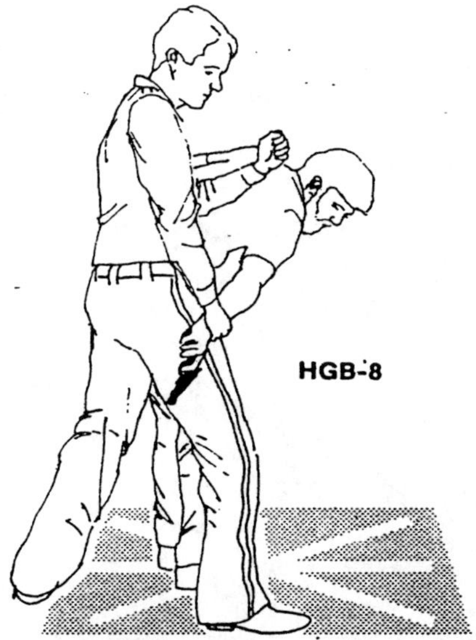

HGB-8

A side view showing the proper position of the person's right wrist against your pelvic area. Using your right hand, rotate the person's right wrist so that his/her elbow is facing you. Raise your left arm in preparation for the delivery of a strike to the person's right elbow.

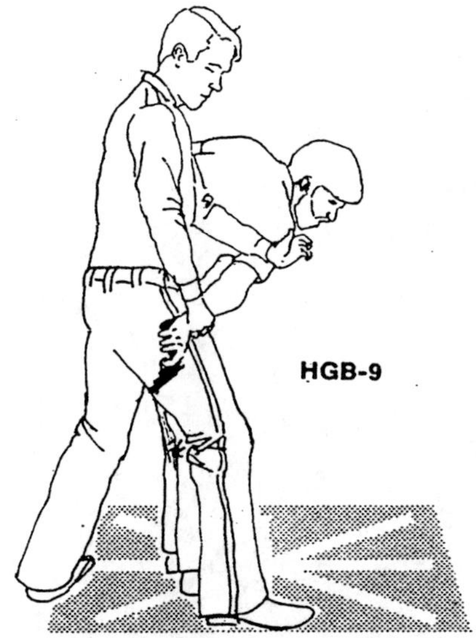

HGB-9

Next, deliver a forceful forearm strike to the person's arm, just above the elbow. This action should break the person's elbow causing him/her to drop the weapon. Use appropriate follow-up procedures.

**Situation:** A person who is holding a handgun in his/her hand places it against the back of your head.

**Action:**

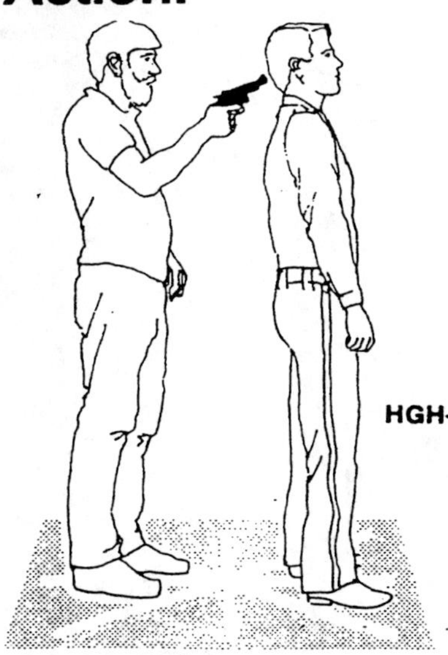

HGH-1

A person places a handgun against the back of your head.

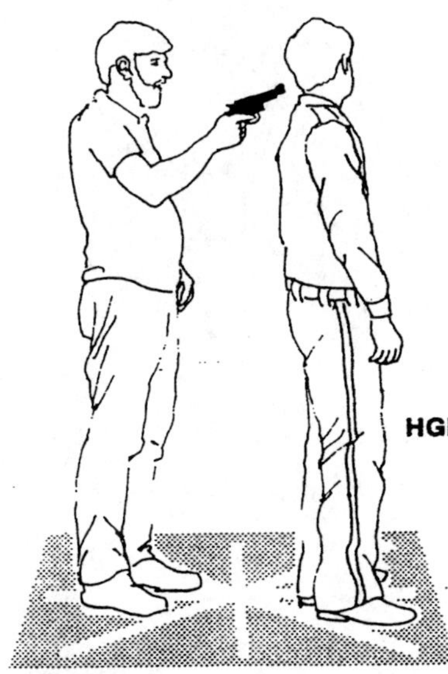

HGH-2

Casually turn your head until you can see which hand is holding the weapon.

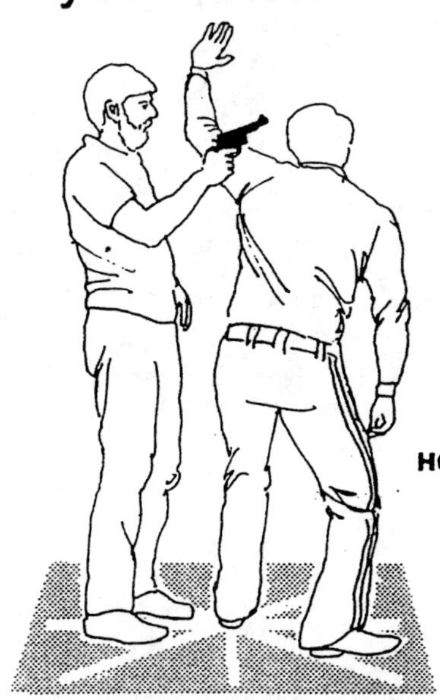

HGH-3

Seeing that it is being held in the right hand, make a quarter turn into the attacker by stepping backward with your left foot. Simultaneously, turn your upper body to the left while raising your left arm over your head. These actions will remove you from the line of fire.

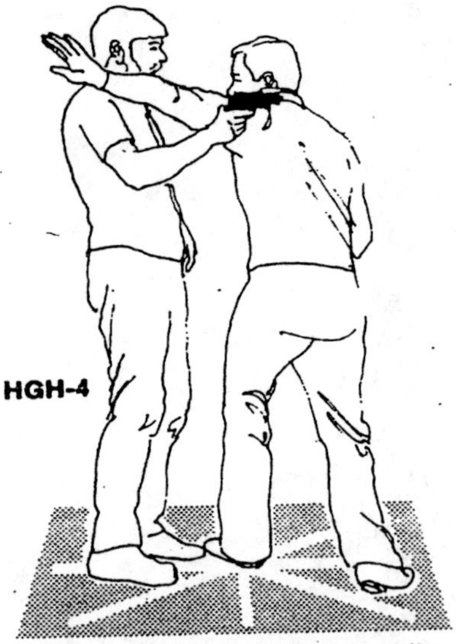

HGH-4

Continue turning to your left while placing your left arm over the person's right arm. Notice that the weapon's barrel is on your left side protruding past your back.

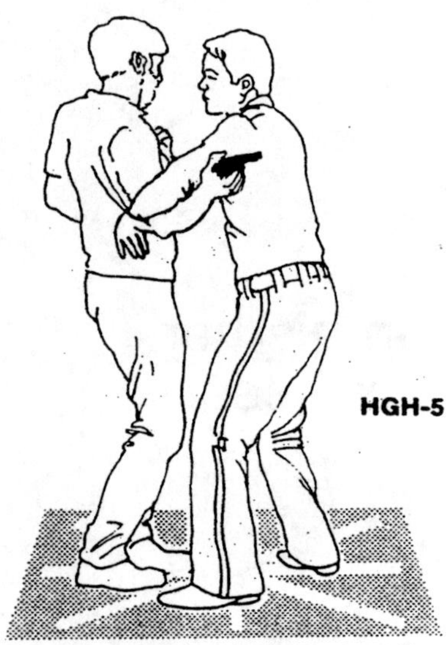

HGH-5

Quickly wrap your left arm over the person's right arm, while simultaneously placing your right hand—palm down—upon the person's right shoulder. Your left forearm must be placed above the person's right elbow for superior leverage.

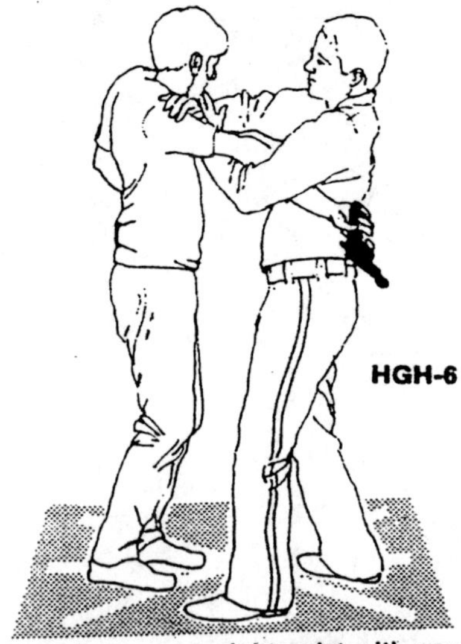

HGH-6

Next, grasp your right wrist with your left hand. Begin to apply upward pressure against the person's right elbow with your left forearm. Remember to keep your left forearm above the person's right elbow causing him/her to drop the weapon.

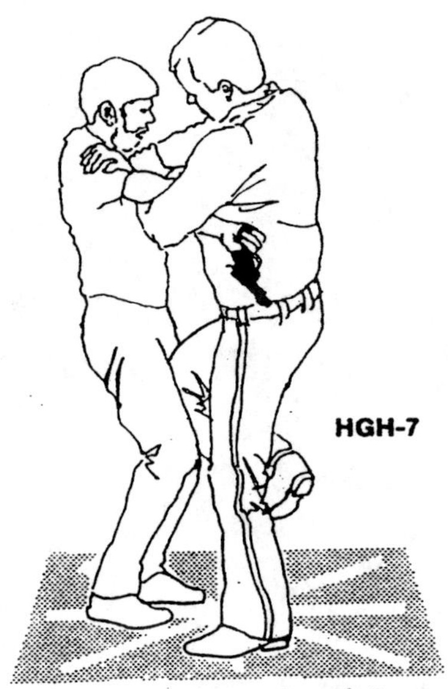

HGH-7

If necessary, you may forcefully strike the person in the groin or in the lower abdominal area with your right knee.

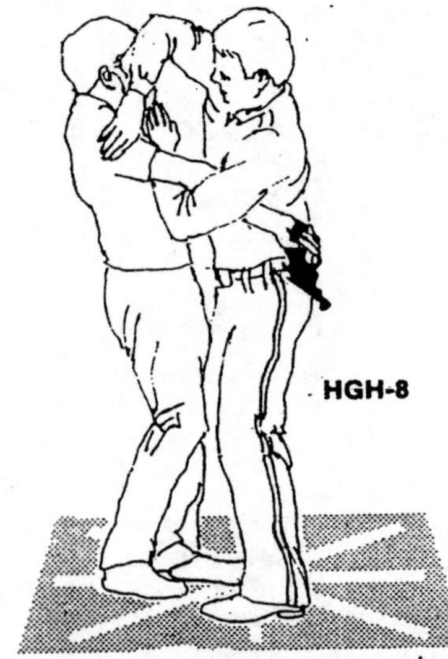

HGH-8

You may also strike the person in the face with your right forearm.

**Situation:** While talking to a suspect, (s)he attempts to draw a weapon.

**Action:**

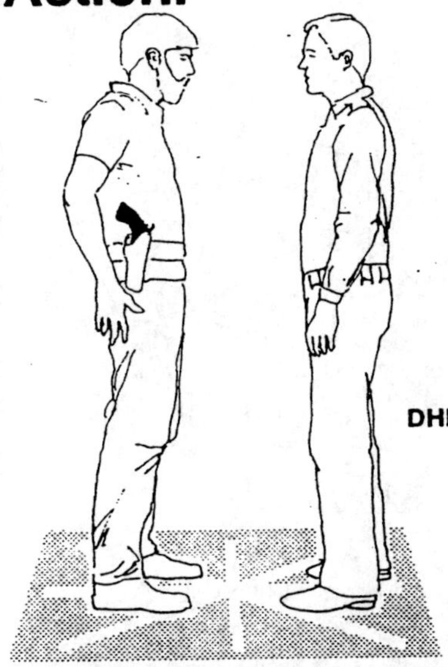

DHL-1

While talking to a suspect, you notice that (s)he is wearing a holstered weapon on his/her right side.

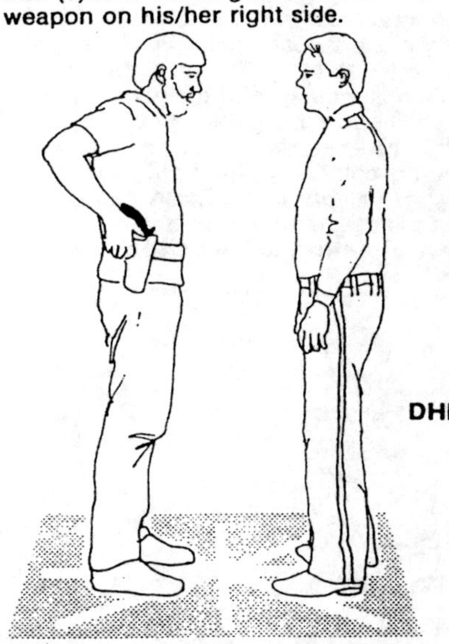

DHL-2

While you are talking, (s)he attempts to draw it from the holster using a right hand.

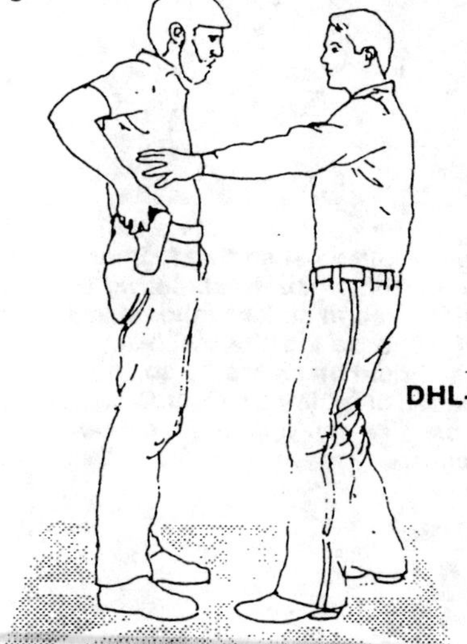

DHL-3

Quickly outstretch your left hand and arm toward the person's wrist.

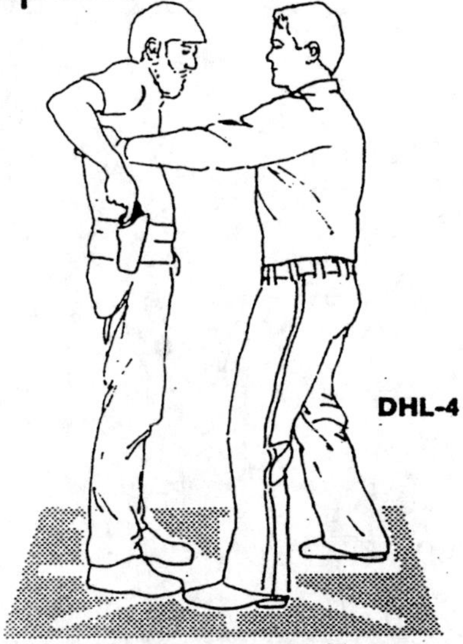

DHL-4

Stepping into the person with your left leg, thrust your left hand and arm between the person's right forearm and right rib cage.

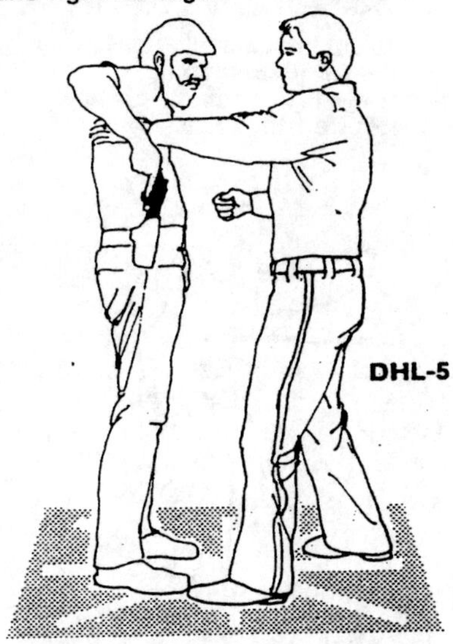

DHL-5

Prepare to place your right hand on the person's right shoulder.

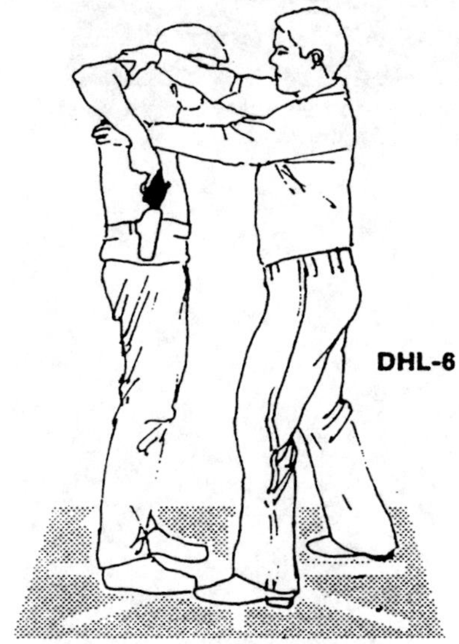

DHL-6

Firmly grasp the person's right shoulder with your right hand.

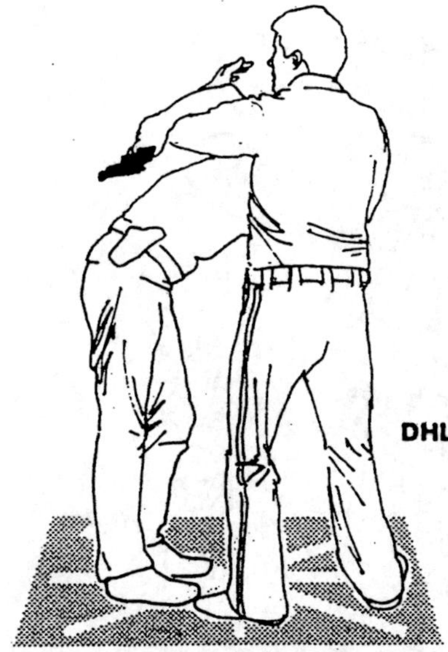

DHL-7

Quickly step to your left while raising your left arm. Notice that the person cannot aim the weapon at you because your left arm is in the way.

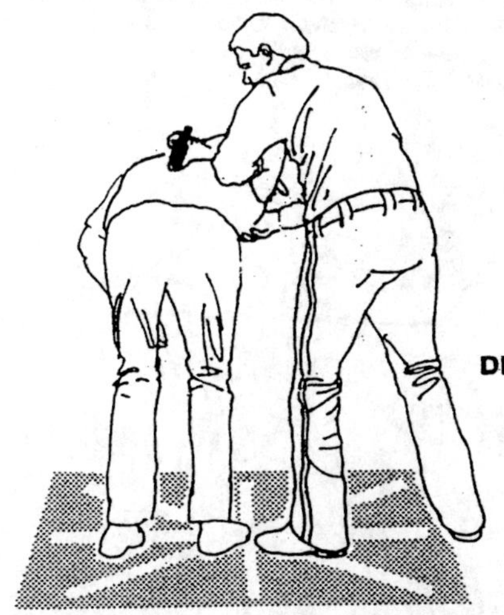

DHL-8

Forcefully lift the suspect's arm using your left arm, causing his/her arm to bend at the elbow. Attempt to cradle the person's forearm in the crook of your left elbow, while pushing down on the person's right bicep area with your left hand. Use appropriate follow-up measures.

**Situation:** While talking to a suspect, (s)he attempts to draw a weapon, cross draw style.

**Action:**

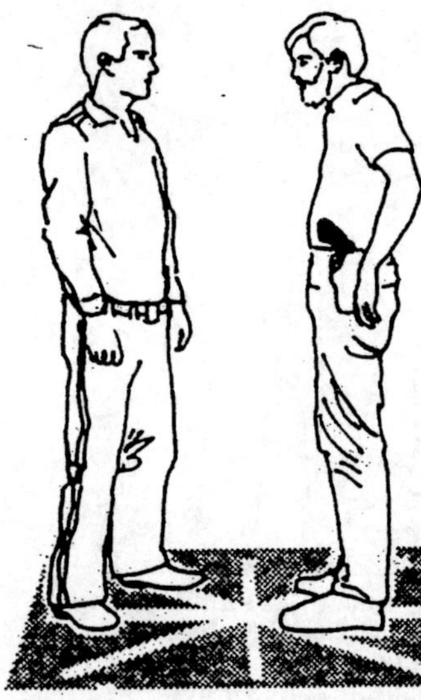

CDL-1

While talking to a suspect you notice that (s)he is wearing a holstered weapon—cross draw style—on his/her left side.

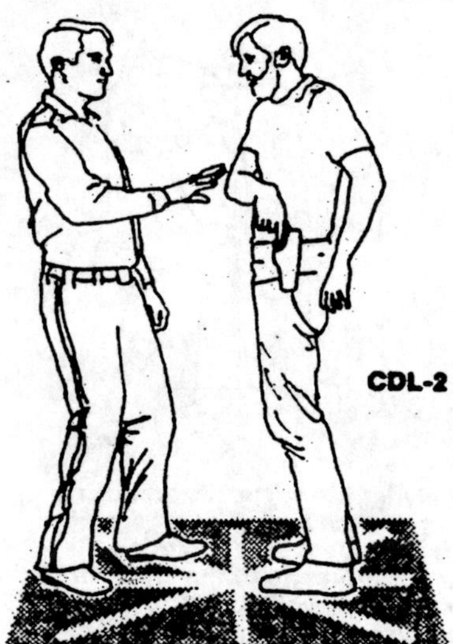

CDL-2

While you are talking (s)he attempts to draw it from the holster using his/her right hand. As the person reaches for the weapon, quickly outstretch your right hand toward his/her right wrist.

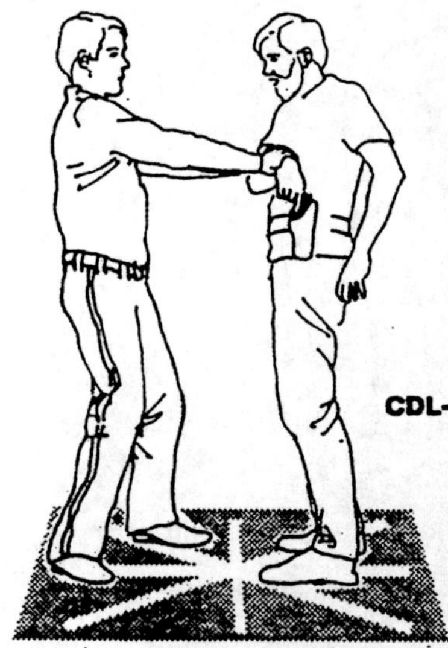

CDL-3

Attempt to pin the person's right arm against his/her midsection by pushing it against him/her. This is only to help slow the draw.

CDL-4

Firmly grasp the person's right wrist with your right hand.

CDL-5

As the weapon clears the holster, quickly make a quarter turn by stepping backward with your right leg. Simultaneously, pull the person's right wrist and arm against your pelvic bone area. Notice that the weapon is pointing to the right, and is away from your body. Raise your left arm in preparation for the delivery of a strike to the person's elbow.

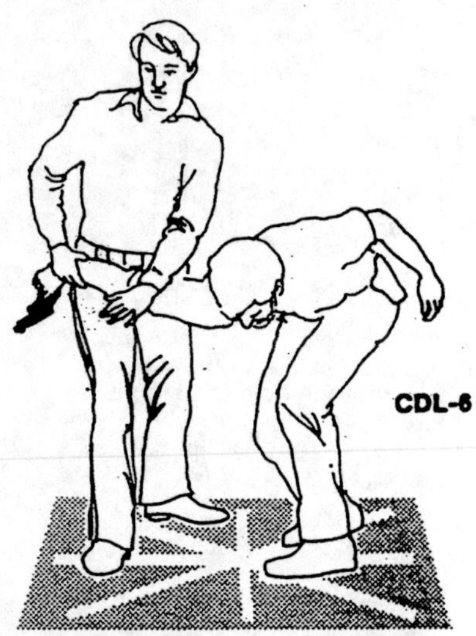

CDL-6

Using your right hand, rotate the person's right wrist so that his/her elbow is facing you. Next, deliver a forceful forearm strike to the person's arm, just above the elbow. This action should break the person's elbow causing him/her to drop the weapon. Use appropriate follow-up procedures.

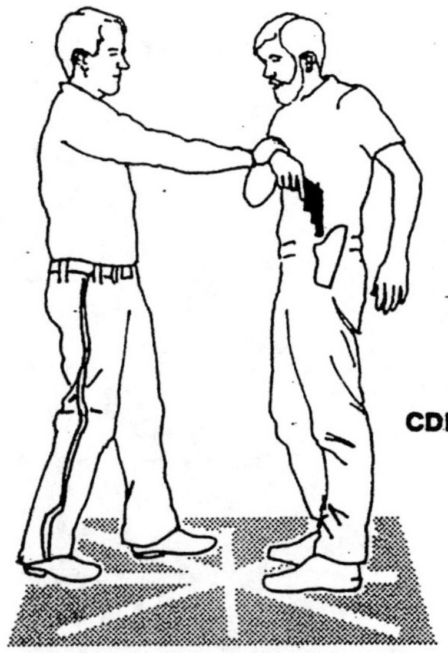

CDL-7

Returning to CDL-4, you may also use a reverse arm lock to disarm the person. As the person draws the weapon, firmly grasp his/her right wrist with your right hand.

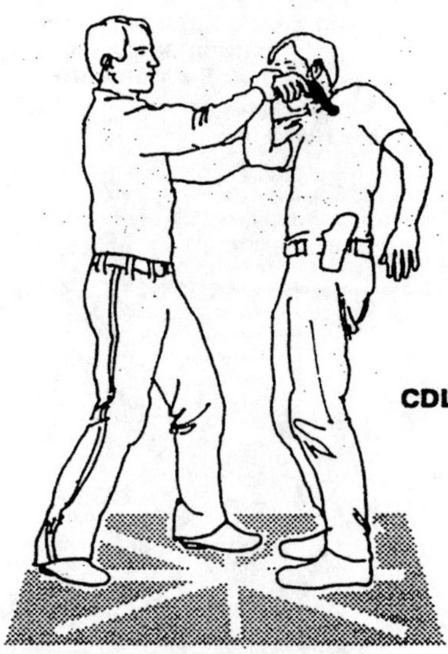

CDL-8

Raising the person's right arm, forcefully place your left forearm into the crook of the person's right arm.

CDL-9

Twist the person's right wrist and hand toward his/her face, while pulling down on the person's right elbow with your left arm.

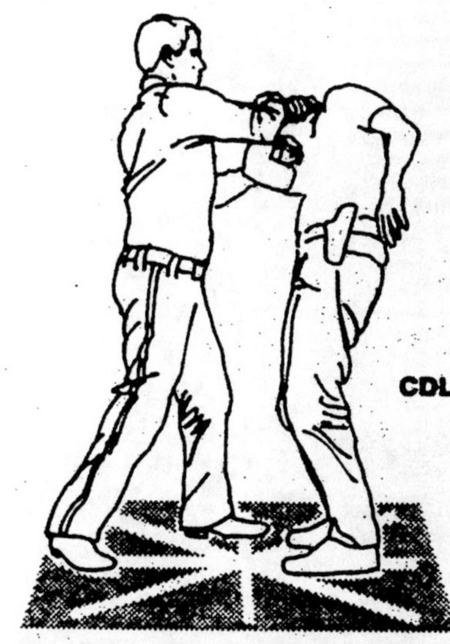

CDL-10

Forcefully strike the person in the face with his/her weapon. Use appropriate follow-up procedures.

**Situation:** A person points a rifle or shotgun at your chest.

**Action:**

LGT-1

A person points a rifle or shotgun at your chest.

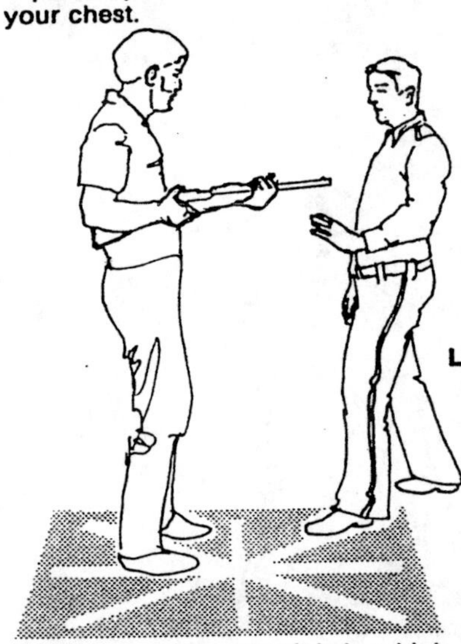

LGT-2

After determining that it is in a high zone, quickly reach for the barrel of the weapon with your left hand. Keep your thumb at a right angle to your hand to ease grasping the barrel.

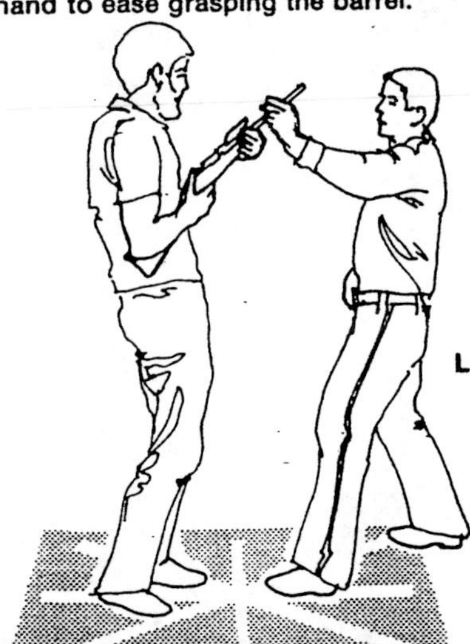

LGT-3

Grasping the barrel tightly, push the barrel upward and away from your head and body.

LGT-4

Pushing the barrel upward, reach for the gun stock with your right hand. NOTE: Your right hand should be prepared to stop a butt strike directed at your groin.

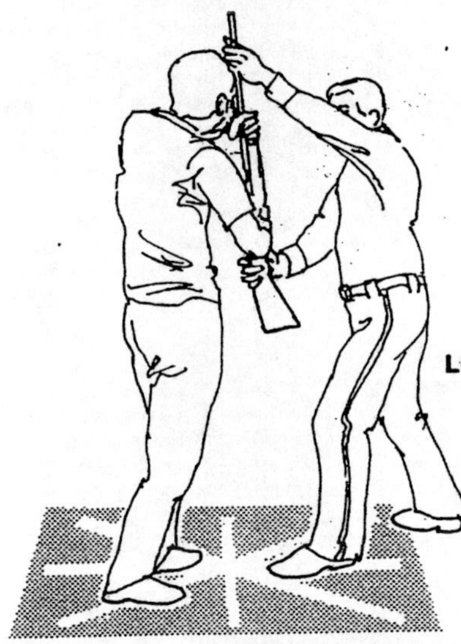

LGT-5

Grasp the stock with your right hand, As you step into the person with your left leg, push the barrel upward with your left hand.

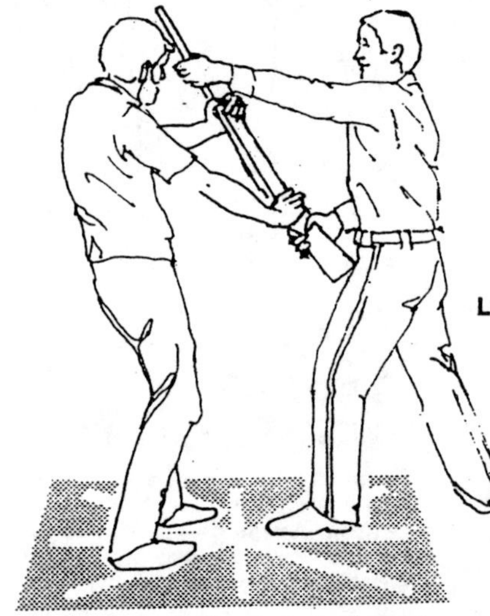

LGT

Forcefully pull the gun stock past your right side using your right hand, causing the gun barrel to strike the person on the head or the collarbone area. For extra impact, forcefully push down on the gun barrel with your left hand as you pull the stock past you.

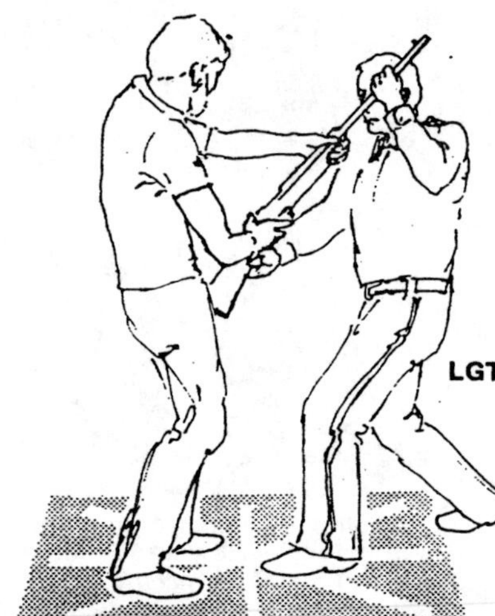

LGT-7

After striking the person on the head or collarbone, forcefully push the gun butt into the person's groin or lower abdominal area. Your right hand will push the gun butt into the person; your left hand will pull the barrel forward and to the left helping to increase the speed and impact of the move. Next, remove the weapon from the person's grip. Use appropriate follow-up procedures.

**Situation:** A person places a rifle or shotgun against your back.

**Action:**

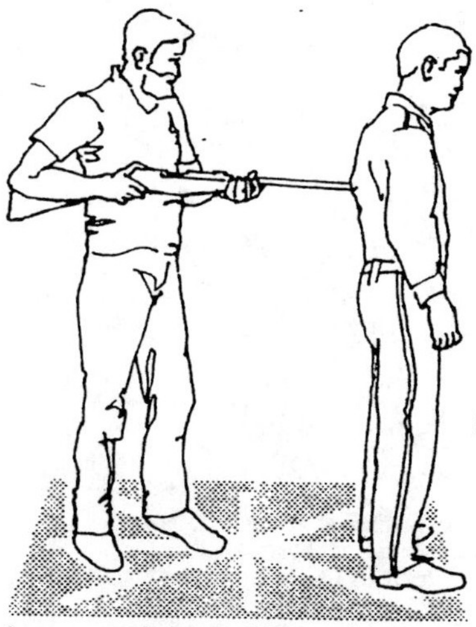

LGB-1

A person places a rifle or shotgun against your upper back.

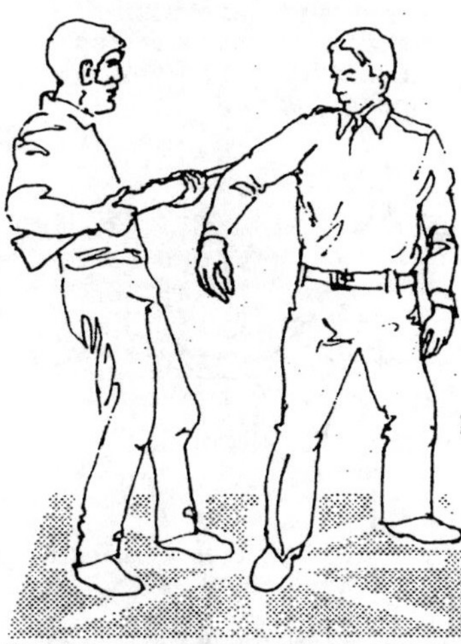

LGB-2

Quickly make a quarter turn to your right by stepping with your right leg, pivoting on your left foot. Simultaneously, position your right arm so that your elbow will "bump" the barrel as you turn. Both actions will remove you from the line of fire.

LGB-3

Firmly grasp the barrel with your right hand, and the weapon (between the person's hands)with your left hand.

LGB-4

Pushing the weapon into the person, forcefully knee the person's groin or lower abdominal areas with your left knee.

LGB-5

Next, forcefully pull the weapon outward--past your body--striking the person's head or collarbone areas with the barrel. Remove the weapon from the person's grasp. Use appropriate follow-up procedures.

**Situation:** A person places a rifle or shotgun against your back.

**Action:**

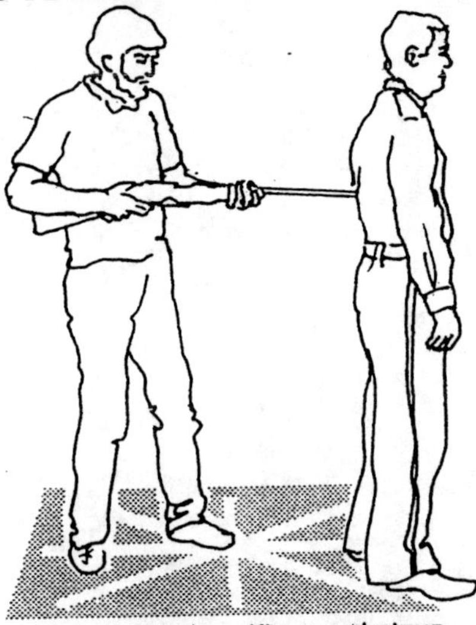

LRB-1

A person places a rifle or a shotgun against your back.

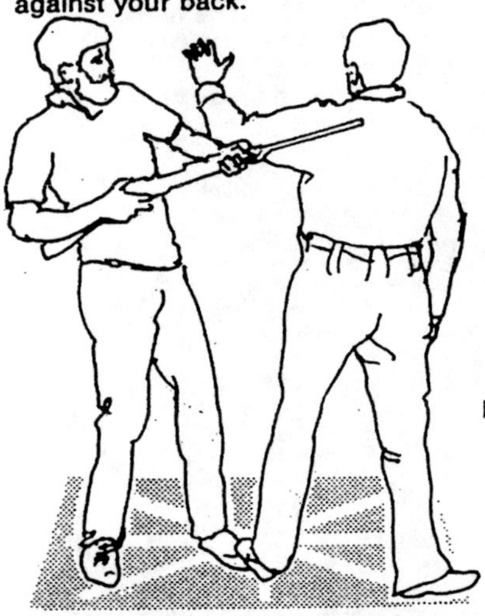

LRB-2

Quickly, make a quarter turn to your left by stepping backward with your left foot. Step on the person's left foot so that (s)he can't move backward. Simultaneously, raise your left arm so that your elbow will bump the barrel as you turn. Both actions will remove you from the line of fire.

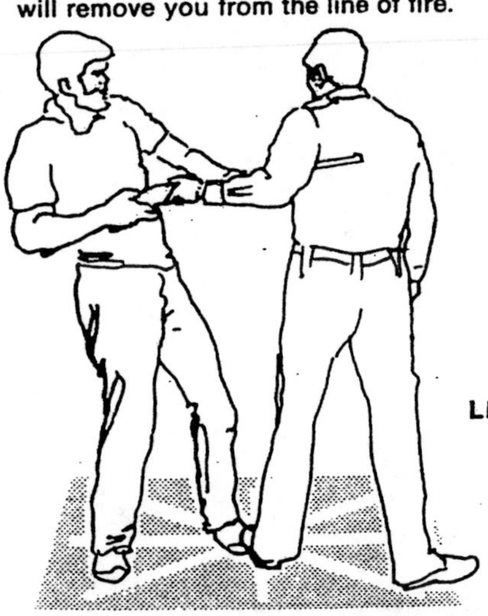

LRB-3

Wrap your left arm over the barrel, firmly grasping the weapon--between the person's two hands--with your left hand. The barrel of the weapon is

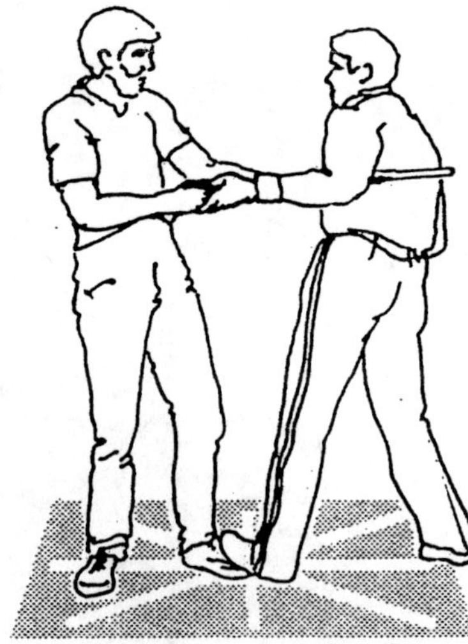

LRB-4

Next, lean backward pulling the person slightly off balance.

LRB-5

Simultaneously, raise your right arm in preparation for striking the person in the facial area.

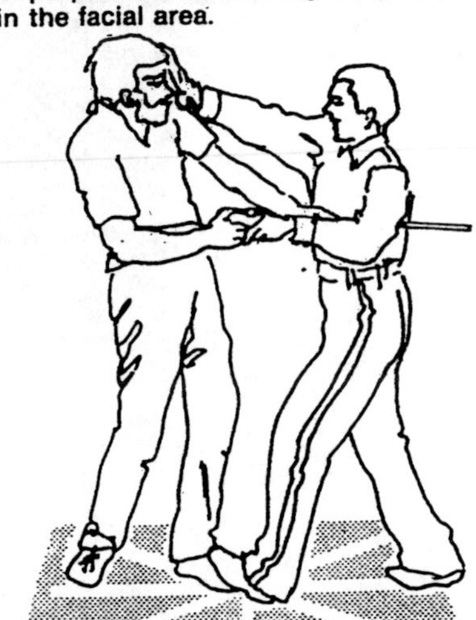

LRB-6

Forcefully, strike the person in the facial area using the palm of your right hand. You may also gouge the person's eyes with your right fingers. These actions should make the person release the weapon. After you obtain the weapon, use appropriate

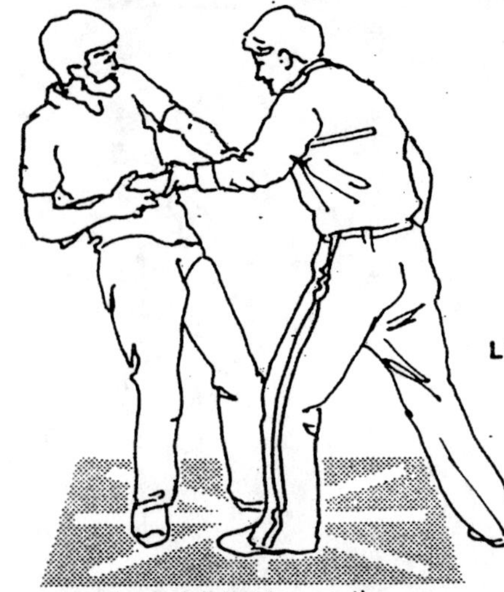

LRB-7

Should you fail to step on the person's foot in LGB-2, don't stop, as you could be seriously injured or killed. Step into the person using your left leg, while firmly grasping the weapon--between the person's hands--with your left hand. Again, the barrel of the weapon is extending past your body, while being firmly held under your left armpit.

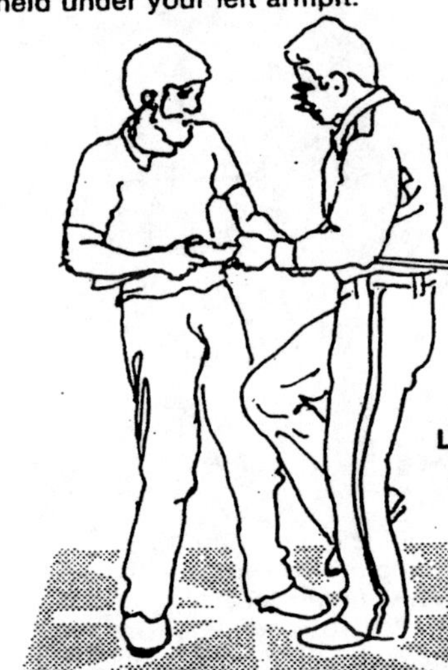

LRB-8

As you pull the person into you, bend your right knee in preparation for striking the person in the lower abdominal area.

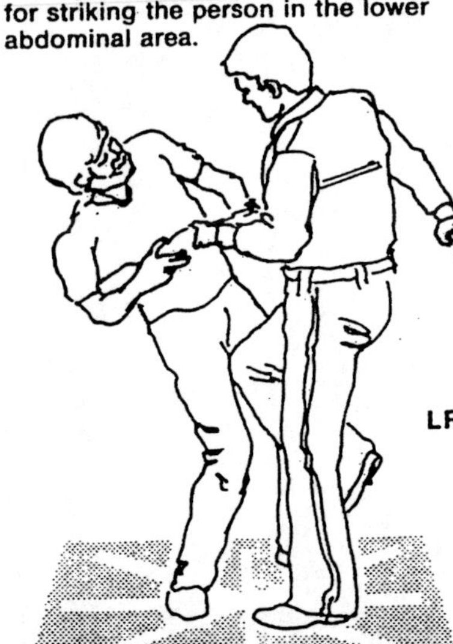

LRB-9

Forcefully strike the person in the

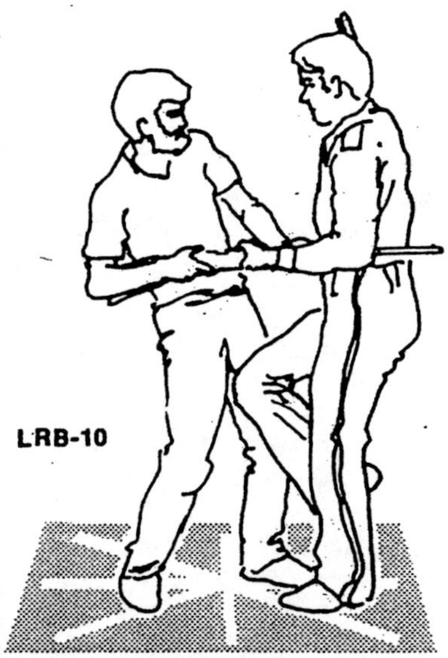

LRB-10

As you strike the person with your knee, begin to raise your right arm.

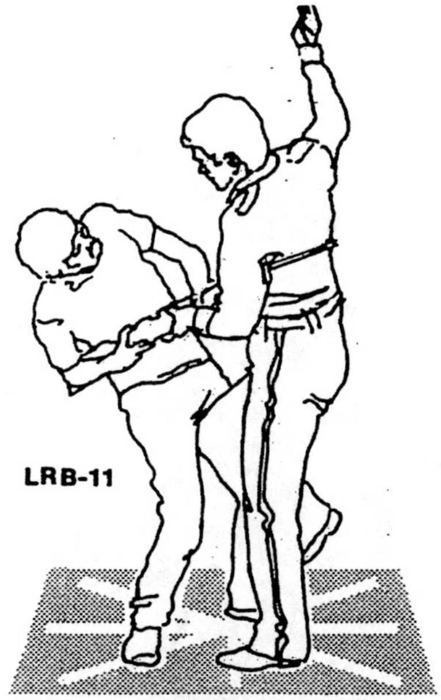

LRB-11

Raise your right arm in preparation for "chopping" the person in the shoulderblade area.

LRB-12

Forcefully strike the person in the neck or the shoulderblade area. This action should make the person release the weapon. After you obtain the weapon, use appropriate follow-up procedures.

**Situation:** A person places a rifle or shotgun against the back of your head.

**Action:**

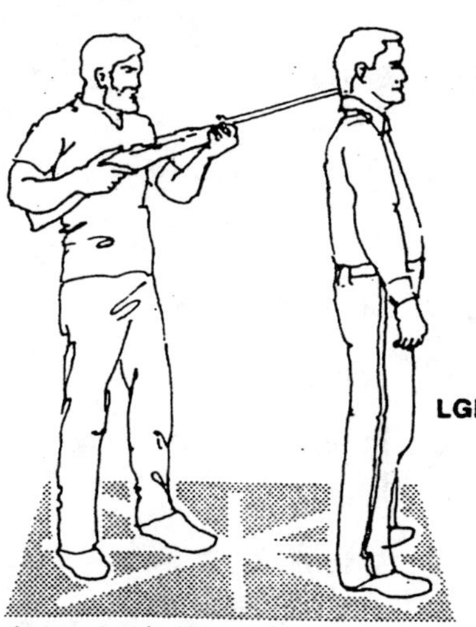

LGH-1

A person places a rifle or shotgun against the back of your head.

LGH-2

Quickly, make a quarter turn to your left by stepping backward with your left foot. If possible, step on the person's foot so (s)he can't move backward. Simultaneously, raise your left arm as if doing a rear choke defense, bumping the barrel as you turn. Both actions will remove you from the line of fire.

LGH-3

Wrap your left arm over the barrel, firmly grasping the weapon—between the person's hands—with your left hand. Next, forcefully strike the person in the face with the heel of your right hand, or eye rake the person with your right fingers.

FIGURE H-1

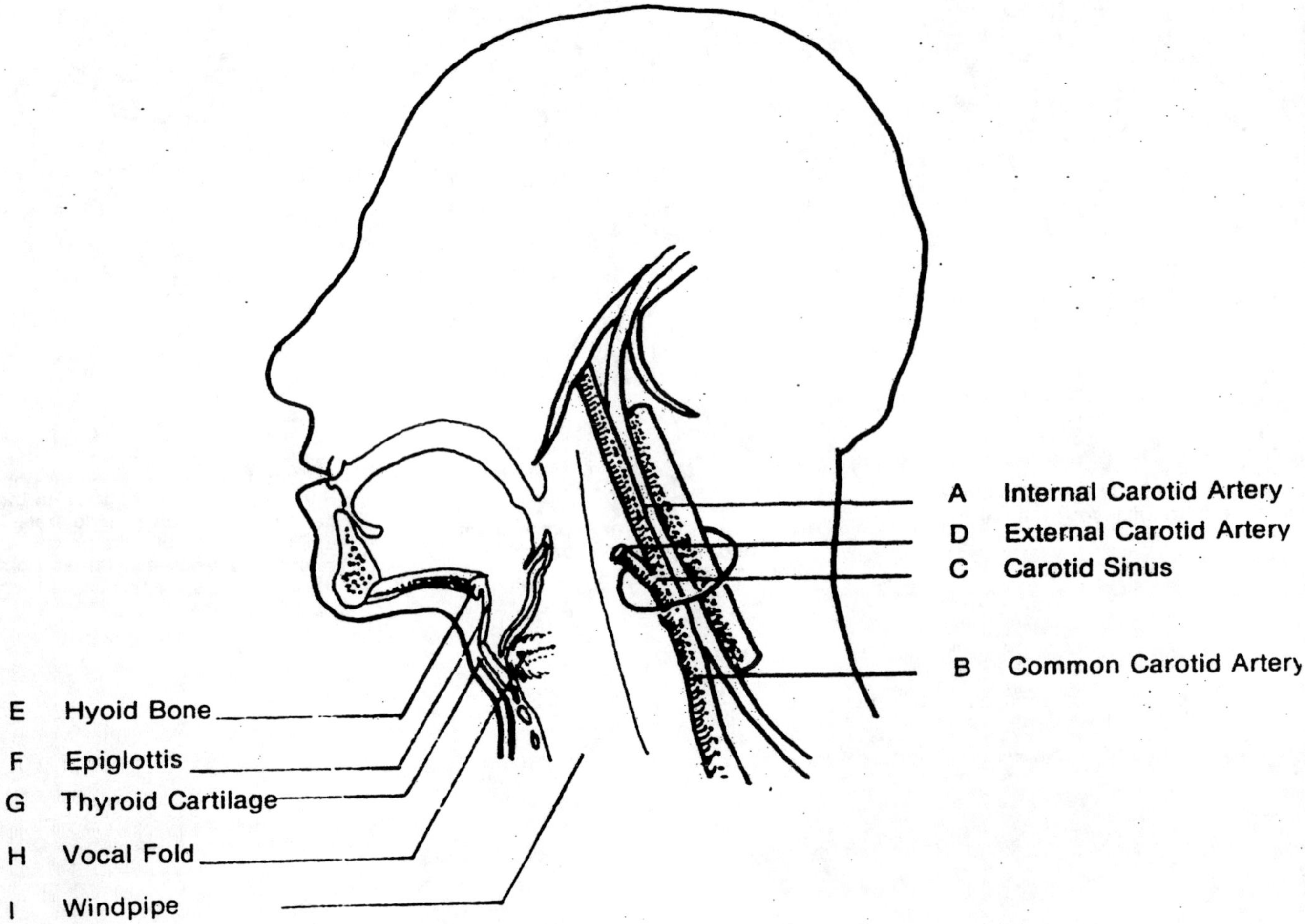


FIGURE T-1

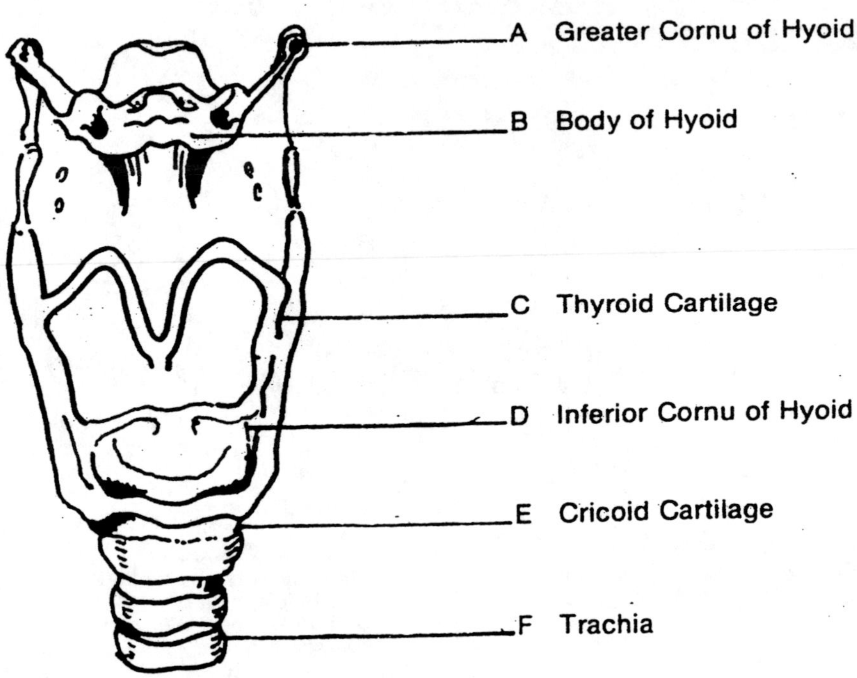

## CHAPTER TEN: THE CAROTID RESTRAINT HOLD

The carotid restraint hold is one of the most effective restraint techniques taught to criminal justice personnel, and also one of the most widely abused techniques when used by these same people. While few people will question its ease of application and extreme effectiveness when used properly, there is a growing concern among judges, prosecutors, defense attorneys and even criminal justice personnel regarding its often unjustified use by street officers.

For example, an officer in the Northwestern part of the United States applied the carotid restraint hold on a driver when he refused to get into the officer's police vehicle. In another case, a correctional officer applied the restraint hold to an inmate who refused to go into his jail cell. In both cases, the victims of the carotid restraint hold died.

In reaction to the growing trend of fatal injuries caused from the application of the carotid restraint hold, many people are microscopically examining the use of this technique. One person who reviewed the use of the carotid restraint hold was U.S. District Judge Robert M. Takasugi. In a 1980 decision, Judge Takasugi said that the carotid restraint hold constituted deadly force as presently applied.

Judge Takasugi issued a preliminary injunction against the police from using the choke hold unless they are confronted by a life or death situation. Although his decision was quickly overturned, it heightened the controversy surrounding this technique. In an effort to better understand the pros and the cons surrounding this technique, let's examine it from a medical and a practical viewpoint.

Before we discuss the practical problems involving the application of the carotid restraint technique, let's first define the carotid restraint hold. When asked how the carotid restraint hold works, the average police officer will tell you that you are stopping the blood flow to the brain by pinching shut the carotid artery. When the flow of blood is stopped, the person will pass out. This description is not entirely correct.

To fully understand the effects of the carotid artery, look at Figure H-1. This figure shows the carotid arteries and the throat area. Studying this figure will help you understand how the carotid restraint hold works.

First, blood containing the necessary oxygen is supplied to your head by the common carotid artery and the vertebral artery. Located on each side of your neck, the two common arteries are connected to the large aorta of the heart. At approximately the height of your Adam's Apple, the artery divides into the external and internal carotid arteries.

Blood is supplied to your face and to your scalp by the external carotid artery, while the internal carotid artery supplies blood to your brain and to your eyes.

Part C on Figure H-1 shows where the carotid artery divides into two parts: part A, the internal carotid artery and part B, the external carotid artery. Where this split takes place is known as the carotid sinus. The carotid sinus will be discussed later.

In addition to the carotid arteries, there are two vertebral arteries which arise from the subclavian arteries. The vertebral arteries are located in the neck and supplement the flow of blood to the brain.

Two large internal jugular veins—one on each side of your neck—carry deoxygenated blood from the brain. The blood flows down your internal jugular veins and is carried back to the heart by other smaller veins. Blood is also collected from other parts of your head by smaller external jugular veins.

This network of arteries and veins contradicts most officers' statements regarding the pinching shut of the carotid artery. As shown, the mere pinching shut of the common carotid artery or the internal carotid arteries does not completely stop the blood flow to the brain. The reason: blood is supplied to the brain via the vertebral arteries. However, pressure on the carotid sinus can produce the responses generally credited to pressing on the carotid artery.

Pressure applied on the carotid sinus generally results in a slowing of the heart. The carotid sinus nerve causes the vagus nerve to engage which causes a person's blood pressure to drop. As a result the brain is not supplied enough oxygen, causing the victim to faint.

Another method to cause a person to faint is through respiratory strangulation. Basically, all you must do is press against the trachia so that the person cannot breath. Unconsciousness will take effect within three minutes.

While few officers would admit to intentionally stranguling a person, a substantial number of "choke-out" deaths are in fact caused by suffocation. While the officer doesn't intend for it to happen, sometimes it cannot be avoided.

For example, while attending the police academy your defensive tactics instructor taught your class the carotid restraint technique. It was shown to you and then you applied it to a classmate who wasn't fighting or struggling. It worked and seemed easy to apply. However, on the street in an actual confrontation the application of the technique isn't so easy.

One of the problems in applying the carotid restraint hold is that the suspect isn't standing still. Instead of cooperating, (s)he is struggling. Hence, when you attempt to apply the carotid restraint hold to the side of the person's neck, your forearm is suddenly against the person's larynx. Unknowingly, you forcefully squeeze your forearm against the person's throat, breaking the hyoid bone. Within three minutes the person dies from suffocation.

In his book, FUNDAMENTALS OF MODERN POLICE IMPACT WEAPONS*, Massad Ayoob mentions some physical after-effects the victim of a carotid restraint or choke hold may develop. For example, some people will vomit when they come too, and may be disoriented for a period of time. There are other possible effects, too.

Ayoob is quick to mention that he sought out a neurosurgeon, a cardiologist, an opthamologist and a specialist in internal medicine to comment on the after-effect of the technique in question. According to Ayoob, all of the doctors were familiar with the various choke-out techniques. They said that a certain percentage of victims would suffer the following: a stroke; a heart attack; convulsive seizures; aspiration of vomit; blindness; ruptured arteries; permanent brain damage; and/or spinal injury. These after-effects are also supported in whole or in part by other medical professionals and researchers*.

For these and other reasons too numerous to discuss, we recommend that the carotid restraint hold not be taught to officers. We agree that the technique will work, but we also agree that the medical implications and the apparent inability of the officer to prudently and judiciously use this technique mandate its deletion from a basic course in defensive tactics.

* For additional reading on this timely subject, see the following.

Ayoob, Massad F. *Fundamentals of Modern Police Impact Weapons* Springfield: Charles C. Thomas, 1978.

Christensen, Loren W. "Chokes and Sleepers." *Black Belt,* September 1981, pp. 40-44.

Endow, Ken. "Danger in the Judo Choke?" *Black Belt,* April 1970, pp. 23-27.

Frohse, Franz; Brodel, Max; and Schlossberg, Leon. *Atlas of Human Anatomy.* 6th ed. New York: Barnes & Noble, 1970.

Koiwai, E.K. *Official Judo Handbook.* Edited by John W. Hunter. El Paso: United States Judo Federation, 1974.

Koiwai, E.K. "How Safe is Choking (Shime-waza) in Judo?" Edited by Donald Pohl. *Official Judo Handbook AAU/USJF.* Detroit: United States Judo Federation, 1970.

Steen, Edwin B., and Mantagu, Ashley. *Anatomy and Physiology.* New York: Barnes & Noble, 1959.

# INTRODUCING . . .